Distributed Graph Coloring

Fundamentals and Recent Developments

Synthesis Lectures on Distributed Computing Theory

Editor
Nancy Lynch, *Massachusetts Institute of Technology*

Synthesis Lectures on Distributed Computing Theory is edited by Nancy Lynch of the Massachusetts Institute of Technology. The series will publish 50- to 150-page publications on topics pertaining to distributed computing theory. The scope will largely follow the purview of premier information and computer science conferences, such as ACM PODC, DISC, SPAA, OPODIS, CONCUR, DialM-POMC, ICDCS, SODA, Sirocco, SSS, and related conferences. Potential topics include, but not are limited to: distributed algorithms and lower bounds, algorithm design methods, formal modeling and verification of distributed algorithms, and concurrent data structures.

Distributed Graph Coloring: Fundamentals and Recent Developments
Leonid Barenboim and Michael Elkin
2013

Distributed Computing by Oblivious Mobile Robots
Paola Flocchini, Giuseppe Prencipe, and Nicola Santoro
2012

Quorum Systems: With Applications to Storage and Consensus
Marko Vukolić
2012

Link Reversal Algorithms
Jennifer L. Welch and Jennifer E. Walter
2011

Cooperative Task-Oriented Computing: Algorithms and Complexity
Chryssis Georgiou and Alexander A. Shvartsman
2011

New Models for Population Protocols
Othon Michail, Ioannis Chatzigiannakis, and Paul G. Spirakis
2011

The Theory of Timed I/O Automata, Second Edition
Dilsun K. Kaynar, Nancy Lynch, Roberto Segala, and Frits Vaandrager
2010

Principles of Transactional Memory
Rachid Guerraoui and Michal Kapalka
2010

Fault-tolerant Agreement in Synchronous Message-passing Systems
Michel Raynal
2010

Communication and Agreement Abstractions for Fault-Tolerant Asynchronous
Distributed Systems
Michel Raynal
2010

The Mobile Agent Rendezvous Problem in the Ring
Evangelos Kranakis, Danny Krizanc, and Euripides Markou
2010

Distributed Graph Coloring: Fundamentals and Recent Developments

Leonid Barenboim and Michael Elkin

ISBN: 978-3-031-00881-8   paperback
ISBN: 978-3-031-02009-4   ebook

DOI 10.1007/978-3-031-02009-4

A Publication in the Springer series
SYNTHESIS LECTURES ON DISTRIBUTED COMPUTING THEORY

Lecture #11
Series Editor: Nancy Lynch, *Massachusetts Institute of Technology*
Series ISSN
Synthesis Lectures on Distributed Computing Theory
Print 2155-1626   Electronic 2155-1634

Distributed Graph Coloring

Fundamentals and Recent Developments

Leonid Barenboim and Michael Elkin
Ben-Gurion University of the Negev

SYNTHESIS LECTURES ON DISTRIBUTED COMPUTING THEORY #11

ABSTRACT

The focus of this monograph is on *symmetry breaking* problems in the *message-passing model* of distributed computing. In this model a communication network is represented by a n-vertex graph $G = (V, E)$, whose vertices host autonomous processors. The processors communicate over the edges of G in discrete rounds. The goal is to devise algorithms that use as few rounds as possible.

A typical symmetry breaking problem is the problem of *graph coloring*. Denote by Δ the maximum degree of G. While coloring G with $\Delta + 1$ colors is trivial in the centralized setting, the problem becomes much more challenging in the distributed one. One can also compromise on the number of colors, if this allows for more efficient algorithms. Other typical symmetry-breaking problems are the problems of computing a *maximal independent set* (MIS) and a *maximal matching* (MM). The study of these problems dates back to the very early days of distributed computing. The founding fathers of distributed computing (see [5, 18, 31, 39, 40, 55, 60, 61]) laid firm foundations for the area of distributed symmetry breaking already in the eighties. In particualr, they showed that all these problems can be solved in randomized logarithmic time. Also, Linial [55] showed that an $O(\Delta^2)$-coloring can be solved very efficiently deterministically.

However, fundamental questions were left open for decades. In particular, it is not known if the MIS or the $(\Delta + 1)$-coloring can be solved in *deterministic polylogarithmic* time. Moreover, until recently it was not known if in deterministic polylogarithmic time one can color a graph with significantly fewer than Δ^2 colors. Additionally, it was open (and still open to some extent) if one can have *sublogarithmic randomized* algorithms for the symmetry breaking problems.

Recently, significant progress was achieved in the study of these questions. More efficient deterministic and randomized $(\Delta + 1)$-coloring algorithms were achieved in [8, 11, 48, 78]. Deterministic $\Delta^{1+o(1)}$-coloring algorithms with polylogarithmic running time were devised in [9]. Improved (and often sublogarithmic-time) randomized algorithms were devised in [11, 47, 78]. Drastically improved lower bounds were given in [50, 52]. Wide families of graphs in which these problems are solvable much faster than on general graphs were identified in [7, 9, 30, 49, 51, 77].

The objective of our monograph is to cover most of these developments, and as a result to provide a treatise on theoretical foundations of distributed symmetry breaking in the message-passing model. We hope that our monograph will stimulate further progress in this exciting area.

KEYWORDS

distributed symmetry breaking, maximal independent set, maximal matching, coloring, deterministic algorithms, randomized algorithms, arboricity

To Lena,
Yonatan and Tal Avraham,
and my parents Leonid Lipman and Marina.

M.E.

To my parents Yevgenia and Michael,
my grandmother Sofia, my uncle Mischa,
Valeria, and Arik.

L.B.

Contents

Acknowledgments

The authors are grateful to Kishore Kothapalli, Alessandro Panconesi and Sriram Pemmaraju for providing them with valuable feedback on a preliminary draft of this monograph.

Leonid Barenboim was supported by the Adams Fellowship Program of the Israel Academy of Sciences and Humanities.

Michael Elkin was supported by the Israeli Science Foundation grant No. 87209011, and by the U.S.-Israel Binational Science Foundation grant No. 2008390.

Leonid Barenboim and Michael Elkin
April 2013

CHAPTER 1

Introduction

Distributed Computing is a large and growing field of study, which is concerned with various settings in which there are several processors working in parallel, typically on a joint problem. The area is roughly forty years old, and by now there are a number of excellent treatises that cover different aspects of Distributed Computing [4, 62, 67, 73].

The most relevant to this monograph is the book of Peleg [67] that describes the *message-passing model* of distributed computation. In this model a communication network is represented by an n-vertex graph $G = (V, E)$, whose vertices host autonomous processors. The processors communicate over the edges of G in discrete rounds.[1] In each of these rounds each processor (equivalently, each vertex) can send messages to all its neighbors in G. The *running time* of an algorithm in this model is the (worst-case) number of rounds of distributed communication that this algorithm requires. Note that local computation comes for free in this model. One also assumes that vertices have distinct identity numbers (or, shortly, Ids) from the range $[n] = \{1, 2, ..., n\}$ at the beginning of the computation. Messages are of unbounded size.[2]

The message-passing model of distributed computing has been a subject of intensive research since the beginning of the eighties. Most important results in this area that were known at the turn of the 21st century were systematically and thoroughly covered in Peleg's book [67]. However, the area has been extremely active since then, and some of the developments in this area call for a new monograph. Most notably, there is an area of *symmetry breaking* and *distributed graph coloring*, within the message-passing model of distributed computing. It deals with problems such as computing a *maximal independent set*, or, shortly, an MIS. A set $U \subseteq V$ of vertices in a graph G is *independent*, if no two vertices $u, v \in U$ are connected by an edge. It is an MIS if $U \cup \{v\}$ is not independent for every vertex $v \in V \setminus U$. Other closely related problems include *Maximal Matching*, which is an edge analogue of MIS, and the coloring problems. In a graph G of maximum degree Δ, in the distributed coloring problem one typically seeks to compute a $(\Delta + 1)$-coloring of G. One is often prepared to compromise on the number of colors, if this allows for more efficient algorithms. One can also aim at $O(a)$-coloring of G, where $a = a(G)$ is the *arboricity* of the graph G.[3]

---

[1]We only describe the *synchronous* variant of the message-passing model here. For details about the *asynchronous* model we refer the reader to [67].

[2]This is the so-called Linial's $\mathcal{LOCAL}$ model of computation [55]. The bounded-message variant of this model is called in [67] $\mathcal{CONGEST}$. In this monograph for simplicity we will always assume the $\mathcal{LOCAL}$ model. On the other hand, most of the algorithms that we will discuss can be implemented within the same running time in the $\mathcal{CONGEST}$ model as well.

[3]The *arboricity* is the minimum number of forests into which the edge-set of G can be decomposed. This parameter will be discussed in Section 2.3. Up to a factor 2 this parameter is equal to the *degeneracy* of the graph G.

The study of these problems was initiated in the very early days of Distributed Computing. Papers by Luby [60, 61], Israeli and Itai [39], Israeli and Shiloach [40], Cole and Vishkin [18], Linial [55], Goldberg, Plotkin and Shannon [31], and by Awerbuch, Goldberg, Luby and Plotkin [5] built the firm foundation of this area back in the eighties. These papers [39, 40, 60, 61] showed that all these problems (we will henceforth call them *the symmetry breaking problems*) can be solved by randomized algorithms that require $O(\log n)$ time. Goldberg et al. [31] also showed that in planar graphs one can solve them in deterministic logarithmic time. Cole and Vishkin [18] devised an algorithm that solves the symmetry breaking problems in deterministic $\log^* n + O(1)$ time on some basic graphs such as paths, rings, rooted trees, and the like.[4] Goldberg et al. [31] extended the result of [18] and showed that the symmetry breaking problems can be solved in deterministic $O(\Delta^2) + \log^* n$ time. Linial [55] devised an $O(\Delta^2)$-coloring algorithm that runs in deterministic $\log^* n + O(1)$ time. He also showed fundamental nearly-tight lower bounds for the symmetry breaking problems in rings, paths and trees. These lower bounds match the upper bounds of Cole and Vishkin [18].

For general graphs Awerbuch et al. [5] and Panconesi and Srinivasan [69] devised deterministic algorithms for these problems that require $2^{O(\sqrt{\log n})}$ time. These algorithms are based on constructions of *ruling sets*. Ruling sets are relaxations of MIS, and can be computed much faster. Specifically, in [5] ruling sets with certain parameters are computed in logarithmic time. Recently, Kothapalli and Pemmaraju [46] devised algorithms for certain ruling sets that require $O(\log \log n)$ time. However, currently it is unknown whether this construction can be used to speed up coloring and MIS computations.

These results (mostly covered in Peleg's monograph [67]) left open a number of fundamental open questions. Among the most notable of them are:

1. Can these problems be solved in deterministic polylogarithmic time?
   In particular, Linial [55] asked whether one can compute a coloring that employs $o(\Delta^2)$ colors in deterministic polylogarithmic time.

2. Can the $O(\log n)$ time bound for randomized algorithms be improved?

3. Are there special graph families for which far more efficient algorithms exist?

4. How fast can these problems be solved in terms of the maximum degree Δ, when the dependence on n is as mild as $O(\log^* n)$?

For all these questions significant progress has been made. Specifically, with regard to the first question Hanckowiack, Karonski and Panconesi [35] showed that the Maximal Matching problem can be solved in deterministic polylogarithmic time. In [9] the authors of this monograph answered Linial's question in the affirmative, and showed that $\Delta^{1+o(1)}$-coloring can be computed in deterministic polylogarithmic time.

---

[4]$\log^* n$ is a very slowly growing function. $\log^{(0)} n = n$, and for $i = 1, 2, ..., \log^{(i)} n = \log_2 \log^{(i-1)} n$. $\log^* n$ is the smallest value of i such that $\log^{(i)} n \leq 2$.

With regard to the second question, Kothapalli et al. [47] came up with a randomized $O(\Delta)$-coloring algorithm that requires $O(\sqrt{\log n})$ time. Their results were improved by Schneider and Wattenhofer [78], and the latter results were subsequently improved by Barenboim et al. [11]. Specifically, Barenboim et al. [11] showed that an MIS can be computed in $O(\sqrt{\log n} \cdot \log \Delta)$ time, a $(\Delta + 1)$-coloring in $2^{O(\sqrt{\log \log n})} + O(\log \Delta)$ time, and a Maximal Matching in $O((\log \log n)^4 + \log \Delta)$ time. (See Sections 10.3 and 10.4 in the current monograph.)

With regard to the third question there were two remarkable developments. First Kuhn et al. [49] identified the family of graphs with *bounded growth*. These are graphs $G = (V, E)$ in which for every vertex $v \in V$, the 2-neighborhood of v (i.e., the set of vertices at distance at most 2 from v) does not contain more than a certain pre-defined number of independent vertices. A sequence of papers [30, 49, 51, 77] that studied the symmetry-breaking problems in these graphs culminated in the work by Schneider and Wattenhofer [77]. The latter authors extended the result of Cole and Vishkin [18], and showed that the aforementioned symmetry-breaking problems can be solved in $O(\log^* n)$ time in graphs of bounded growth.

The second development in the context of the third question was the study of graphs with *bounded arboricity* (see Chapter 5), initiated in [7]. We showed there that symmetry breaking problems can be solved in $O(\frac{\log n}{\log \log n})$ deterministic time in graphs of constant arboricity (including planar graphs), and in deterministic polylogarithmic time whenever arboricity is at most polylogarithmic in n. The methodology developed in [7] was also used in [9] for devising a $\Delta^{1+o(1)}$-coloring in deterministic polylogarithmic time.

With regard to the fourth question Szegedy and Vishwanathan [74] proved a lower bound that shows that any coloring algorithm of a certain type (called a *locally-iterative*[5] algorithm) requires $\Omega(\Delta \log \Delta + \log^* n)$ rounds for $(\Delta + 1)$-coloring. The state-of-the-art $(\Delta + 1)$-coloring algorithm at that time was a locally-iterative algorithm by [31], that requires $O(\Delta^2) + \log^* n$ time. This result was improved to $O(\Delta \log \Delta) + \log^* n$ by Kuhn and Wattenhofer [53]. The algorithm in [53] can also be viewed as locally-iterative, and thus their result is tight for locally-iterative algorithms. However, recently the authors of the current monograph [8] and independently Kuhn [48] devised $(\Delta + 1)$-coloring algorithms that run in $O(\Delta) + \log^* n$ time, breaking the barrier of Szegedy and Vishwanathan [74]. The algorithms of [8] and [48] are not locally-iterative. Instead they are based on the notion of *defective coloring* (see Section 2.4, and Chapter 6).

The goal of the current monograph is to cover most of these developments, and as a result to provide a treatise on theoretical foundations of distributed graph coloring, MIS, and related problems. To make the monograph suitable also for readers that are not familiar with the field of distributed coloring, we provide the required background in the first chapters. We start (Chapter 2) with providing some basics of Graph Theory that are necessary for understanding the following chapters. We then proceed (Chapter 3) to describing the basic distributed graph coloring

---

[5] Roughly speaking, an algorithm in which every vertex v in every round selects a new color based only on its previous color and on colors of its neighbors is called *locally-iterative*. See also Section 3.8.

algorithms, such as the algorithms of Cole and Vishkin [18], Goldberg et al. [31] and Linial's algorithm [55]. This chapter also contains a section about more recent Kuhn-Wattenhofer's color reduction technique. Even though it was discovered in the last decade, we feel that it "morally" belongs to the basics of distributed graph coloring theory. Additional fundamental results are discussed in Chapter 4 which deals with Linial's lower bounds [55].

The rest of the monograph deals with recent developments. Chapter 5 is devoted to algorithms that compute forest decompositions, and use them for coloring graphs of bounded arboricity. It is mostly based on the paper [7] by the authors of the current monograph. Chapter 6 is devoted to *defective coloring*, and to its applications to the computation of $(\Delta + 1)$-coloring in $O(\Delta) + \log^* n$ time. This chapter is based on the papers [8, 48]. In Chapter 7 we introduce the notion of *arbdefective coloring*, which is an extension of the notion of defective coloring. We then show how to compute arbdefective coloring efficiently, and how to use them to compute a $\Delta^{1+o(1)}$-coloring in deterministic polylogarithmic time. As was mentioned above, this result answers Linial's open question in the affirmative. This chapter is based on our paper [9].

In Chapter 8 we turn our attention to *edge-coloring*. We start with presenting the classical algorithm by Panconesi and Rizzi [68] that computes $(2\Delta - 1)$-edge-coloring and maximal matching in $O(\Delta) + \log^* n$ time. We then show that in graphs with bounded arboricity these objects can be computed in $O(\frac{\log n}{\log \log n})$ time [7]. Finally, we describe our $\Delta^{1+o(1)}$-edge-coloring algorithm from [10] that requires $O(\log \Delta) + \log^* n$ time. The latter algorithm is based on the notions of defective and arbdefective colorings, described in Chapters 6 and 7. Another feature of this algorithm is the utilization of the notion of "bounded neighborhood independence". This graph parameter is presented and discussed in Section 8.2.

In Chapter 9 we describe the *Network-Decomposition* technique that was introduced by Awerbuch et al. [5] and its applications. Roughly speaking, network-decompositions are partitions of the input graph into a bounded number of subgraphs with bounded diameters. These partitions turned out to be extremely useful for solving a variety of problems including $(\Delta + 1)$-coloring and MIS. Currently, the best-known deterministic algorithms for these problems in general graphs are based on network-decompositions [69]. We describe algorithms for computing network-decompositions and for using them to solve coloring problems.

While Chapters 3–9 deal with deterministic algorithms, in Chapter 10 we turn our attention to *randomized* ones. We start with presenting some classical logarithmic algorithms [60, 61]. Next we describe a more recent $O(\Delta)$-coloring algorithm that runs in $O(\sqrt{\log n})$ time. This algorithm is a variant of an algorithm presented by Kothapalli et al. [47]. We then proceed to more advanced distributed MIS and maximal matching algorithms, that are based on the recent work by Barenboim et al. [11]. Finally, in Chapter 11 we overview the numerous open problems in this field.

Distributed graph coloring and symmetry breaking is a vast area, and we could not cover it entirely in this monograph. The most notable omissions are:

1. We do not present the recent lower bounds by Kuhn, Moscibroda and Wattenhofer [50, 52]. In a major breakthrough, Kuhn et al. [50, 52] showed that MIS and maximal matching require $\Omega\left(\min\{\sqrt{\log n}, \log \Delta\}\right)$ time.

2. The entire theory of distributed symmetry breaking in graphs of bounded growth [30, 49, 51, 77] was left out of our monograph. We feel that this subject justifies a separate monograph.

3. The string of beautiful papers of Panconesi and his co-authors [24, 32, 33, 70, 71] and by Chierichetti and Vattani [16] about randomized edge-coloring and Brooks-Vizing vertex coloring is not covered in our monograph. This fascinating subject is, however, partially covered in the excellent monograph by Dubhashi and Panconesi [25].

In part, the monograph evolved from lectures that the second-named author gave in Ben-Gurion University in the Distributed Algorithms class in Autumn 2012. However, it contains more material than can be covered in one semester. Depending on the level of the course and the teacher's taste, one can skip Chapter 4 or/and Chapters 6–8, and still give the students quite a coherent picture of the field. Our intention is that the monograph will be used both for self-study and for teaching graduate courses. We hope that it will further stimulate the progress in this vivid research area.

CHAPTER 2

Basics of Graph Theory

In this chapter we provide the background in Graph Theory which is most relevant to this monograph. We make no attempt to survey this entire area. Many books are devoted to this subject. See, e.g., [13, 23].

2.1 GRAPHS WITH LARGE GIRTH AND LARGE CHROMATIC NUMBER

The girth of a graph $G = (V, E)$ is the minimum length of a simpe cycle in G. A *legal coloring* φ of a graph $G = (V, E)$ is a function $\varphi : V \to \mathbb{N}$ from its vertex set to natural numbers that satisfy that $\varphi(v) \neq \varphi(u)$, for every edge $(v, u) \in E$. The coloring φ is called a *k-coloring*, for an integer $k \geq 2$, if the image of φ is the set $\{1, 2, ..., k\} = [k]$.

The *chromatic* or *coloring* number of a graph G, denoted $\chi(G)$, is the minimum k for which there exists a legal k-coloring of G. The problem of finding an optimal legal coloring (a legal coloring that employs $\chi(G)$ colors) is NP-hard [29, 43]. Moreover, providing even a loose $n^{1-\epsilon}$-approximation to this problem is NP-hard as well [12, 38, 79]. In the context of distributed algorithms we are mostly interested in a much simpler problem, specifically, in $(\Delta + 1)$-coloring, where $\Delta = \Delta(G)$ is the maximum degree of a vertex in G.

Lemma 2.1 *For every graph $G = (V, E)$, it holds that $\chi(G) \leq \Delta + 1$.*

Proof. Let $V = (v_1, v_2, ..., v_n)$ be an arbitrary ordering of vertices of G. The proof is by induction on n. The base ($n = 1$) is immediate. For the induction step suppose that $v_1, v_2, ..., v_{n-1}$ are already legally $(\Delta + 1)$-colored. The vertex v_n has at most Δ neighbors, and thus, there are at most Δ forbidden colors for v_n. Therefore, there always exists an available color for v_n (which is different from the colors of all neighbors of v_n) from the set $[\Delta + 1]$. □

The algorithm described in this proof is inherently sequential. One of the main challenges of distributed graph algorithms is to devise efficient distributed algorithms for $(\Delta + 1)$-coloring. Another closely related challenge is to construct a *Maximal Independent Set* (henceforth, *MIS*). A set $U \subseteq V$ of vertices is *independent* if there is no edge $(u, w) \in E$ with $u, w \in U$. An independent set U is said to be *maximal* if for every vertex $v \in V \setminus U$, the set $U \cup \{v\}$ is not an independent set.

Note that similarly to $(\Delta + 1)$-coloring, an MIS can also be constructed greedily. To describe a greedy algorithm for computing an MIS we need to introduce some notation. For a vertex v, denote by $\hat{\Gamma}(v)$ (respectively, $\Gamma(v)$) the set of neighbors of v including (resp., not including) v. For a vertex set $U \subseteq V$, let $\hat{\Gamma}(U) = \bigcup_{u \in U} \hat{\Gamma}(u)$. To compute an MIS, initialize $U = \emptyset$. Pick an arbitrary vertex $v \in V \setminus \hat{\Gamma}(U)$, and add it to U. Continue as long as $V \setminus \hat{\Gamma}(U) \neq \emptyset$. It is easy to verify that this simple algorithm constructs an MIS. However, it is also inherently sequential. Finding efficient distributed MIS and coloring algorithms is the subject of this monograph.

A natural way to construct a graph with chromatic number k is to use a k-clique K_k. This example suggests that the requirement to have large chromatic number is contradictory to having large girth. (The *girth* of a graph G is the length of the shortest cycle in G.) Nevertheless, we will next show that one can construct graphs which simultaneously have arbitrarily large girth and chromatic number. We will start with explicit constructions of triangle-free graphs with arbitrarily large chromatic number. We will then proceed to constructing graphs with girth at least 6 and arbitrarily large chromatic number. Finally, we will describe Erdős' classical proof that graphs with arbitrarily large girth and chromatic number exist. The latter proof is a celebrated example of using the Probabilistic Method. See [2] for a comprehensive treatis on this subject.

It is easy to construct a triangle-free graph (i.e., a graph with girth at least 4) with chromatic number 3. This is a 5-cycle C_5, or, more generally, any odd cycle. Constructing a triangle-free graph with chromatic number 4 is already more challenging. See Figure 2.1 for the Grotzsch graph [34]. The Grotzsch graph $\mathcal{G} = (V, E)$ has 11 vertices. It consists of a 5-cycle $(x_1, x_2, x_3, x_4, x_5)$. For every pair $i, j \in [5]$, $i \neq j$, of distinct not consecutive indices (5 and 1 are consecutive), add a vertex y_{ij}, and connect it to x_i and to x_j by two edges (x_i, y_{ij}), (y_{ij}, x_j). Finally, add a vertex z and connect it to all the five vertices y_{ij}. It is easy to verify that $\mathcal{G}$ is triangle-free.

Lemma 2.2 $\chi(\mathcal{G}) = 4$.

Proof. To show that $\chi(\mathcal{G}) \leq 4$ it is enough to construct a legal 4-coloring ρ of $\mathcal{G}$. This is a straightforward exercise.

Next we argue that $\chi(\mathcal{G}) \geq 4$. Any legal 3-coloring φ of the cycle $C = (x_1, x_2, x_3, x_4, x_5)$ is such that one vertex is colored by a unique color, and each of the other two colors is employed by two vertices. Denote the unique color by 3, and suppose without loss of generality that $\varphi(x_5) = 3$. Then $\varphi(y_{14}) = 3$, as $\{\varphi(x_1), \varphi(x_4)\} = \{1, 2\}$. If $\varphi(x_1) = 1$ and $\varphi(x_4) = 2$ then $\varphi(y_{25}) = 1$, $\varphi(y_{35}) = 2$, and $\varphi(y_{14}) = 3$. Hence $\varphi(z) \notin \{1, 2, 3\}$. Similarly, if $\varphi(x_1) = 2$ and $\varphi(x_4) = 1$ then $\varphi(y_{35}) = 1$, $\varphi(y_{25}) = 2$, and $\varphi(y_{14}) = 3$, and so $\varphi(z) \notin \{1, 2, 3\}$. Hence φ employs at least 4 colors. $\square$

Next we describe Mycielski's construction [64]. This construction generalizes Grotzsch graph. It provides a way to obtain triangle-free graphs with $\chi(G) = k$, for an arbitrarily large integer k. Suppose that we are given a triangle-free graph $G = G_k$ with $\chi(G) = k$. Let $V = \{v_1, v_2, ..., v_n\}$ denote its vertex set. We construct the graph $G' = G_{k+1}$ in the following way.

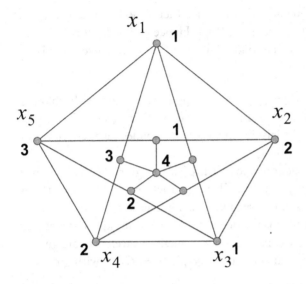

Figure 2.1: Grotsch graph.

Let $V' = V \cup U \cup \{u\}$, $U = \{u_1, u_2, ..., u_n\}$. The vertex u is called the *center* vertex of G_{k+1}. The graph $G(V)$ is isomorphic to G. Also, we add a star (u, u_i), for every $i \in [n]$. Finally, each vertex u_i is connected to all vertices in $\Gamma(v_i)$. Observe that Grotzsch graph is obtained from Mycielski's construction applied to C_5.

Lemma 2.3 G' *is triangle-free.*

Proof. The center vertex is not a part of any triangle, because it is connected only to vertices of U, and there are no edges between vertices of U. Triangles that contain a single U-vertex (i.e., (u_i, v_p, v_q)) are impossible, because if such a triangle exists then $v_p, v_q \in \Gamma(v_i)$, i.e., there is a triangle in G. This is a contradiction. Triangles that contain a single vertex from V are impossible, because there are no edges between U-vertices. □

Obviously, $\chi(G_{k+1}) \leq k + 1$. Indeed, we can color G with k colors. Each u_i can be colored by the same color as v_i, and then the center u can be colored by the color $k + 1$.

Lemma 2.4 $\chi(G') \geq k + 1$.

Proof. Suppose for contradiction that there exists a legal k-coloring φ of G'. Suppose without loss of generality that $\varphi(u) = k$. Denote by $\tilde{V}$ the subset of V with vertices colored by color k. For each vertex $v_i \in \tilde{V}$ we recolor it by setting $\varphi'(v_i) = \varphi(u_i)$. All other vertices retain their colors, i.e., set $\varphi'(w) = \varphi(w)$. Consider an edge $(v_i, v_j) \in E$. If $v_i, v_j \notin \tilde{V}$, then $\varphi'(v_i) = \varphi(v_i) \neq \varphi(v_j) =$

$\varphi'(v_j)$. Otherwise, suppose without loss of generality that $v_i \in \tilde{V}$. Then $v_j \notin \tilde{V}$. Since (u_i, v_j) is an edge in G', it follows that $\varphi'(v_i) = \varphi(u_i) \neq \varphi(v_j) = \varphi'(v_j)$. Hence φ' is a legal coloring of G, and it employs at most $k - 1$ colors. This is a contradiction to $\chi(G) = k$. Hence there is no legal k-coloring of G', i.e., $\chi(G') \geq k + 1$.   □

To summarize, we have shown that $G' = G_{k+1}$ is a triangle-free graph with coloring number $k + 1$. Denote by n_k the number of vertices in G_k. It follows that $n_{k+1} = 2 \cdot n_k + 1$, i.e., $n_k = 6 \cdot 2^{k-3} - 1$, for $k \geq 3$. Therefore, Mycielski's construction provides (explicit) n-vertex triangle-free graphs with chromatic number $\Omega(\log n)$.

Next we describe another explicit construction, due to Tutte [22], of graphs G with girth at least 6, and arbitrarily large chromatic number $\chi(G) = k$. This construction will be referred to as Descartes' construction.[1] The number of vertices in these graphs is, however, very large in terms of k. (Even much larger than exponential in k, which is the dependence in Mycielski' construction.) Similarly to Mycielski's construction, Descartes' construction is inductive as well. We are given a graph $G = G_k$ with girth$(G) \geq 6$, $\chi(G) = k$, and construct a graph $G' = G_{k+1}$ with girth(G') ≥ 6 and $\chi(G') = k + 1$.

Denote $n = n_k = |V(G_k)|$ the number of vertices in G_k. Let $T, T \gg n$, be a number that will be determined in the sequel. Let U be a set of T vertices, which we will call "*groundset.*" For every n-vertex subset of the groundset, we create a (new) copy of G. The n vertices of the copy are connected to the vertices of the subset via an arbitrary perfect matching. This completes the description of the graph $G' = G_{k+1}$. Its chromatic number is obviously at most $k + 1$. (Just color all copies of G by k colors, and use color $k + 1$ for vertices in the groundset U.)

Also, the shortest cycles that cross between different copies of G are of the form $(v_i, v_j, u_1, v'_p, v'_q, u_2, v_i)$, with v_i, v_j belonging to one copy of G, v'_p and v'_q belonging to another copy, and $u_1, u_2 \in U$. (See Figure 2.3.) Hence girth$(G') \geq 6$. It remains to argue that G' cannot be colored by k colors.

Lemma 2.5   *For $T \geq (n - 1) \cdot k + 1$, it holds that $\chi(G') \geq k + 1$.*

Proof. Consider a k-coloring φ of G'. There exists a subset $U' \subseteq U$ of the groundset U with $|U'| \geq \lceil T/k \rceil$ vertices, that are all colored by φ with the same color. Set $T = (n - 1) \cdot k + 1$, i.e., $|U'| = \lceil T/k \rceil = n$. (If $|U'| > n$, remove arbitrary $|U'| - n$ vertices from U'.) Suppose without loss of generality that all vertices of U' are colored by k. There is a copy of G that corresponds to the subset U'. This copy is connected to U' via a perfect matching. Thus, no vertex in this copy is colored by color k. Thus, vertices of this copy are colored by colors from the palette $[k - 1]$. However, $\chi(G) \geq k$, and thus φ is not a legal coloring of this copy. Hence φ is not a legal coloring of G'.   □

---

[1] Tutte used the pseudonym "Descartes" in his note [22] which described this construction.

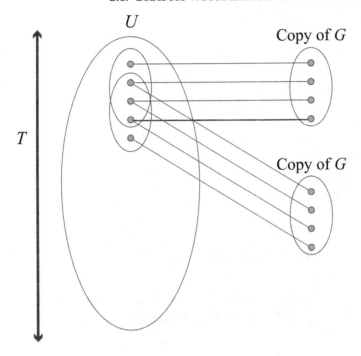

Figure 2.2: Descartes' construction.

The number of vertices in G' satisfies the recursion $n_{k+1} \approx \binom{n_k \cdot k}{n_k} \cdot n_k \approx k^{n_k} \cdot n_k$. In other words, it is a huge number that can be expressed by a tower function. To summarize:

Theorem 2.6   *Descartes' constructions provides (explicit) n–vertex graphs G with girth$(G) \geq 6$ and $\chi(G) = \omega(1)$.*

There are known much better (and far more complicated) explicit constructions of graphs with high girth and chromatic number. (See [59]. They are based on Ramanujan graphs, and are outside the scope of this monograph.) Next, we describe Erdős' probabilistic (and, therefore, not explicit) proof of existence of such graphs.

Theorem 2.7   *[26]: For every k, ℓ, there exists a graph G with girth$(G) > k$ and $\chi(G) \geq \ell$.*

Remark: This theorem means that chromatic number is not a local property. Indeed, a graph with high girth looks locally like a tree. On the other hand, a tree has chromatic number 2, while a graph with high girth may have an arbitrarily large chromatic number.

Proof. Set $\vartheta < 1/k$, and $p = n^\vartheta/n$. Consider the distribution $\mathcal{G}(n, p)$ of n-vertex graphs, in which every edge appears with probability p, independently of other edges. (We refer the readers

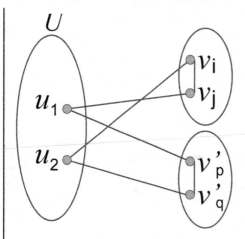

Figure 2.3: Shortest cycles in a graph G', obtained via Descartes' construction.

to [14, 41] for extensive treatment of random graph theory.) Denote by X the random variable that counts cycles of length at most k in a graph G selected from the distribution $\mathcal{G}(n, p)$. Then the expectation $\mathbb{E}(X)$ of X is given by

$$\mathbb{E}(X) = \sum_{i=3}^{k} \frac{(n)_i}{2i} \cdot p^i.$$

Here $(n)_i$ is the number of possibilities to choose i vertices from n vertices, where the order is important. The expression is divided by i because any sequence of i distinct vertices can be arbitrarily rotated, and the rotated sequence gives rise to the same cycle. Similarly, it is divided by 2, because any such sequence can be reversed, while still giving rise to the same cycle in the n-clique K_n. Hence

$$\mathbb{E}(X) \leq \sum_{i=3}^{k} \frac{n^i}{2i} \cdot n^{(\vartheta-1)i} = \frac{1}{2} \sum_{i=3}^{k} \frac{n^{\vartheta i}}{i} = o(n),$$

because $\vartheta < 1/k$. By Markov's inequality, $\mathbb{P}(X \geq n/2) = \mathbb{P}(X \geq \frac{n/2}{o(n)} \cdot o(n)) < \frac{o(n)}{n/2} = o(1)$. In other words, with high probability, the selected graph has only a small number of short cycles.

The second part of the proof shows that with high probability there are no large independent sets, and thus, the chromatic number is not too small. Set $x = \left\lceil \frac{3}{p} \cdot \ln n \right\rceil = \left\lceil 3 \cdot n^{1-\vartheta} \cdot \ln n \right\rceil$. Denote by $\alpha(G)$ the size of the *maximum* independent set in the graph G. (Notice that in contrast to a maximal independent set, a maximum independent set is an independent set of maximum cardinality in G.) For a given set $Q \subseteq V$ of x vertices, denote by $I(Q)$ the indicator random variable of the event $\{Q$ is an independent set$\}$. Then

$$\mathbb{P}(\alpha(G) \geq x) \leq \sum_{Q \subseteq V, |Q| = x} \mathbb{P}(I(Q)).$$

Also, $\mathbb{P}(I(Q)) = (1 - p)^{\binom{x}{2}}$. (For each of the $\binom{x}{2}$ pairs of vertices from Q, there is no edge between them with probability $(1 - p)$, independently of other pairs.) Hence,

$$\mathbb{P}(\alpha(G) \geq x) \leq \binom{n}{x} \cdot (1 - p)^{\binom{x}{2}} \leq \left(\frac{e \cdot n}{x}\right)^x \cdot e^{-p \cdot x \cdot (x-1)/2} < \left(n \cdot e^{-p \cdot (x-1)/2}\right)^x.$$

(The last inequality requires $x = \lceil 3 \cdot n^{1-\vartheta} \ln n \rceil > e$, which, of course, holds for a sufficiently large n.) Since $p \cdot (x - 1)/2 > \frac{3}{2} \ln n - p/2 \geq \frac{4}{3} \ln n$, it also holds that $n \cdot e^{-p \cdot (x-1)/2} \leq 1/n^{1/3}$.

Thus $\mathbb{P}(\alpha(G) \geq x) \leq (1/n^{1/3})^x = o(1)$, and $\mathbb{P}(\chi(G) \leq \frac{n}{x}) \leq \mathbb{P}(\alpha(G) \geq x) = o(1)$. Hence $\mathbb{P}((\alpha(G) \geq x)$ or $(X \geq n/2)) = o(1)$, and so $\mathbb{P}((\alpha(G) < x)$ and $(X < n/2)) = 1 - o(1) > 0$. Consider a graph G that satisfies these two properties, i.e., $\alpha(G) < x = \lceil 3n^{1-\vartheta} \ln n \rceil$, and it has less than $n/2$ short cycles (i.e., cycles of length at most k). Remove one vertex from each of these short cycles. Denote the graph induced on surviving vertices by G'. The number n' of vertices in G' satisfies $n' > n/2$. Moreover, girth$(G') > k$. Finally, any independent set in G' is an independent set in G too, and so $\alpha(G') < x = \lceil 3n^{1-\vartheta} \ln n \rceil \leq \lceil 6n'^{(1-\vartheta)} \cdot (\ln n' + 1) \rceil = O(n'^{(1-\vartheta)} \ln n')$. Hence $\chi(G') = \Omega(\frac{n'^{\vartheta}}{\ln n'})$, as required. $\square$

Therefore, we proved that for every positive integer k there exists an n-vertex graph G with girth$(G) > k$ and chromatic number almost $n^{1/k}$. (Specifically, $\Omega(\frac{n^{\vartheta}}{\ln n})$, for $\vartheta < 1/k$ being arbitrarily close to $1/k$.) By a more careful analysis one can also guarantee $\chi(G) = \Omega(\frac{n^{1/k}}{k})$ in this proof. By modifying the construction slightly one can also ensure that the maximum degree $\Delta(G)$ of this graph is upper bounded by $O(n^{1/k})$.

We finish this section by showing that any graph G with girth$(G) > k$ is quite sparse. We will later use this lemma to show that the condition girth$(G) > k$ implies $\chi(G) \leq O(n^{2/k})$, i.e., the dependencies between girth and chromatic number in Erdős' theorem is in the right ballpark.

Before stating the lemma we introduce a few definitions.

Definition 2.8   *In an unoriented graph* $G = (V, E)$*, the* distance *between a pair of vertices* $u, v \in V$*, denoted* $dist_G(u, v)$*, is the number of edges in the shortest path connecting* u *and* v *in* G*. Denote also by* $\delta(G)$ *the minimum degree of a vertex in* G*. For a vertex* v*, denote by* $\deg(v) = \deg_G(v) = |\Gamma(v)|$ *the* degree *of a vertex* v*. Then* $\delta(G) = \min\{\deg(v) \mid v \in V\}$ *and* $\Delta(G) = \max\{\deg(v) \mid v \in V\}$*. Also, for a positive integer* ℓ*, let* $\hat{\Gamma}_\ell(v)$ *(respectively,* $\Gamma_\ell(v)$*) denote the* ℓ*-neighborhood of a vertex* v *including (resp., not including)* v*, i.e., the set of all vertices at distance at most* ℓ *including* v *(resp., not including* v*).*

Lemma 2.9   *For an even positive integer k, and a graph $G = (V, E)$ with girth$(G) > k$, it holds that $m \leq n^{1+2/k} + n$, where $m = |E|, n = |V|$.*

Proof. We argue that for any graph G, there exists an induced subgraph G' with $\delta(G') \geq \lfloor \frac{m}{n} \rfloor + 1$. If $\delta(G) \geq \lfloor \frac{m}{n} \rfloor + 1$ then we are done. Otherwise iteratively remove from G a vertex v with $\deg(v) \leq \lfloor \frac{m}{n} \rfloor$. We stop if $\delta(G') \geq \lfloor \frac{m}{n} \rfloor + 1$; otherwise continue removing vertices. Suppose for contradiction that we removed all vertices. Observe that after $(n - 1)$ iterations, all edges are eliminated. Thus the number of iterations is at most $n - 1$. In each iteration we removed at most $\lfloor \frac{m}{n} \rfloor$ edges. Hence $m \leq (n - 1) \cdot \lfloor \frac{m}{n} \rfloor$, contradiction. Therefore, G' does contain some vertices. Hence G' is a non-empty graph with $\delta(G') \geq \lfloor \frac{m}{n} \rfloor + 1$. Also, since G' is an induced subgraph of G, it follows that girth$(G') \geq$ girth$(G) > k$. Denote by n' the number of vertices in G'. To provide a lower bound for n', consider a $\frac{k}{2}$-neighborhood of a vertex v in G'. Since girth$(G') > k$, it follows that $n \geq n' \geq |\hat{\Gamma}_{k/2}(v)| \geq (\delta(G') - 1)^{k/2} = \lfloor \frac{m}{n} \rfloor^{k/2}$. Hence $n^{2/k} \geq \frac{m}{n} - 1$, and the lemma follows.   □

2.2   PLANAR GRAPHS

In this section we provide some background about planar graphs. This is a large area; see, e.g., [63] for an extensive treatise. The discussion below follows to a large extent, the monograph of Bollobas [13], Chapter I.4.

Definition 2.10   *A planar graph is a graph that can be drawn on the surface of a sphere in such a way that no two edges of it intersect (except for intersections in vertices).*

Definition 2.11   *A plane graph is a specific drawing of a planar graph.*

A *face* of a plane graph G is a polygon whose boundary is a chordless cycle, i.e., a cycle $(v_0, v_1, ..., v_\ell = v_0)$ in G, such that there is no edge (v_i, v_j) between a pair of non-consecutive v_i and v_j which crosses the cycle. See Figure 2.4.

It is often more convenient to think about planar graphs as drawn in the plane, rather than on a sphere. When a planar graph is drawn in a plane one of its faces becomes the *outer face*. On the other hand, in a drawing on a sphere, all faces play the same role.

Observation 2.12   *A subgraph of a planar graph is a planar graph as well.*

Theorem 2.13   *(Euler's formula) In a connected plane graph with n vertices, m edges, and f faces, it holds that $n - m + f = 2$.*

Before we prove the theorem, we provide one more definition and observation.

outer face

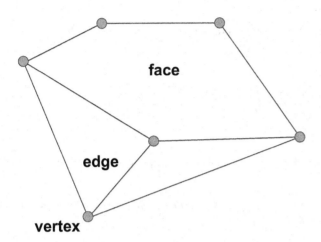

face

edge

vertex

Figure 2.4: An example of a plane graph drawn in the plane.

Definition 2.14   *An edge e is a* bridge edge *in a graph G if $G \setminus \{e\}$ is not connected.*

Observation 2.15   *In a bridgefree plane graph, every edge is adjacent to exactly two faces. On the other hand, a bridge edge is adjacent only to the outer face.*

Proof. (of Theorem 2.13) The proof is by induction on the number of faces f.
Base: If $f = 1$ then G has no cycles. (Its only face is the outer face.) Hence G is a tree, i.e., $n = m + 1$, and $n - m + f = 2$.
Step: Suppose that $f \geq 2$. Then G contains a cycle. Let $e = (u, v)$ be an edge in some cycle in G. The edge lies on a boundary of two faces, S and T. If the edge e is removed from the graph G, we obtain a graph $G' = G \setminus \{e\}$ with $f' = f - 1$ faces, $n' = n$ vertices, and $m' = m - 1$ edges. By the induction hypothesis, $n' - m' + f' = 2$, and so $n - (m - 1) + (f - 1) = n - m + f = 2$.
$\square$

An interesting consequence of Euler's characteristic is that every drawing of a planar graph (such that no two edges intersect) has exactly the same number of faces.

Fix a plane graph G. Denote by f_i, for every $i \geq 1$, the number of faces α in G that have exactly i edges on their boundaries, i.e., $F_i = \{\alpha$ is a face of G: α has i edges on its boundary$\}$, and $f_i = |F_i|$. Obviously $\sum_{i \geq 1} f_i = f$. Denote by F the set of all faces of G.

Lemma 2.16   *Suppose that G is bridgefree. Then $\sum_{i \geq 3} i f_i = 2m$.*

Proof. Let N denote the number of pairs (e, α) such that the edge e lies on the boundary of the face α. Denote also by $I(e, \alpha)$ the indicator variable of the event $\{e$ lies on the boundary of $\alpha\}$. Then, since G is bridgefree,

$$N = \sum_{\alpha \in F} \sum_{e \in E} I(e, \alpha) = \sum_{e \in E} \sum_{\alpha \in F} I(e, \alpha) = \sum_{e \in E} 2 = 2m.$$

Also,

$$N = \sum_{\alpha \in F} \sum_{e \in E} I(e, \alpha) = \sum_{i \geq 3} \sum_{\alpha \in F_i} \sum_{e \in \alpha} I(e, \alpha) = \sum_{i \geq 3} \sum_{\alpha \in F_i} i = \sum_{i \geq 3} i f_i.$$

$\square$

Next, we prove a useful bound on the number of edges in a planar graph.

Theorem 2.17   *In an n-vertex planar graph G, $n \geq 3$, the number of edges m satisfies $m \leq 3n - 6$. Moreover, if girth$(G) \geq g$ (and $g \geq 3$), then $m \leq \max\{\frac{g}{g-2} \cdot (n-2), n-1\}$.*

Proof. The proof is by induction on n.

Base: If $n \leq g - 1$, then the graph G has no cycles. In this case $m \leq n - 1$, as required. Suppose now that $n \geq g$.

Step: First consider the case that G contains a bridge $e = (u, v)$. Then $G \setminus \{e\}$ is a union of two vertex-disjoint graphs G_1, G_2. Denote $n_1 = |V(G_1)|$, $n_2 = |V(G_2)|$, $m_1 = |E(G_1)|$, $m_2 = |E(G_2)|$. By induction hypothesis

$$m = m_1 + m_2 + 1 \leq \max\{\frac{g}{g-2}(n_1 - 2), n_1 - 1\} + \max\{\frac{g}{g-2}(n_2 - 2), n_2 - 1\} + 1. \quad (2.1)$$

The proof splits into three cases.

Case 1: $\frac{g}{g-2}(n_1 - 2) \leq n_1 - 1$ and $\frac{g}{g-2}(n_2 - 2) \leq n_2 - 1$. Then the right-hand-side of (2.1) is equal to $n - 1$, as required.

Case 2: $\frac{g}{g-2}(n_1 - 2) > n_1 - 1$ and $\frac{g}{g-2}(n_2 - 2) > n_2 - 1$. Then the right-hand-side of (2.1) is equal to $\frac{g}{g-2}(n - 4) + 1 = \frac{g}{g-2}(n - 2) - \frac{g+2}{g-2} < \frac{g}{g-2}(n - 2)$, as required.

Case 3: $\frac{g}{g-2}(n_1 - 2) > n_1 - 1$ and $\frac{g}{g-2}(n_2 - 2) \leq n_2 - 1$. (The remaining case is symmetric to Case 3.) Then the right hand side of (2.1) is equal to $\frac{g}{g-2}(n_1 - 2) + n_2 = n + \frac{2}{g-2}n_1 - \frac{2g}{g-2} \leq \frac{g}{g-2}(n - 2) = \frac{g}{g-2}n - \frac{2g}{g-2}$. This completes the analysis of the case that G contains a bridge. Next, we turn to the complimentary case (that G is bridgefree).

In this case, by Lemma 2.16, $2m = \sum_{i \geq 3} i f_i = \sum_{i \geq g} i f_i$, because there are no faces with less than g edges incident on them. It holds that $\sum_{i \geq g} i f_i \geq g \sum_{i \geq g} f_i = g \cdot f$, and so $f \leq \frac{2}{g} \cdot m$. By Euler's formula (Theorem 2.13), $2 = n - m + f \leq n - m + \frac{2}{g}m = n - \frac{g-2}{g}m$, and so $m \leq \frac{g}{g-2}(n - 2)$. In particular, for $g = 3$ we get the bound $m \leq 3n - 6$. $\square$

The upper bound from Theorem 2.17 on the number of edges of a planar graph has an important application to colorability of planar graphs.

Theorem 2.18   *Every planar graph is 6-colorable.*

Proof. Observe that there exists a vertex v with $\deg(v) \leq 5$. Indeed, otherwise all vertices have degree at least 6, and so $2|E| = \sum_{v \in V} \deg(v) \geq 6n$, i.e., $|E| \geq 3n$. The latter, however contradicts Euler's formula.

Denote the vertex v as above by v_n. Let $G = G_n$, and $G_{n-1} = G_n \setminus \{v_n\}$. G_{n-1} is a planar graph as well. Let v_{n-1} be a vertex of degree at most 5 in G_{n-1}, etc. We end up constructing a sequence of vertices $v_1, v_2, ..., v_n$, so that for every index $i \in [n]$, v_i has at most 5 neighbors v_j with index $j < i$. Now we color the vertices one after another using the palette $[6] = \{1, 2, ..., 6\}$. Suppose we have already colored $v_1, v_2, ..., v_{i-1}$, for some i, $1 \leq i \leq n$. To color v_i we note that it has at most 5 neighbors that are already colored, and thus, there is necessarily a color in our palette which is available for v_i. We color v_i by this color.   □

It is known that any planar graph is, in fact, 4-colorable [3]. The proof of this is, however, far beyond the scope of this monograph.

2.3   ARBORICITY

In this section we introduce the graph parameter called *arboricity*, and prove some basic properties of this parameter. As we shall see in the sequel (Chapters 5 and 7), arboricity and its properties play a central role in the theory of distributed graph coloring.

2.3.1   NASH-WILLIAMS THEOREM

There are two ways to define arboricity. The *density* of a graph $G = (V, E)$, denoted $\rho(G)$ is defined by

$$\rho(G) = \max_{H \subseteq V, |H| > 2} \left\lceil \frac{|E(H)|}{|H| - 1} \right\rceil,$$

where the maximum is over all possible subsets $H \subseteq V$ with at least 2 vertices. The second (and the more intuitive) way to define *arboricity* $a(G)$ of a graph $G = (V, E)$ is the following one. The arboricity $a(G)$ is the minimum number a of edge-disjoint forests $F_1, F_2, ..., F_a$, whose union covers the entire edge set E of the graph $G = (V, E)$. Such a decomposition is called an a-forest-decomposition of G.

A classical result in Graph Theory, which was proved by Nash-Williams [66] in 1961, states that the two notions are equivalent.

Theorem 2.19   *[66] For every graph $G = (V, E)$, $\rho(G) = a(G)$.*

We start with proving a straightforward direction of this theorem.

Lemma 2.20 $a(G) \geq \rho(G)$

Proof. Consider the subset $H \subseteq V$ of vertices that maximizes $\left\lceil \frac{|E(H)|}{|H|-1} \right\rceil$, i.e., $\rho(G) = \left\lceil \frac{|E(H)|}{|H|-1} \right\rceil$.
$a = a(G)$ edge-disjoint forests restricted to the vertex set H contain at most $a \cdot (|H|-1)$ edges. Since the union of some a edge-disjoint forests covers the entire edge set E, it follows that $|E(H)| \leq a \cdot (|H|-1)$. Hence $a \geq \frac{|E(H)|}{|H|-1}$. Since a is an integer it follows that $a \geq \left\lceil \frac{|E(H)|}{|H|-1} \right\rceil = \rho(G)$. $\qquad\square$

Before we turn to the proof of the non-trivial direction of the Nash-Williams theorem, we prove a number of basic properties of arboricity.

Lemma 2.21   *The subset $H \subseteq V$ with at least two vertices which maximizes $\frac{|E(H)|}{|H|-1}$, is contained in a single connected component of G.*

Proof. Suppose that $G(H)$ decomposes into connected components $G(H_1), G(H_2), ..., G(H_t)$, for some integer $t \geq 1$. Then we argue that

$$\frac{|E(H)|}{|H|-1} = \frac{\sum_{i=1}^{t} |E(H_i)|}{\left(\sum_{i=1}^{t} |H_i|\right) - 1} \leq \max_{1 \leq i \leq t} \left\{ \frac{|E(H_i)|}{|H_i|-1} \right\}, \tag{2.2}$$

and, moreover, the equality is attained only if $t = 1$. (Observe that each H_i contains at least two vertices. Otherwise single-vertex components can be removed, and as a result a subset $H' \subseteq H$ with a larger ratio $\frac{|E(H')|}{|H'|-1}$ will be obtained, contradiction.)

Denote $|E(H_i)| = \alpha_i$, $|H_i| = \beta_i$, $|H_i| - 1 = \gamma_i$, for every $i \in [t]$. Suppose without loss of generality that $\max_{1 \leq i \leq t} \left\{ \frac{\alpha_i}{\gamma_i} \right\} = \frac{\alpha_1}{\gamma_1}$. The proof that $\frac{\sum_{i=1}^{t} \alpha_i}{\sum_{i=1}^{t} \gamma_i} \leq \frac{\alpha_1}{\gamma_1}$ is by induction on i. The base is trivial. For the induction step write

$$\frac{\sum_{i=1}^{t+1} \alpha_i}{\sum_{i=1}^{t+1} \gamma_i} = \frac{\sum_{i=2}^{t+1} \alpha_i + \alpha_1}{\sum_{i=2}^{t+1} \gamma_i + \gamma_1},$$

and denote $\alpha_2' = \sum_{i=2}^{t+1} \alpha_i$, $\gamma_2' = \sum_{i=2}^{t+1} \gamma_i$. Now the right-hand side is equal to $\frac{\alpha_1 + \alpha_2'}{\gamma_1 + \gamma_2'}$. By induction hypothesis, $\frac{\alpha_2'}{\gamma_2'} \leq \frac{\alpha_2}{\gamma_2}$. Without loss of generality, let $\frac{\alpha_2}{\gamma_2} = \max_{2 \leq i \leq t+1} \left\{ \frac{\alpha_i}{\gamma_i} \right\}$. Hence $\frac{\alpha_1}{\gamma_1} \geq \frac{\alpha_2}{\gamma_2} \geq \frac{\alpha_2'}{\gamma_2'}$, and so $\frac{\alpha_1 + \alpha_2'}{\gamma_1 + \gamma_2'} \leq \frac{\alpha_1}{\gamma_1}$. This completes the proof of inequality (2.2). Moreover, for $t > 1$,

$$\frac{\sum_{i=1}^{t} \alpha_i}{\left(\sum_{i=1}^{t} \beta_i\right) - 1} < \frac{\sum_{i=1}^{t} \alpha_i}{\sum_{i=1}^{t} (\beta_i - 1)} \leq \frac{\alpha_1}{\beta_1 - 1}.$$

Hence the equality in (2.2) is attained only if $t = 1$.

Hence if $G(H)$ consists of more than one connected component then there exists a connected components $G(H_1)$ of $G(H)$ that satisfies

$$\frac{\sum_{i=1}^{t} |E(H_i)|}{(\sum_{i=1}^{t} |H_i|) - 1} < \frac{|E(H_1)|}{|H_1| - 1},$$

contradicting the maximality of H.   □

Note that Lemma 2.21 implies that $\rho(G) = \max_{1 \le i \le t} \rho(G_i)$, where $G_1, G_2, ..., G_t$ are connected components of G. Next we prove the non-trivial direction of the Nash-Williams theorem. Our proof is based on [15].

Lemma 2.22 $\rho(G) \ge a(G)$,

Proof. Let G be a counter-example that minimizes $|V| + |E|$. G satisfies $a(G) > \rho(G)$.

Claim 2.23 G is connected.

Proof. Suppose for contradiction that G consists of $t > 1$ connected components $G_1, G_2, ..., G_t$. We have seen that $\rho(G) = \max_{1 \le i \le t} \rho(G_i)$. Also, clearly, $a(G) = \max_{1 \le i \le t} a(G_i)$. If $\rho(G_i) \ge a(G_i)$ for every $i \in [t]$, then $a(G) = \max_{1 \le i \le t} a(G_i) \le \max_{1 \le i \le t} \rho(G_i) = \rho(G)$. This is a contradiction to $a(G) > \rho(G)$.

Hence there exists an index $i \in [t]$ with $a(G_i) > \rho(G_i)$, contradicting the minimality of G. This completes the proof of the claim that G is connected.   □

Observe that $|V| > 1$, because otherwise $a(G) = 0$.

Claim 2.24 G is critical with respect to arboricity, i.e., $a(G \setminus e) < a(G)$ holds for every edge $e \in E$.

Proof. Indeed, otherwise, there exists an edge $e \in E$ such that $a(G \setminus e) = a(G)$. Also, $\rho(G \setminus e) \le \rho(G)$. Hence $a(G \setminus e) = a(G) > \rho(G) \ge \rho(G \setminus e)$, contradicting the maximality of G. This completes the proof of the claim that G is critical with respect to arboricity.   □

For a graph G' that satisfies the assertion of Claim 2.24, we will say that G' is $a(G)$-arb-critical. For a graph $G' = (V', E')$ and its forest-decomposition $\mathcal{E} = (F_1, F_2, ..., F_t)$, $E' = \bigcup_{i=1}^{t} F_i$, and $F_i \cap F_j = \emptyset$ for every $i \ne j$, we say that $\mathcal{E}$ is a t-forest-decomposition of G'.

Claim 2.25   Let $G = (V, E)$ be a connected and $a(G)$-arb-critical graph, and $|V| > 1$. Let $a = a(G)$. Then for every edge $e \in E$, any $(a - 1)$-forest-decomposition of $(G \setminus e)$ is a decomposition into $(a - 1)$ spanning trees of G.

Before we prove this claim, we argue that it implies Lemma 2.22. Denote $n = |V|$. Since $(a - 1)$ edge-disjoint spanning trees contain $(n - 1)(a - 1)$ edges, it follows that $|E| - 1 = |E(G \setminus e)| = (n - 1) \cdot (a - 1)$, for every edge e. But,

$$a(G) > \rho(G) = \max_{H \subseteq V, |H| \geq 2} \left\lceil \frac{|E(H)|}{|H| - 1} \right\rceil.$$

Hence $a = a(G) > \left\lceil \frac{|E|}{n-1} \right\rceil = \left\lceil \frac{(n-1)(a-1)+1}{n-1} \right\rceil = a$. This is a contradiction to $a(G) > \rho(G)$. So we only need to prove Claim 2.25 to complete the proof of Lemma 2.22 (and of Nash-Williams theorem).

Proof. (of Claim 2.25): Suppose for contradiction that there exists an edge $e = (u, v) \in E$ and the decomposition of the edge set $E \setminus e$ into $(a - 1)$ edge-disjoint forests $E_1, E_2, ..., E_{a-1}$ in which E_1 is not a spanning tree.

The edge set $E_1 \cup \{e\}$ contains a cycle, as otherwise we get a decomposition of E into $a - 1$ edge disjoint forests, $E_1 \cup \{e\}, E_2, ..., E_{a-1}$. (This is, however, a contradiction to the assumption that $a(G) = a$.) Hence both endpoints u and v of e are in a connected component T of E_1. Let $U = G(V(T))$ be the subgraph induced by $V(T)$ in G. Note that $e \in E(U)$. Since E_1 is not a spanning tree, $V(T) \neq V(G)$. Since G is connected, $E(G) \setminus E(U) \neq \emptyset$. Since G is a-arb-critical, it follows that U has a decomposition into $(a - 1)$ edge-disjoint forests $E(U) = A_1 \cup A_2 \cup ... \cup A_{a-1}$.

Consider the set $\mathcal{S}$ of all a-forest-decompositions of G of the form $(E_1', ..., E_{a-1}', \{e'\})$, with $e' \in E(U)$ and such that a connected component of E_1' is a spanning tree of U. Observe that $(E_1, ..., E_{a-1}, \{e\}) \in \mathcal{S}$. Let $\mathcal{E} = (\bar{E}_1, ..., \bar{E}_{a-1}, \{\bar{e}\}) \in \mathcal{S}$ be an a-forest-decomposition of G that maximizes

$$\mathcal{J}(\mathcal{E}) = \sum_{i=1}^{a-1} |A_i \cap \bar{E}_i|.$$

Recall that $(A_1, A_2, ..., A_{a-1})$ is a fixed $(a - 1)$-forest-decomposition of U. Since $\bar{e} \in E(U)$, it follows that $\bar{e} \in A_t$ for some $t \in [a - 1]$. Fix an index t such that $\bar{e} \in A_t$. The edge set $\bar{E}_t \cup \{\bar{e}\}$ contains a cycle C which contains the edge $\bar{e}$. (Indeed, otherwise $(\bar{E}_1, ..., \bar{E}_{t-1}, \bar{E}_t \cup \{\bar{e}\}, \bar{E}_{t+1}, ..., \bar{E}_{a-1})$ is an $(a - 1)$-forest-decomposition of G, contradiction.)

Claim 2.26 *All edges of C are in $E(U)$, i.e., $E(C) \subseteq E(U)$.*

Proof. The proof splits into two cases, depending on the volume of t.
Case 1: $(t = 1)$. Since $\mathcal{E} \in \mathcal{S}$, it follows that a connected component T of $\bar{E}_1$ is a spanning tree for U. Also, $\bar{E}_1 \cup \{\bar{e}\}$ contains the cycle C, with $\bar{e} \in C$. Hence $T \cup \{\bar{e}\}$ contains C. Finally, $\bar{e} \in E(U)$. Hence $E(C) \subseteq T \subseteq E(U)$.
Case 2: $(t \neq 1)$. Suppose that $E(C)$ is not contained in $E(U)$. $\mathcal{E} = (\bar{E}_1, \bar{E}_2, ..., \bar{E}_{a-1}, \{\bar{e}\})$ is an a-forest-decomposition of G. A connected component T of $\bar{E}_1$ is a spanning tree for U, and

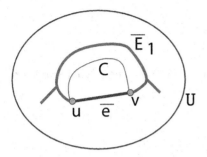

Figure 2.5: An illustration for Case 1 (i.e., $t = 1$).

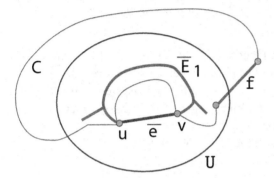

Figure 2.6: An illustration for Case 2 (i.e., $t \neq 1$).

$\bar{e} \in E(U)$. Also $\bar{e} \in A_t$ for some $t \in [a-1]$, where $E(U) = A_1 \cup ... \cup A_{a-1}$. Finally, $\bar{E}_t \cup \{\bar{e}\}$ contains a cycle C, $\bar{e} \in C$. Let $f \in E(C)$ be an edge with one endpoint in $V(U) = T$ and the other point in $V(G) \setminus V(U)$. (It exists because $E(C) \not\subseteq E(U)$.)

Since a connected component of $\bar{E}_1$ spans U, it follows that $\bar{E}_1 \cup \{f\}$ is acyclic. Thus $(\bar{E}_1 \cup \{f\}, ..., \bar{E}_{t-1}, \bar{E}_t \cup \{e\} \setminus \{f\}, \bar{E}_{t+1}, ..., \bar{E}_{a-1})$ is an $(a-1)$-forest-decomposition of G, contradiction. This completes the proof of Claim 2.26. □

Now we return to the proof of Claim 2.25. Recall that $\bar{e} \in A_t$, and $(A_1, A_2, ..., A_{a-1})$ is an $(a-1)$-forest-decomposition of U. Since A_t is a forest (i.e., acyclic), there exists an edge $f \in E(C) \setminus A_t \subseteq E(U)$. But $\tilde{\mathcal{E}} = (\bar{E}_1, ..., \bar{E}_{t-1}, \tilde{E}_t = \bar{E}_t \cup \{\bar{e}\} \setminus \{f\}, \bar{E}_{t+1}, ..., \bar{E}_{a-1}, \{f\})$ is a decomposition in $\mathcal{S}$. Note that

$$\mathcal{J}(\tilde{\mathcal{E}}) = \mathcal{J}(\mathcal{E}) + 1. \tag{2.3}$$

To see it, observe that $\tilde{E}_t \cap A_t$ contains also the edge $\bar{e}$ (which also belongs to A_t), while $\bar{e} \notin \bar{E}_t$.
But (2.3) is a contradiction to the maximality of $\mathcal{J}(\mathcal{E})$. □

This completes the proof of Claim 2.25, and hence of Nash-Williams theorem. □

Next, we present several bounds on the number of edges and high-degree vertices in graphs of bounded arboricity. We need the following definition.

Definition 2.27 *For a pair of vertex sets $A, B \subseteq V$ in a graph $G = (V, E)$, denote by $E(A, B)$ the set of edges $\{(a, b) \in E \mid a \in A, b \in B\}$.*

Lemma 2.28 *Let G be a graph with m edges, n vertices and arboricity a. Then*
(1) $m \leq a \cdot n$.
(2) The number of vertices with degree at least $t \geq a + 1$ is at most $\frac{m}{t-a} \leq \frac{a \cdot n}{t-a}$.
(3) The number of edges whose endpoints both have degree at least $t \geq a + 1$ is at most $\frac{a \cdot m}{t-a}$.

Proof. (1) follows from the definition of arboricity. Denote $U = \{u \mid \deg(u) \geq t\}$. By definition of arboricity, $|E(U)| \leq a \cdot |U|$. Thus, (1) and (2) implies (3). So it remains to prove (2). Also by definition of U, it holds that $\sum_{u \in U} \deg(u) \geq t \cdot |U|$. For a fixed vertex $u \in U$, let $\deg(u, U)$ denote the number of neighbors it has in U. Since $\deg(u) \geq t$, it follows that

$$\deg(u, V \setminus U) = \deg(u) - \deg(u, U) \geq t - \deg(u, U).$$

Hence

$$|E(U, V \setminus U)| = \sum_{u \in U} \deg(u, V \setminus U) \geq \sum_{u \in U} (t - \deg(u, U)).$$

Also,

$$m \geq |E(U, V \setminus U)| + |E(U)| \geq \sum_{u \in U} (t - \deg(u, U)) + \frac{1}{2} \sum_{u \in U} \deg(u, U)$$

$$= t \cdot |U| - \frac{1}{2} \sum_{u \in U} \deg(u, U) = t \cdot |U| - |E(U)| \geq (t - a)|U|.$$

Since $a \cdot n \geq m$, we conclude that $U \leq \frac{a \cdot n}{t-a}$, as required. $\square$

2.3.2 DEGENERACY AND ARBORICITY

In this section we define the notion of *degeneracy*, which is closely related to the notion of arboricity.

Definition 2.29 *For a graph $G = (V, E)$, the degeneracy $degen(G)$ is the minimum integer number d so that there exists an ordering of the vertex set of G, $V = (v_1, v_2, ..., v_n)$, such that for every index $i \in [n-1]$, v_i has at most d neighbors with greater index. For a vertex v and a vertex set U, let $\deg(v, U)$ denote the number of neighbors that v has in U.*

By a previous argument (see Theorem 2.18), $\chi(G) \leq degen(G) + 1$. (Once $\{v_2, v_3, ..., v_n\}$ are all colored by $d + 1$ colors, $d = degen(G)$, there is necessarily an available color for v_1 in the palette $[d + 1]$.) We have seen (Section 2.2) that for a planar graph G, $degen(G) \leq 5$, and thus, $\chi(G) \leq 6$.

Also, there exist graphs G with $degen(G) = d$ and $\chi(G) = d + 1$, for every value of d. A clique K_{d+1} with $d + 1$ vertices is an example of such a graph. Next, we analyze the relationship between arboricity and degeneracy in general.

Lemma 2.30 *For a graph $G = (V, E)$, $degen(G) \leq 2a(G) - 1$.*

Proof. Consider the following process. If there exists a vertex v with $deg_G(v) \leq 2a(G) - 1$, set $v_1 = v$, and remove v (and all edges incident on v) from G. Iterate up until there is no vertex with degree at most $2a(G) - 1$. (Each new vertex that we add was appended to the end of the sequence.) If this process eliminated all graph vertices, then we have obtained an ordering $(v_1, v_2, ..., v_n)$, such that for every $i \in [n - 1]$, the vertex v_i has at most $2a(G) - 1$ neighbors with greater index. This proves that $degen(G) \leq 2a(G) - 1$.

Hence it remains to consider the case that some vertices are left. In this case there exists a subset $U \subseteq V$ of vertices such that the minimum degree $\delta(G(U))$ of a vertex in the graph $G(U)$ induced by U is at least $2a(G)$. Note that $|U| \geq 2$. But then

$$\left\lceil \frac{|E(U)|}{|U| - 1} \right\rceil \geq \left\lceil \frac{2a(G) \cdot |U|/2}{|U| - 1} \right\rceil = \left\lceil \frac{a(G) \cdot |U|}{|U| - 1} \right\rceil \geq a + 1.$$

But

$$a(G) = \max_{H \subseteq V, |H| \geq 2} \left\lceil \frac{|E(H)|}{|H| - 1} \right\rceil,$$

contradiction. $\square$

Lemma 2.30 implies that $\chi(G) \leq degen(G) + 1 \leq 2a(G)$. The inequality $degen(G) \leq 2a(G) - 1$ is tight, because $degen(K_{2a}) = 2a - 1$ and $a(K_{2a}) = \left\lceil \frac{2a \cdot (2a-1)/2}{2a-1} \right\rceil = a$. Also, $\chi(K_{2a}) = 2a$. The next lemma provides a lower bound on the degeneracy in terms of the arboricity.

Lemma 2.31 *For every graph $G = (V, E)$, it holds that $degen(G) \geq a(G)$.*

Proof. Let $U \subseteq V$, $|U| \geq 2$, be a subset of vertices. Let $\sigma = (v_1, v_2, ..., v_n)$ be an ordering of vertices which satisfies that v_i has at most d neighbors with greater index, for every $i \in [n - 1]$.

Let $U = (u_1, u_2, ..., u_k)$ be the set U ordered according to σ. Denote by $\deg(u, U)$ the number of neighbors that a vertex u has within a vertex set U. It follows that

$$|E(U)| = \sum_{i=1}^{k-1} \deg(u_i, \{u_{i+1}, u_{i+2}, ..., u_k\}) \leq d \cdot (k-1).$$

Hence $\frac{|E(U)|}{|U|-1} \leq \frac{d(k-1)}{k-1} = d$. Hence

$$a(G) = \max_{U \subseteq V, |U| \geq 2} \left\lceil \frac{|E(U)|}{|U|-1} \right\rceil \leq d = \operatorname{degen}(G).$$

$\square$

This inequality is also tight as long as $a(G) \leq c\sqrt{n}$, for a sufficiently small constant c. To summarize, $a(G) \leq \operatorname{degen}(G) \leq 2a(G) - 1$, i.e., these two parameters are equivalent up to a factor of 2. An example with $a(G) = \operatorname{degen}(G)$ is the graph $G = (V, E)$, $V = (v_1, v_2, .., , v_n)$, in which each vertex v_i is connected to $v_{i-1}, v_{i-2}, ..., v_{\max\{1,i-a\}}$, for every $i \in [n]$. Its degeneracy is clearly a. Its arboricity is given by

$$a(G) = \left\lceil \frac{1 + 2 + ... + (a-1) + (n-a) \cdot a}{n-1} \right\rceil = \left\lceil \frac{(n-1)a - (a-1)a/2}{n-1} \right\rceil = a - \left\lfloor \frac{(a-1)a}{2(n-1)} \right\rfloor.$$

For $a < c\sqrt{n}$, for a sufficiently small constant c, it holds that $(a-1)a < 2(n-1)$, and the right-hand-side is equal to a.

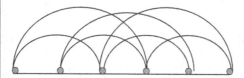

Figure 2.7: An example of a graph G with $\operatorname{degen}(G) = a(G)$. Here both parameters are equal to 3.

The next simple lemma provides an upper bound for arboricity in terms of the maximum degree.

Lemma 2.32 $a(G) \leq \Delta(G)$, *for every graph G.*

Proof. For a set $U \subseteq V$, $|U| \geq 2$, it holds that $\left\lceil \frac{|E(U)|}{|U|-1} \right\rceil = \left\lceil \frac{\Delta \cdot |U|}{2(|U|-1)} \right\rceil \leq \Delta$. $\square$

It is equally easy to see that $\operatorname{degen}(G) \leq \Delta(G)$. Indeed, there is clearly an ordering $(v_1, v_2, ..., v_n)$ such that $\deg(v_i, \{v_{i+1}, ..., v_n\}) \leq \Delta$ for all $i \in [n-1]$.

2.4   DEFECTIVE COLORING

In this section we introduce and discuss a relaxed notion of coloring, called *defective coloring*. It was formally defined in the mid-eighties by [19, 20, 36], but was implicitly studied already in the mid-sixties [58]. Quite recently defective coloring was shown to be very useful for computing legal colorings in the distributed setting [8, 9, 10, 48]. We will discuss this relationship in detail in Chapters 6–7, and in Section 8.2.

Definition 2.33   *For a coloring φ of a graph $G = (V, E)$, the* defect *of a vertex $v \in V$ under the coloring φ, denoted $def_\varphi(v)$, is the number of neighbors $u \in \Gamma(v)$ that satisfy $\varphi(u) = \varphi(v)$.*

Note that for any vertex v and any coloring φ, $def_\varphi(v) \leq \deg(v) \leq \Delta$. Observe also that for a legal coloring φ, every vertex v has defect zero under φ.

Definition 2.34   *The* defect *of a coloring φ of a graph $G = (V, E)$ is the maximum defect of its vertices, i.e., $def(\varphi) = \max_{v \in V} def_\varphi(v)$.*

For a pair of non-negative integer parameters p, q, a coloring φ is said to be q-defective p-coloring if it employs colors only from the palette $[p]$ and its defect is at most q.

We next state and prove a fundamental (though very simple) fact (due to Lovasz [58]) about defective colorings.

Lemma 2.35   *For a graph $G = (V, E)$ with maximum degree Δ and an integer parameter $p \in [\Delta]$, there exists a $\frac{\Delta}{p}$-defective p-coloring of G.*

Proof. We describe an iterative process that, as we argue, ends up producing a desired coloring. It starts with an arbitrary p-coloring φ_0 of G. Let B_0 denote the set of edges $e = (u, v)$ which are colored monochromatically (i.e., $\varphi(u) = \varphi_0(v)$) by φ_0. For $i = 1, 2, \ldots$, let φ_i denote the coloring produced by this iterative process after i^{th} iteration, and B_i be the set of edges colored monochromatically by φ_i.

The iteration i of the process, for $i = 1, 2, \ldots$, proceeds as follows. If for every vertex $v \in V$, $def_{\varphi_i}(v) \leq \frac{\Delta}{p}$, then the process terminates, and returns the coloring φ_i. Otherwise we pick an arbitrary vertex $v \in V$ with $def_{\varphi_i}(v) > \frac{\Delta}{p}$. Denote $\alpha = \varphi_i(v)$. There exists a color $\beta \in [p] \setminus \{\alpha\}$ such that at most $\frac{\Delta}{p}$ neighbors u of v satisfy $\varphi_i(u) = \beta$. We recolor v by the color β. In other words, the new coloring φ_{i+1} agrees with φ_i in every vertex, except for the vertex v. The new color $\varphi_{i+1}(v)$ is set to β. This completes the description of the iterative process.

Denote by v_i, for $i = 1, 2, \ldots$, the vertex which is recolored in the ith iteration of the process. Let $A(v_i) = \{(v_i, u) \in E \mid \varphi_i(v_i) = \varphi_i(u)\}$ (respectively, $A'(v_i) = \{(v_i, u) \in E \mid \varphi_{i+1}(v_i) = \varphi_{i+1}(u)\}$) denote the set of edges incident on v_i which are colored monochromatically by φ_i (resp., φ_{i+1}). Observe that $B_{i+1} = (B_i \setminus A(v_i)) \cup A'(v_i)$. Moreover, $A(v_i) \cap$

$A'(v_i) = \emptyset$, and thus $|B_{i+1}| = |B_i| - |A(v_i)| + |A'(v_i)|$. Recall that $|A(v_i)| > \frac{\Delta}{p}$, and $|A'(v_i)| \leq \frac{\Delta}{p}$. Hence $|B_{i+1}| < |B_i|$. Since both $|B_{i+1}|$ and $|B_i|$ are integers, $|B_{i+1}| \leq |B_i| - 1$. Recall that $|B_0| \leq |E|$, and thus the process cannot continue for more than $|E|$ iterations. Hence after at most $|E|$ iterations the cardinality of the set B_i cannot decrease further, and the process returns a $\frac{\Delta}{p}$-defective coloring. Note also that all the colorings $\varphi_0, \varphi_1, \varphi_2, ...,$ employ p colors, and we are done. $\qquad\square$

Next we present a notion of *arbefective coloring*, which is closely related to defective coloring. It was introduced in [9] in the context of distributed graph coloring. (See Chapter 7.)

Definition 2.36 *Consider a graph $G = (V, E)$ with arboricity a, and a pair of integer non-negative parameters p and q. A p-coloring φ of G is called q-arbdefective if for every index $i \in [p]$, the subset $V_i = \{v \in V \mid \varphi(v) = i\}$ induces a subgraph $G(V_i)$ of arboricity at most q.*

Lemma 2.37 *Let d and p be a pair of positive integers, $p \leq d$. For a graph $G = (V, E)$ with degeneracy d, there exists a p-coloring φ that satisfies that for every index $i \in [p]$, the subset $V_i = \{v \in V \mid \varphi(v) = i\}$ induces a subgraph $G(V_i)$ with degeneracy at most $\frac{d}{p}$.*

Proof. Let $V = (v_1, v_2, ..., v_n)$ be an ordering of the vertex set of G that satisfies that for every index $j \in [n]$, $\deg(v_j, \{v_1, v_2, ..., v_{j-1}\}) \leq d$. Such an ordering exists because G has degeneracy at most d. Suppose that we have already computed a p-coloring φ of $\{v_1, v_2, ..., v_{j-1}\}$ that satisfies that for every index $k \in [j-1]$, the vertex v_k has at most $\frac{d}{p}$ neighbors in $\{v_1, v_2, ..., v_{k-1}\}$ with the same φ-color. (The induction base, $j = 1$, holds vacuously.) By pigeonhole principle there exists a color $\alpha \in [p]$ such that v_j has at most $\frac{d}{p}$ neighbors in $\{v_1, v_2, ..., v_{j-1}\}$ colored by α. We set $\varphi(v_j) = \alpha$.

For some index $i \in [p]$, consider the subsequence $U = (u_1, u_2, ..., u_h)$ of $(v_1, v_2, ..., v_n)$ which contains only the vertices of V_i (i.e., vertices φ-colored by the color i). Each vertex u_j, $j \in [h]$, in this subsequence has at most $\frac{d}{p}$ neighbors with smaller index in U. Thus $G(V_i)$ has degeneracy at most $\frac{d}{p}$, for every $i \in [p]$. $\qquad\square$

Consider a graph $G = (V, E)$ with arboricity a, and an integer parameter p, $p \in [2a - 1]$. By Lemma 2.30, $\deg\text{en}(G) \leq 2a - 1$. Hence, by Lemma 2.37, there exists a p-coloring φ of G such that for every index $i \in [p]$, $\deg\text{en}(G(V_i)) \leq \frac{2a-1}{p}$. Hence $a(G(V_i)) \leq \deg\text{en}(G(V_i)) \leq \frac{2a-1}{p}$.

Corollary 2.38 *For a graph $G = (V, E)$ with arboricity $a = a(G)$, and an integer parameter $p \in [2a - 1]$, there exists a $(\frac{2a-1}{p})$-arbdefective p-coloring φ of G.*

2.5   EDGE-COLORING AND MATCHINGS

In this section we describe some basic results concerning edge-coloring. Edge-coloring is closely related to vertex-coloring, and it is an interesting primitive on its own right. Given a graph $G = (V, E)$, an *edge-coloring* $\varphi : E \rightarrow \{1, 2, ...\}$ is a function from the edges set E of the graph to positive integers. It is called *legal* if any two adjacent edges e_1 and e_2 (i.e., $e_1 \cap e_2 \neq \emptyset$) are colored by different colors. Observe that each color class of a legal edge-coloring is a matching. (An edges set $M \subseteq E$ is called a *matching* if for every pair of edges $e, e' \in M$, $e \neq e'$ implies $e \cap e' = \emptyset$. A matching M is called *maximal* if $M \cup \{e\}$ is not a matching, for every edge $e \in E \setminus M$.)

A useful notion in this context is the notion of *line graphs*. For the graph $G = (V, E)$, the line graph $L(G) = (E, \mathcal{E})$ is defined as follows. The vertices of the line graph correspond to edges of the original graph. Two distinct vertices $e, e' \in E$ of $L(G)$ are connected by an edge in $L(G)$ if the respective edges e, e' in G incident to one another (i.e., $(e, e') \in \mathcal{E}$ if $e \cap e' \neq \emptyset$). Observe that an MIS in $L(G)$ is a maximal matching (shortly, MM) in G. Also, a legal vertex-coloring of $L(G)$ is a legal edge-coloring of G. The *chromatic index* $\chi'(G)$ of a graph $G = (V, E)$ is the minimum possible number of colors in a legal edge-coloring of G. It is straightforward to verify that $\chi'(G) = \chi(L(G))$.

Consider a graph $G = (V, E)$ with maximum degree Δ. Every edge $e \in E$ is incident on up to $2(\Delta - 1)$ other edges of G. Hence the maximum degree $\Delta(L(G))$ of the line graph $L(G)$ is $\Delta(L(G)) \leq 2(\Delta - 1)$. (See Figure 2.8.) Hence the chromatic number $\chi(L(G))$ of the line graph satisfies $\chi'(G) = \chi(L(G)) \leq \Delta(L(G)) + 1 \leq 2\Delta - 1$. On the other hand, obviously $\chi'(G) \geq \Delta$. (Because for a vertex $v \in V$ with degree $\deg(v) = \Delta$, the Δ edges incident on v require Δ distinct colors.)

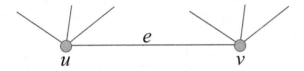

Figure 2.8: Each of the endpoints of e is incident to up to $\Delta - 1$ edges other than e.

Therefore, $\Delta \leq \chi'(G) \leq 2\Delta - 1$. However, a stronger bound is known. A seminal theorem by Vizing [75] states that $\chi'(G) \leq \Delta + 1$. The proof can be found e.g., in [13] pages 153-154. As a corollary of Vizing's theorem, for every graph G either $\chi'(G) = \Delta$ or $\chi'(G) = \Delta + 1$. Distinguishing between these two cases is NP-hard even for cubic (i.e., 3-regular) graphs. However, interestingly, for many families of graphs it holds that $\chi'(G) = \Delta$. In particular, this is the case for bipartite graphs (see, e.g., [13] page 152), and for planar graphs with $\Delta \geq 7$. (The latter was shown by Vizing [76] for $\Delta \geq 8$. He also showed that this is not the case for $\Delta \leq 5$. The case $\Delta = 7$ was settled by Sanders and Zhao [72]. Finally, the case $\Delta = 6$ is open. See [17], and the reference therein.)

CHAPTER 3

Basic Distributed Graph Coloring Algorithns

In this section we turn to the distributed model, and describe the classical algorithms for graph coloring and computing an MIS. We start with the formal definition of the model.

3.1 THE DISTIRUBUTED MESSAGE-PASSING $\mathcal{LOCAL}$ MODEL

In the message-passing $\mathcal{LOCAL}$ model of distributed computing a communication network is modeled by an n-vertex undirected unweighted graph $G = (V, E)$. The network is static, and so its topology does not change during an execution of an algorithm. The processors in the network are represented by the vertices of G. For each two vertices $u, v \in V$, there is an edge $(u, v) \in E$ if and only if the two processors corresponding to u and v in the network are connected by a communication link. Each vertex has a unique identity number. These numbers are assumed to belong to the range $\{1, 2, ..., n\}$. (However, all algorithms described in this monograph are applicable also for wider ranges of identity numbers. Specifically, it is sufficient that the identity number can be represented as a bit sequence of length $O(\log n)$.)

Initially, each vertex v knows only its identity number $Id(v)$. The vertices communicate over the edges of E in the *synchronous manner*. Specifically, a computation (or equivalently, an algorithm) starts simultaneously in all vertices, and proceeds in discrete rounds. In each round each vertex v is allowed to send a message (of unbounded size) to each of its neighbors. A vertex is allowed to send distinct messages to distinct neighbors. All messages that are sent in a certain round arrive to their destinations before the next round starts. The number of rounds that elapse from the beginning of the algorithm until its end is called the *running time* of the algorithm. Vertices are allowed to perform unbounded local computations. Computations that are performed locally are not taken into account in the running time analysis of distributed algorithms in this model.

3.2 BASIC COLOR REDUCTION

In this section we describe a few simple and most fundamental algorithms for coloring and computing a maximal independent set. Suppose we have a graph $G = (V, E)$ with maximum degree Δ, which is legally α-colored by a coloring φ, for some $\alpha \geq \Delta + 1$. The following routine reduces the number of colors to $(\Delta + 1)$ within $\alpha - (\Delta + 1)$ rounds. In the beginning of each round each vertex sends its current color to all its neighbors. In the first round each vertex v of color α recolors itself in parallel into an available color from the palette $[\Delta + 1]$. Specifically, the set $\Gamma(v)$ of neighbors of v is colored with at most Δ colors, i.e., $|\varphi(\Gamma(v))| \leq \Delta$. Hence there exists an available color $\beta \in [\Delta + 1] \setminus \{\varphi(\Gamma(v))\}$. Observe that the set of vertices that are colored by color α form an independent set. Thus, the resulting coloring φ_1 is legal as well, and it employs just $\alpha - 1$ colors. (The coloring φ_1 is legal since for each edge $(u, v) \in E$, at most one endpoint has selected a new color. Suppose without loss of generality that this endpoint is u. Then $\varphi_1(u) \neq \varphi(v) = \varphi_1(v)$.) Repeating this procedure for colors $\alpha - 1, \alpha - 2, ..., \Delta + 2$ results in a legal $(\Delta + 1)$-coloring $\psi = \varphi_{\alpha-(\Delta+1)}$. This coloring is computed within $\alpha - (\Delta + 1)$ rounds.

A similar procedure enables one to use an α-coloring φ for computing an MIS within α rounds. Initialize a set U as an empty set. For $i = 1, 2, ..., \alpha$, each vertex v with $\varphi(v) = i$ checks in parallel if it has a neighbor in U. If it does not, it joins U, and sends a message to its neighbors to inform them about this. By induction on i, it is easy to verify that after i rounds the set U is an MIS for the graph $G(\{v \mid 1 \leq \varphi(v) \leq i\})$, for each $i \leq \alpha$. Hence after α rounds, U is an MIS for G. Moreover, it is possible to employ an α-*edge*-coloring ψ for computing a maximal matching within α rounds using the same idea. Specifically, for $i = 1, 2, ..., \alpha$, in round i all edges e with $\psi(e) = i$ that have no incident edges in the matching join it. It is easy to verify that after α rounds a maximal matching is constructed. (The last procedure is, essentially, an MIS computation on the line graph that is initially α-*vertex*-colored. See Chapter 2.5 for the definition of line graphs, and more details.)

3.3   ORIENTATIONS

An orientation μ is an assignment of directions to the edges of G, where each edge (u, v) is directed either toward u or toward v. If an orientation does not contain any consistently oriented cycles (i.e., simple cycles in which each vertex has out-degree 1 and in-degree 1) it is said to be an *acyclic orientation*. Acyclic orientations turn out to be very useful for graph coloring. In this section we present several helpful properties of acyclic orientations.

Definition 3.1   *(1) The* out-degree *of an acyclic orientation μ of G (or, shortly, μ-out-degree) is the maximum out-degree of a vertex in G with respect to μ.*
(2) The length *of an acyclic orientation μ of G is the length of the longest directed (with respect to μ) path in G. (A directed path is a path $P = \langle v_0, v_1, ..., v_\ell \rangle$, such that for all $i \in \{1, 2, ..., \ell\}$, the edge (v_{i-1}, v_i) is oriented toward v_i.)*
(3) For an edge (u, v) oriented toward v by μ, the vertex v is called the parent *of u under μ. The vertex u is called the* child *of v under μ.*

Property 3.2   *[28] A graph G with an acyclic orientation μ of length k can be colored using $k + 1$ colors in $k + 1$ rounds.*

Proof. In round i, for $i = 1, 2, ..., k + 1$, we color by color i the vertices all of whose parents have been already colored in previous rounds. Since the orientation is acyclic, in each round at least one vertex is colored. (In particular, in the first round there must be a vertex with no outgoing edges, and it is colored by color 1.) Since each edge is oriented, its endpoints are colored in different rounds. The parent endpoint is colored before the child endpoint. Thus the endpoints are colored with different colors. Consequently, in the end of this procedure, if all vertices are colored then we obtain a legal $(k + 1)$-coloring.

Next, we argue that indeed all vertices obtain a color within $k + 1$ rounds. Consider any vertex $v \in V$. Each directed path that emanates from this vertex has length at most k. By induction on i it is easy to see that if all paths that emanate from a vertex v have length at most i, then v is colored in round $i + 1$ or before. Hence all vertices obtain a color within $k + 1$ rounds.   □

Property 3.3   *[28] A graph G with an acyclic orientation μ of length k and out-degree d can be colored with $d + 1$ colors in $k + 1$ rounds.*

Proof. Similarly to the proof of Property 3.2, in round i, for $i = 1, 2, ..., k + 1$, we color the vertices all of whose parents have been already colored in previous rounds. However, the color of a vertex v is selected in a different way. Specifically, it is a color from the range $\{1, 2, ..., d + 1\}$ which is not used by any of the parents of v. Since v has at most d parents, such a color can always be found. The resulting coloring is legal, since for any pair of neighbors u and v, the child endpoint selects a color that is different from its parent's color. Similarly to the argument in the proof of Property 3.2, all vertices obtain a color within $k + 1$ rounds.   □

Properties 3.2–3.3 demonstrate that acyclic orientations are very helpful for computing colorings. But the opposite direction is also true: colorings can be used for computing acyclic orientations.

Property 3.4   *A graph G with a legal k-coloring φ can be assigned an acyclic orientation μ with length $k - 1$.*

Proof. We orient each edge $(u, v) \in E$ toward the endpoint which is colored by a greater color. (Since the coloring is legal, the color of u is necessarily different from the color of v.) Now each directed path contains vertices whose colors appear in (strictly) ascending order. Therefore, the orientation is acyclic. Moreover, each directed path contains at most k vertices, i.e., its length is at most $k - 1$.   □

For an orientation μ which was obtained from a coloring φ by the rule described in the proof of Property 3.4, we say that μ is an *induced orientation* of the coloring φ. Consider a graph $G = (V, E)$ in which some of the edges are oriented. Denote by $E' \subseteq E$ the subset of oriented edges. The edges from $E \setminus E'$ are not oriented. Such an orientation is called a *partial orientation* of G. If there are no consistently oriented cycles, the orientation is called *acyclic partial orientation.* Such orientations turn out to be very useful as well. We demonstrate how to use them in Chapters 7 and 8, but for now we provide several definitions.

Definition 3.5   *Suppose that μ is an acyclic orientation of a subset $E' \subseteq E$. Then μ is an* acyclic partial orientation *of $G = (V, E)$, and it holds that:*
(1) The out-degree *of μ is the maximum out-degree of a vertex in G with respect to μ.*
(2) The length *of μ is the length of the longest directed path in $G' = (V, E')$.*
(3) The deficit *of μ is the maximum number of edges in $E \setminus E'$ (i.e., unoriented edges) that share a common vertex in V.*
(4) For an edge (u, v) oriented toward v by μ, we say that v is a parent *of u under μ, or shortly μ-parent, and that u is a* child *of v under μ, or shortly, μ-child.*

3.4   THE ALGORITHM OF COLE AND VISHKIN

One of the simplest configurations in the distributed setting is an *oriented tree*. An oriented tree $T = (V, E)$ is rooted at a vertex $r \in V$, and every vertex $v \in V$, $v \neq r$, knows the identity of its parent $\pi(v)$ in the rooted tree (T, r). On the other hand, in an *unoriented tree* there is no distinguished root, and there is no parent-child relationship between neighbors. Notice that in oriented trees each vertex has information that allows it to orient the edges adjacent on it toward the parents. (For each edge (u, v) exactly one of the endpoints is the parent of the other one. Thus each edge can be oriented toward the parent endpoint.) Consequently, an acyclic orientation of out-degree at most 1 is obtained. Therefore, an oriented tree can be 2-colored using property 3.3. Unoriented trees can be 2-colored as well, since trees are bipartite. However, 2-coloring a tree (even an oriented one) in the distributed model requires $\Omega(n)$ time [55]. (See also Section 4.2.) Moreover, if the tree is unoriented, then even with a larger number of colors one still needs at least $\Omega(\log n)$ time to color a tree [55]. (We provide a proof of this in Section 4.2.) However, an *oriented* tree can be 3-colored within just $\log^* n + O(1)$ time. (See the definition of $\log^* n$ function below.) This is a fundamental result by Cole and Vishkin [18], and Goldberg, Plotking and Shannon [31].

For a parameter n, $\log^* n$ stands for the number of times that one needs to apply the logarithm on the base 2 starting with n before reaching a number smaller or equal than 2, i.e., $\log^* n = \min\{i \mid \log^{(i)} n \leq 2\}$. (Here $\log^{(0)} n = n$ and $\log^{(i+1)} n = \log_2 \log^{(i)} n$, for any nonnegative integer i.) This is a very slowly growing function. For example, $\log^* 2^{16} = 1 + \log^* 16 = 2 + \log^* 4 = 3$. Hence for every $n \leq 2^{2^{16}}$, $\log^* n \leq 4$. The threshold $2^{2^{16}}$ is much larger than the number of particles in the known universe.

We start with describing a 6-coloring algorithm for oriented trees. It will be later refined to a 3-coloring one. Initially, each vertex v has an identity number $Id(v)$ from the set $[n]$, where n is the number of vertices. It initializes its color φ_v to be equal to its identity number $Id(v)$. Denote by $|\varphi_v|$ the number of bits used to represent the color φ_v of v, i.e., $|\varphi_v| = \lceil \log_2 \varphi_v \rceil$. Also, for each index i, $1 \le i \le |\varphi_v|$, let $\varphi_v[i]$ denote the ith leftmost bit of the bit string φ_v.

The algorithm works iteratively. In each iteration each vertex $v \ne r$ compares the bit string φ_v which represents its current color with the bit string $\varphi_{\pi(v)}$ which represents the color of its parent. It finds an index i such that $\varphi_v[i] \ne \varphi_{\pi(v)}[i]$, and sets $\varphi_v' = \langle i, \varphi_v[i] \rangle$. Specifically, φ_v' is the new color of the vertex v, and it consists of two fields. The first field contains the binary representation of the bit string i, and the second field contains the single bit $\varphi_v[i]$. The color φ_v' is the concatenation of these two fields. The root r of the tree T picks an arbitrary index i and sets $\varphi_r' = \langle i, \varphi_r[i] \rangle$. The algorithm is executed for $\log^* n$ iterations. (For simplicity we assume that all vertices know the value of n. However, this assumption can be omitted using a slightly more delicate argument.)

Next we analyze the algorithm.

Lemma 3.6   *Given a legal coloring φ, the resulting coloring φ' is legal as well.*

Proof. Consider an edge $(v, u) \in E$, and suppose without loss of generality that $u = \pi(v)$. By the assumption of the lemma, $\varphi_v \ne \varphi_u$. Let $i(v)$ (respectively, $i(u)$) be the index selected by v (resp., by u). If $i(v) \ne i(u)$ then the first fields of φ_v' and φ_u' are different. Otherwise, by the choice of $i = i(v)$, it holds that $\varphi_v[i] \ne \varphi_u[i]$. Hence in this case the second fields of φ_v' and φ_u' are different. In either case $\varphi_v' \ne \varphi_u'$.

Denote by α and β the first and the second fields of φ_v', respectively. Analogously, let γ and δ be the first and the second fields of φ_u', respectively. A priori it can happen that $\alpha \ne \gamma$, $\beta \ne \delta$, but the concatenations $\alpha \circ \beta$ and $\gamma \circ \delta$ of the respective bit strings are equal. However, both β and δ are one-bit strings, and thus ($\alpha \ne \gamma$ or $\beta \ne \delta$) implies that $\varphi_v' = \alpha \circ \beta \ne \gamma \circ \delta = \varphi_u'$. $\square$

Denote by N_j, for every $j = 1, 2, \ldots$, the maximum number of bits used by a color φ_v, for some $v \in V$, after iteration j. For convenience, let $N_0 = \lceil \log n \rceil$ denote the number of bits used for the initial coloring of the algorithm. Then $N_{j+1} \le \lceil \log N_j \rceil + 1 \le \log N_j + 2$. Hence $N_1 \le \log N_0 + 2$, and $N_2 \le \log(\log N_0 + 2) + 2 \le \log \log N_0 + 3$, assuming that $\log N_0 \ge 2$. Also, $N_3 \le \log N_2 + 2 \le \log(\log \log N_0 + 3) + 2 \le \log^{(3)} N_0 + 3$, assuming that $\log \log N_0 \ge 3$. Generally, for $j = 1, 2, \ldots$, such that $\log^{(j)} N_0 \ge 3$, it holds that $N_j \le \log^{(j)} N_0 + 3$. In particular, for $j = \log^* N_0$ we get $N_j \le 5$. Since $N_0 = \lceil \log n \rceil$, it follows that after at most $\log^* n$ iterations the number $|\varphi_v|$ of bits used in each color φ_v is at most 5. At this point two more iterations of the algorithm decrease the maximum number of bits used for the color to 3, i.e., the palette size reduces to 8. Moreover, one more iteration of the algorithm reduces the palette size further to 6, because the first field of the color has just 3 possible values.

Next, the number of colors is further reduced to 3 by a different technique, called the *shift-down*. This phase of the algorithm requires 3 additional iterations, with $O(1)$ rounds each. (Generally, it can be used to reduce the number of colors from α to 3 within $\alpha - 3$ iterations, for any α. This implies Theorem 3.8.) In each iteration the number of colors is reduced by 1 within two steps. Denote by φ the initial 6-coloring. In the first step of the first iteration each vertex $v \neq r$ adopts the color $\varphi(\pi(v))$ of its parent $\pi(v)$, i.e., it sets $\varphi'(v) \to \varphi(\pi(v))$. The root changes its color to an arbitrary color from $\{1, 2, 3\}$, different from the color it used to have.

Lemma 3.7 φ' *is a legal 6-coloring.*

Proof. Consider an edge $(v, \pi(v))$ in the tree. First, suppose that $\pi(v) = r$ is the root of the tree. Then $\varphi'(v) = \varphi(r)$, and $\varphi'(r) \neq \varphi(r)$, as desired. Otherwise, denote $u = \pi(v)$. Then $\varphi'(v) = \varphi(u)$, $\varphi'(u) = \varphi(\pi(u))$, and $\varphi(u) \neq \varphi(\pi(u))$, because φ is a legal coloring.   □

The new coloring φ' satisfies a helpful property: for each vertex v, all its children are colored by the same color. Hence the number of forbidden (i.e., not available) colors for u is at most 2. In the second step of the first iteration each vertex v with $\varphi'(v) = 6$ finds in parallel an available color from $\{1, 2, 3\}$, and colors itself by this color. As a result we obtain a legal 5-coloring. Two more iterations (each with two steps) reduce the number of colors to 3.

We summarize this section by the following theorem.

Theorem 3.8   *[18, 31] An oriented n–vertex tree can be 3-colored within* $\log^* n + O(1)$ *time.*

Interestingly, for oriented paths and cycles the running time can be further improved to $\frac{1}{2}\log^* n + O(1)$ [74]. This result is tight up to the additive term $O(1)$, in view of Linial lower bound [55]. Specifically, Linial showed that $O(1)$-coloring an oriented path requires $\frac{1}{2}\log^* n - O(1)$ rounds. (See Section 4.2.) The tightness of these bounds is remarkable. In particular, it shows that the $\log^*$ function is not an artifact of the specific algorithm of Cole and Vishkin [18] or its analysis, but rather it is inherent in the complexity of this problem.

3.5   EXTENSIONS TO GRAPHS WITH BOUNDED MAXIMUM DEGREE

In this section we describe a few extensions of the Cole-Vishkin algorithm (henceforth, the CV algorithm) to graphs with maximum degree at most Δ. In the first extension, each vertex v views each of its $d = \deg(v) \leq \Delta$ neighbors $u_1, u_2, ..., u_d$ as its parents (in the sense of the CV algorithm). Specifically, suppose that we are given a legal coloring φ of the graph. The new coloring φ' is formed in the following way. The new color $\varphi'(v)$ of v will consist of d fields, $\varphi'(v) = \langle \varphi_1'(v), \varphi_2'(v), ..., \varphi_d'(v) \rangle$. For each $j \in [d]$, the field $\varphi_j'(v)$ is the new color that the vertex v would get in Cole-Vishkin's algorithm if u_j were the parent of v. In other words, $\varphi_j'(v) = \langle i, \varphi(v)[i] \rangle$, i.e., φ_j' consists of two subfields. The first subfield is an index $i = i(j)$ of a bit such that $\varphi(v)[i] \neq \varphi(u_j)[i]$, and the second subfield is the bit $\varphi(v)[i]$. For now the reader can think of different fields and subfields as being concatenated one after another. Later we will specify some special delimiters that separate various fields. These delimiters will guarantee that if $\varphi'(x) = \varphi'(y)$ for some two vertices x and y, then necessarily $\varphi'(x)$ and $\varphi'(y)$ have the same number d of fields, and for every $j \in [d]$, it holds that $\varphi'_j(x) = \varphi'_j(y)$.

Lemma 3.9 φ' is a legal coloring.

Proof. Consider an edge $(v, w) \in E$, and suppose that $w = u_j$ is the jth neighbor of v. Consider the jth fields $\varphi'_j(v)$ and $\varphi'_j(w)$ in the two new colors $\varphi'(v)$ and $\varphi'(w)$, respectively. (If $\varphi'(w)$ has less than j fields, then $\varphi'(v) \neq \varphi'(w)$.) Let i_v (respectively, i_w) be the index selected by v (resp., by w) for its jth field. If $i_v \neq i_w$ then the first subfield of $\varphi'(v)$ is different from the first subfield of $\varphi'_j(w)$. Otherwise their second subfields are different. In any case $\varphi'_j(v) \neq \varphi'_j(w)$, and so $\varphi'(v) \neq \varphi'(w)$.   □

Denote by N_i, $i = 1, 2, ...$, the maximum number of bits used by a color after the ith recoloring phase of this algorithm. Denote also by N_0 the number of bits used for colors before the algorithm starts. Since initially the identity numbers serve as colors, it follows that $N_0 = \lceil \log n \rceil$. By Lemma 3.9, $N_{i+1} \leq \Delta \cdot (\lceil \log N_i \rceil + 1)$. It is straightforward to verify that for $i = \log^* n + O(1)$, $N_i \leq \Delta \cdot (\log \Delta + O(\log \log \Delta))$. At this point the maximum color used by a vertex is at most $\exp\{\Delta \cdot (\log \Delta + O(\log \log \Delta))\}$, i.e., at most $\Delta^{O(\Delta)}$.

Corollary 3.10   *An extension of the CV algorithm computes a $\Delta^{O(\Delta)}$-coloring within $\log^* n + O(1)$ time.*

Finally, we address the subtlety that has to do with bit representations. Specifically, since fields may have different lengths, it may happen that for a pair of vertices v, u, and an index j, $\varphi'_j(v) \neq \varphi'_j(u)$, but still $\varphi'(v) = \varphi'_1(v) \circ ... \circ \varphi'_{deg(v)}(v) = \varphi'_1(u) \circ ... \circ \varphi'_{deg(u)}(u) = \varphi'(u)$, where $\circ$ stands for concatenation between bit strings. One way to handle this issue is by encoding each bit in $\varphi'(x)$, for every vertex $x \in V$, by two bits. Specifically, 0 will be encoded as 00, and 1 as 01. On the other hand, as a delimiter between different fields we use 10, and at the end of the bit sequence we write 11. With these delimiters, if $\varphi'_j(v) \neq \varphi'_j(u)$ for some index j and pair of vertices v and u then $\varphi'(v) \neq \varphi'(u)$, as desired.

The number of bits in the resulting bit strings will grow by a factor of 2, i.e., the number of colors used will grow quadratically. However, this is swallowed in the (giant) estimation of $\Delta^{O(\Delta)}$ for the number of colors (see Corollary 3.10). Observe that Corollary 3.10 with the trivial color reduction technique that reduces one color in each round (see Section 3.2) provides a $(\Delta + 1)$-coloring algorithm which requires $\Delta^{O(\Delta)} + \log^* n$ time.

3.6   AN IMPROVED COLORING ALGORITHM FOR GRAPHS WITH BOUNDED MAXIMUM DEGREE

In this section we demonstrate that the CV algorithm can be used in a different, more efficient, way to compute a coloring of a graph $G = (V, E)$ with maximum degree at most Δ. The new algorithm starts with computing a decomposition $\mathcal{F} = (F_1, F_2, ..., F_\Delta)$ into Δ forests. This decomposition, due to Panconesi and Rizzi [68], is computed within $O(1)$ time, and it is valuable for a variety of applications, in addition to the one that we will describe in the current section. In the first step of the forest-decomposition procedure every vertex v orients all edges (v, u) such that $Id(v) < Id(u)$ toward the endpoint with the greater Id (that is, the vertex u). In the second step each vertex v labels all outgoing edges (v, u) incident on v by distinct labels $1, 2, ...$. The two steps can be executed within one single round of communication.

Lemma 3.11   *For each* $i \in [\Delta]$, *the set* F_i *of edges labeled by* i *is acyclic.*

Proof. Suppose for contradiction that F_i contains a cycle C. Let v be the vertex with the smallest identity in C, and let u, u' be its two distinct neighbors in C. Then both edges $(v, u), (v, u')$ are oriented outwards from v. Hence v oriented two distinct outgoing edges $e = (v, u)$ and $e' = (v, u')$ incident on it by the same label i, contradiction.   □

The number of labels that are used by the algorithm is obviously at most Δ. Observe also that each of the trees in the forest-decomposition $\mathcal{F} = (F_1, F_2, ..., F_\Delta)$ is oriented. Specifically, for each edge $(v, u) \in F_i$, for some $i \in [\Delta]$, oriented from v to u, the vertex u is designated as the parent $\pi(u)$ of v. A vertex r that has no outgoing edges in F_i is a root of one of the trees of the forest F_i. Since each vertex v in F_i has at most one outgoing edge, it follows that each tree (connected component) T in F_i has exactly one root r, and all oriented paths in T lead to r.

To summarize:

Theorem 3.12   *[68] For a graph* $G = (V, E)$ *with maximum degree* Δ, *a forest-decomposition* $\mathcal{F}$ *with at most* Δ *oriented forests can be computed within one communication round.*

Remark: An *oriented forest* is a collection of vertex-disjoint oriented trees.

Given this forest-decomposition, the algorithm proceeds as follows. In each forest $F_i \in \mathcal{F}$ in parallel we run the CV algorithm. This algorithm produces a 3-coloring φ_i of the forest F_i within $\log^* n + O(1)$ rounds. Finally, each vertex v forms its color $\varphi(v) = \langle \varphi_1(v), \varphi_2(v), ..., \varphi_\Delta(v) \rangle$. That is, $\varphi(v)$ consists of Δ fields each of which is from $\{1, 2, 3\}$. For an index $i \in [\Delta]$ with no incident edges in the forest F_i, the vertex v can be seen as a single-vertex tree in F_i. Thus $\varphi_i(v)$ can be set to an arbitrary color from $\{1, 2, 3\}$.

Lemma 3.13 φ *is a legal* 3^Δ-*coloring of* G.

Proof. Consider an edge $(v, u) \in E$. Since $\mathcal{F}$ is a forest-decomposition of G, there exists an index $i \in [\Delta]$ such that $(v, u) \in E(F_i)$. Hence $\varphi_i(v) \neq \varphi_i(u)$, i.e., $\varphi(v) \neq \varphi(u)$. Finally, φ consists of Δ fields, with 3 options for each field. Hence φ employs 3^Δ colors.   □

Corollary 3.14 3^Δ-*coloring of an n–vertex graph with maximum degree Δ can be computed within* $\log^* n + O(1)$ *time.*

By the basic color reduction technique, this corollary also implies that a $(\Delta + 1)$-coloring can be computed within $3^\Delta + \log^* n + O(1)$ time. This improves upon the result derived in Section 3.5.

3.7   A FASTER $(\Delta + 1)$-COLORING

In sections 3.5 and 3.6 we analyzed algorithms that produce $\Delta^{O(\Delta)}$- and 3^Δ- colorings, respectively, in $\log^* n + O(1)$ time. As a corollary we concluded that $(\Delta + 1)$-coloring can be computed within $3^\Delta + \log^* n + O(1)$ time. In this section we present a much faster $(\Delta + 1)$-coloring algorithm due to Goldberg, Plotkin and Shannon [31].

The algorithm starts with computing a forest $\mathcal{F} = (F_1, F_2, ..., F_\Delta)$ of the input graph $G = (V, E)$. Each F_i is an oriented forest, and so Cole-Vishkin's algorithm is applicable to it. It is applied in parallel in each forest, to obtain a 3-coloring φ_i for each forest F_i. Next, the colorings $\varphi_1, \varphi_2, ..., \varphi_\Delta$ are merged into a unified coloring $\hat{\varphi}$ for G in Δ iterations. In the first iteration, $\hat{\varphi}(v) = \hat{\varphi}_1(v)$ is set as $\varphi_1(v)$, for every $v \in V$. (We assume here that every vertex v belongs to each forest F_i. If there are no edges of a forest F_i adjacent on v, then v is considered to be a single-vertex tree in F_i.) Consider the ith iteration, for some $i \in [2, \Delta]$. Every vertex v forms a color $\psi(v) = \langle \hat{\varphi}_{i-1}(v), \varphi_i(v) \rangle$, where $\hat{\varphi}_{i-1}(v)$ is the coloring $\hat{\varphi}$ which was formed in the previous iteration. Inductively we will guarantee that $\hat{\varphi}_{i-1}(v) \in [\Delta + 1]$, for every $v \in V$, and that $\hat{\varphi}_{i-1}$ is a legal coloring of $\bigcup_{j=1}^{i-1} F_j$. Also, $\varphi_i(v) \in \{1, 2, 3\}$. Hence ψ is a legal $3(\Delta + 1)$-coloring of $\bigcup_{j=1}^{i} F_j$. The maximum degree of $\bigcup_{j=1}^{i} F_i$ is at most Δ. Thus, in $2(\Delta + 1)$ rounds the coloring ψ can be converted into a legal $(\Delta + 1)$-coloring $\hat{\varphi}_i$ for $\bigcup_{j=1}^{i} F_j$ via the basic color reduction technique (see Section 3.2). This completes the description of the ith iteration, and thus, of the entire algorithm.

The running time of this algorithm consists of three parts. In the first part of the algorithm the forest-decomposition is computed within $O(1)$ time. The second part, i.e., the application of the CV algorithm in each forest, requires $\log^* n + O(1)$ time. Finally, each of the $\Delta - 1$ iterations of the recoloring step requires $2(\Delta + 1)$ rounds. Hence the overall running time is $O(\Delta^2) + \log^* n$.

To summarize:

Corollary 3.15   *[31] $(\Delta + 1)$-coloring of an n–vertex graph $G = (V, E)$ can be computed within* $O(\Delta^2) + \log^* n$ *time.*

This result does not improve the bound of Corollary 3.14 that says that 3^Δ-coloring can be computed within $\log^* n + O(1)$ time. Improving this bound will be the subject of Chapter 3.10.

3.8   KUHN-WATTENHOFER COLOR REDUCTION TECHNIQUE AND ITS APPLICATIONS

In Section 3.2 we presented the basic color reduction technique. This technique converts an α-coloring φ of a graph $G = (V, E)$ with maximum degree Δ into a $(\Delta + 1)$-coloring, within $\alpha - (\Delta + 1)$ rounds. In this section we describe a far more efficient technique due to Kuhn and Wattenhofer [53] for this task. This technique requires $O\left(((\log \frac{\alpha}{\Delta+1}) + 1) \cdot \Delta\right)$ time. Suppose that $\alpha \geq 2(\Delta + 1)$. Otherwise a $(\Delta + 1)$-coloring can be computed within $(\Delta + 1)$ rounds via the standard color reduction technique.

Kuhn-Wattenhofer (henceforth, KW) reduction technique starts with partitioning the vertex set V of G into $k = \lceil \frac{\alpha}{\Delta+1} \rceil$ sets $V_1, V_2, ..., V_k$ in the following way. For each $i \in [k]$, V_i will contain the vertices v with $(i - 1)(\Delta + 1) + 1 \leq \varphi(v) \leq i \cdot (\Delta + 1)$. Consider the coloring φ restricted to the vertex set $V_1 \cup V_2$. It is a $(2(\Delta + 1))$-coloring of $G(V_1 \cup V_2)$. By the standard color reduction technique, it can be converted into a $(\Delta + 1)$-coloring ψ_{12} for $G(V_1 \cup V_2)$ within $(\Delta + 1)$ rounds. The same applies to the set $V_3 \cup V_4$, and the set $V_5 \cup V_6$, etc. (In case that k is odd, we group the last three sets V_{k-2}, V_{k-1} and V_k, rather than leaving the set V_k ungrouped.) In all these sets the standard reduction technique is applied in parallel. As a result we obtain a $(\Delta + 1)$-coloring ψ_{12} for $V_1 \cup V_2$, a $(\Delta + 1)$-coloring ψ_{34} for $V_3 \cup V_4$, etc. Overall, the number of colors used by all the colorings $\psi_{12}, \psi_{34}, \psi_{56}, ...$ is at most $\alpha/2$. (Because in each vertex set $V_i \cup V_{i+1}$, $i = 1, 3, 5, ...$, the palette size decreased from at least $2(\Delta + 1)$ to $(\Delta + 1)$. In the last vertex set, if k is odd, it decreased by an even greater factor than 2.) Note also that the new coloring of G can use the palette $[1, \alpha/2]$. Specifically, $V_1 \cup V_2$ uses the palette $[1, \Delta + 1]$, and $V_3 \cup V_4$ uses the palette $[\Delta + 2, 2(\Delta + 1)]$, etc. The running time of this halving step is $O(\Delta)$.

Theorem 3.16   *Given a graph $G = (V, E)$ and an α-coloring φ of G, with $\alpha \geq 2(\Delta + 1)$, an $(\alpha/2)$-coloring ψ of G can be computed within at most $2(\Delta + 1)$ rounds.*

This halving step is applied repeatedly, up until the resulting number of colors is smaller than $2(\Delta + 1)$. At that point the coloring can be converted into a $(\Delta + 1)$-coloring within additional at most $\Delta + 1$ rounds. The number of times that the halving step is invoked is at most $\lceil \log k \rceil = \lceil \log \lceil \frac{\alpha}{\Delta+1} \rceil \rceil$. Hence the overall running time is $O(\Delta \cdot \log \frac{\alpha}{\Delta+1})$.

Corollary 3.17   *[53] An α-coloring can be converted into a $(\Delta + 1)$-coloring within $O(\Delta \cdot \log \frac{\alpha}{\Delta+1})$ deterministic time.*

One simple application of this result is the following one. As was mentioned above, the identities of vertices can be used as an initial n-coloring of the input graph. Apply Corollary 3.17 to this initial coloring. We obtain a $(\Delta + 1)$-coloring in $O(\Delta \log n)$ time. This result is due to Goldberg, Plotkin and Shannon [31]. Also we saw (Corollary 3.14) that 3^Δ-coloring can be computed within $\log^* n + O(1)$ time. By using this coloring as an input to Corollary 3.17 we obtain a $(\Delta + 1)$-coloring within $O(\Delta^2)$ additional time. The overall time for $(\Delta + 1)$-coloring in this algorithm is $O(\Delta^2) + \log^* n$, that matches the one that was achieved in Section 3.7 by a different technique. Moreover, in Chapter 3.10 we will see an algorithm for $O(\Delta^2)$-coloring that requires only $\log^* n + O(1)$ time, due to Linial [55]. The KW color reduction technique in conjunction with Linial's algorithm produces a $(\Delta + 1)$-coloring within $O(\Delta \log \Delta) + \log^* n$ time.

In the sequel we will refer to the algorithm that computes a $(\Delta + 1)$-coloring from scratch in $O(\Delta \log \Delta) + \log^* n$ time as the *Kuhn and Wattenhofer algorithm*, or shortly, the KW algorithm. On the other hand, the variant that starts from a legal α-coloring and produces a $(\Delta + 1)$-coloring within $O(\Delta \cdot \log \frac{\alpha}{\Delta+1})$ time (Corollary 3.17) will be referred to as the *KW iterative procedure*.

We finish this section by presenting a slightly different view of the KW iterative procedure. Consider again the CV algorithm. It starts with an α_1-coloring, for some number α_1. After one iteration (that lasts for one round) it produces an α_2-coloring, for some $\alpha_2 \le \alpha_1$. After one more iteration it produces an α_3-coloring, $\alpha_3 \le \alpha_2 \le \alpha_1$, etc.

Szegedy and Vishwanathan [74] identified the family of algorithms that on each round gradually improve the coloring at hand, where each vertex selects a new color based only on its current color, and the current colors of its neighbors. Such algorithms are called *locally-iterative* coloring algorithms. Not only the CV algorithm is of this kind, but also the aforementioned Linial's $O(\Delta^2)$-coloring algorithm for general graphs. Szegedy and Vishwanathan showed that any $(\Delta + 1)$-coloring locally-iterative algorithm requires $\Omega(\Delta \log \Delta)$ time.

Interestingly, Linial's algorithm can be combined with the KW iterative procedure to produce a locally-iterative $(\Delta + 1)$-coloring algorithm that requires $O(\Delta \log \Delta) + \log^* n$ time. This result is tight in view of the lower bound of [74]. On the other hand, in Chapter 6 we will show (the results are due to [8, 48]) that by algorithm of a different type one can break the Szegedy-Vishwanathan's barrier of $\Omega(\Delta \log \Delta)$, and obtain a $(\Delta + 1)$-coloring in $O(\Delta) + \log^* n$ time. (In fact, even $O(\Delta) + \frac{1}{2}\log^* n$ time. The term $\frac{1}{2}\log^* n$ is tight in view of Linial's lower bound from [55]. See Chapter 4.)

Next, we show how the KW iterative procedure can be stated as a locally-iterative algorithm. (The fact that Linial's algorithm is locally-iterative will be apparent when we describe it in Chapter 3.10.) Consider the α-coloring φ, which is the input for the KW iterative procedure. Suppose that the colors are in the range $[0, \alpha - 1]$. Group all vertices of colors $[0, \Delta + 1]$ into the set V_1, all vertices of colors $[\Delta + 2, 2\Delta + 3]$ into the set V_2, etc. Within each vertex set V_j, $j = 1, 2, ..., \lceil \frac{\alpha}{\Delta+2} \rceil$, for each index $i \in [0, \Delta + 1]$, let $U_j^i = \{v \in V_j \mid \varphi(v) \equiv i \pmod{\Delta + 2}\}$.

In each vertex set V_j in parallel all vertices of the set $U_j^{\Delta+1}$ recolor themselves into an available color for them from the palette $[(j - 1)(\Delta + 2), j(\Delta + 2) - 2]$. Such available colors necessarily exist, because the palette is of size $(\Delta + 1)$, while the maximum degree in each $G(V_j)$ is at most $\Delta(G) = \Delta$. Hence, roughly speaking, in each round the employed number of colors decays by a factor $\frac{\Delta+1}{\Delta+2}$. (We suppress here some technical details regarding the way to "eliminate spaces" from the resulting coloring ψ. The latter is required to guarantee that ψ is a $\frac{\Delta+1}{\Delta+2} \cdot \alpha$-coloring. Other suppressed technicalities have to do with the fact that, in general, α need not be divisible by $\Delta + 2$.) Applying this recoloring iteratively to the $O(\Delta^2)$-coloring produced by Linial's algorithm results in a $(\Delta + 1)$-coloring within $O(\Delta \log \Delta)$ additional rounds (i.e., total of $O(\Delta \log \Delta) + \log^* n$ rounds).

3.9   A REDUCTION FROM $(\Delta + 1)$-COLORING TO MIS

In Section 3.2 we showed that given an α-coloring of a graph $G = (V, E)$ one can compute an MIS of G within α rounds. In this section we show a reduction in the opposite direction: given an algorithm for computing an MIS we show how it can be translated into an algorithm with the same running time for employing a $(\Delta + 1)$-coloring. This reduction is due to Luby [60] (see also [55].)

Denote by $K_{\Delta+1}$ the clique with $\Delta + 1$ vertices, and by $G' = G \times K_{\Delta+1}$ the Cartesian product of G by $K_{\Delta+1}$. The vertex set V' of G' is $V' = V \times [\Delta + 1]$, i.e., every vertex $v \in V$ translates into $(\Delta + 1)$ vertices $(v, 1), (v, 2), ..., (v, \Delta + 1)$. All vertices $(v, i), (v, j)$ are interconnected, and so essentially each vertex $v \in V$ is replaced by a clique that connects its $(\Delta + 1)$ copies. For distinct vertices $v, u \in V$, connect (v, i) and (v, j) in G' ($i, j \in [\Delta + 1]$) iff $((v, u) \in E$ and $(i = j))$. This completes the description of the graph $G' = G \times K_{\Delta+1}$. See Figure 3.1 for an illustration.

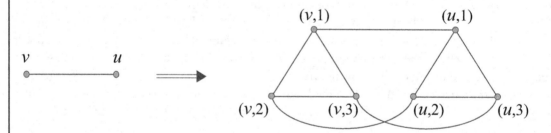

Figure 3.1: A Cartesian product of an edge (v, u) with K_3.

Consider an MIS $U' \subseteq V'$ in G'.

Lemma 3.18   *U' contains exactly one vertex from each clique $\{(v, 1), (v, 2), ..., (v, \Delta + 1)\}$.*

Proof. Since vertices of $\{(v, 1), (v, 2), ..., (v, \Delta + 1)\}$ form a clique, U' cannot contain two of them. Suppose for contradiction that $U' \cap \{(v, 1), (v, 2), ..., (v, \Delta + 1)\} = \emptyset$ for some vertex $v \in V$. Then for each index $i \in [\Delta + 1]$ there exists a vertex $u_i \in U$ such that $((v, i), (u_i, i)) \in E'$ and $(u_i, i) \in U'$. Moreover, for distinct indices $i, j \in [\Delta + 1]$, it holds that $(u_i, i), (u_j, j) \in U'$, and so $u_i \neq u_j$. (Because otherwise there would be two representatives $(u_i, i), (u_i, j)$ in U' from the clique of u_i.) Hence $(v, u_i) \in E$, for every $i \in [\Delta + 1]$, and the vertices $u_1, u_2, ..., u_{\Delta+1}$ are distinct. This contradicts the assumption the the graph G has maximum degree Δ.   □

Given an MIS U' for G' one can determine the $(\Delta + 1)$-coloring φ for G in the following way: for a vertex $v \in V$, let $i \in [\Delta + 1]$ be the unique index such that $(v, i) \in U'$. (The index exists and it is unique by Lemma 3.18). Set $\varphi(v) = i$.

Lemma 3.19   *The $(\Delta + 1)$-coloring φ is a legal coloring of G.*

Proof. Consider an edge $(v, u) \in E$. The vertices $(v, \varphi(v)), (u, \varphi(u))$ both belong to the MIS U', and so these vertices are not connected in E'. Since $(v, \varphi(v))$ and $(u, \varphi(v))$ are connected in E', it holds that $(u, \varphi(u)) \neq (u, \varphi(v))$. Thus $\varphi(u) \neq \varphi(v)$.   □

Now we are ready to describe the reduction from $(\Delta + 1)$-coloring to MIS. Given a graph $G = (V, E)$, every vertex $v \in V$ simulates the $\Delta + 1$ vertices of the clique $(v, 1), (v, 2), ..., (v, \Delta + 1)$ of G'. The network runs an algorithm $\mathcal{A}$ for MIS, which is provided to the reduction as input. Whenever a vertex (v, i) wishes to send a message to a vertex (u, i), in the simulation the vertex v sends the appropriately labeled message to u. Whenever (u, i) wishes to send a message to (u, j), this is performed locally within the vertex v. Once the algorithm $\mathcal{A}$ completes the computation of the MIS U', every vertex v locally checks what is the index i such that $(v, i) \in U'$, and sets $\varphi(v) = i$. By Lemmas 3.18 and 3.19, the resulting coloring is a legal $(\Delta + 1)$-coloring. The running time of this computation is the running time of the algorithm $\mathcal{A}$.

Corollary 3.20   *[60] Given an algorithm $\mathcal{A}$ that computes an MIS for general n-vertex graphs with maximum degree Δ within time $T(n, \Delta)$, the reduction which was described above provides a $(\Delta + 1)$-coloring algorithm with running time $T((\Delta + 1) \cdot n, 2\Delta)$.*

We remark that the simulation which was described above increases the message size by a factor of $(\Delta + 1)$. Also, note that this reduction is not applicable to graphs of bounded arboricity. Specifically, even if the arboricity of G is $a < \Delta$, the arboricity of G' is $\Theta(\Delta)$. To the best of our knowledge it is open whether a similar reduction that does not blow up the message size exists.

3.10 LINIAL'S ALGORITHM

In Section 3.6 we saw that a 3^{Δ}-coloring can be computed within $\log^* n + O(1)$ time. Also, in Section 3.7 we saw that $(\Delta + 1)$-coloring can be computed within $O(\Delta^2) + \log^* n$ time. This section is devoted to a stronger result (due to Linial [55]), which states that an $O(\Delta^2)$-coloring can be computed within $\log^* n + O(1)$ rounds. The proof relies on the following purely combinatorial lemma due to Erdős et al. [27]. See also [55].

Lemma 3.21   *For two integers n and Δ, $n > \Delta \geq 4$, there exists a family $\mathcal{J}$ of n subsets of the set $\{1, 2, ..., m\}$, $m = 5 \cdot \lceil \Delta^2 \cdot \ln n \rceil$, such that if $F_0, F_1, ..., F_\Delta \in \mathcal{J}$ then*

$$F_0 \nsubseteq \bigcup_{i=1}^{\Delta} F_i.$$

Remark: A set system $\mathcal{J}$ that satisfies the assertion of the lemma is called Δ-*cover-free*.

Proof. We build a random collection $\mathcal{J}$ of subsets of $[m]$ in the following way. For every element $x \in [m]$, and for every index $i \in [n]$, we insert x into the set S_i with probability $1/\Delta$, independently of other pairs $(x', i') \neq (x, i)$. For a fixed element x, $x \in [m]$, and fixed distinct indices $i_0, i_1, ..., i_\Delta \in [n]$, it holds that

$$\mathbb{P}\left(x \in S_{i_0} \setminus \bigcup_{j=1}^{\Delta} S_{i_j} \right) = \frac{1}{\Delta} \cdot \left(1 - \frac{1}{\Delta} \right)^{\Delta} \geq \frac{1}{4\Delta}.$$

Hence

$$\mathbb{P}\left(x \notin \left(S_{i_0} \setminus \bigcup_{j=1}^{\Delta} S_{i_j} \right) \right) \leq 1 - \frac{1}{4\Delta}.$$

The probability that for every x, $x \in [m]$, $x \notin S_{i_0} \setminus \cup_{j=1}^{\Delta} S_{i_j}$ is

$$\mathbb{P}\left(\forall x, x \notin S_{i_0} \setminus \bigcup_{j=1}^{\Delta} S_{i_j} \right) \leq \left(1 - \frac{1}{4\Delta} \right)^{m} \leq e^{-(5/4)\Delta \ln n} = n^{-(5/4)\Delta}.$$

Hence

$$\mathbb{P}\left(S_{i_0} \subseteq \bigcup_{j=1}^{\Delta} S_{i_j} \right) \leq n^{-(5/4)\Delta}.$$

The probability that there will be $(\Delta + 1)$ indices $i_0, i_1, ..., i_\Delta$, such that $S_{i_0} \subseteq \cup_{j=1}^{\Delta} S_{i_j}$ is, by union-bound, at most the number of ways to choose these indices multiplied by $n^{-(5/4)\Delta}$. There are $\binom{n}{\Delta+1}$ ways to choose the $(\Delta + 1)$ distinct indices, and $(\Delta + 1)$ ways to choose i_0 from the selected $(\Delta + 1)$-tuple of indices. Hence

$$\mathbb{P}\left(\exists i_0, i_1, ..., i_\Delta \text{ such that } S_{i_0} \subseteq \bigcup_{j=1}^{\Delta} S_{i_j} \right) \leq (\Delta + 1) \binom{n}{\Delta + 1} \cdot n^{-(5/4)\Delta}$$

$$\leq \left(\frac{e}{\Delta + 1} \right)^{\Delta} \cdot e \cdot n^{-(1/4)\Delta + 1}.$$

The right-hand-side is strictly smaller than 1, for $\Delta \geq 4$. We remark that to fix the cases of $\Delta \in \{1, 2, 3\}$ one should increase the leading constant in the definition of m from 5 to 8, i.e., set $m = 8 \cdot \lceil \Delta^2 \cdot \log n \rceil$. Hence

$$\mathbb{P}\left(\forall \text{ distinct } i_0, i_1, ..., i_s, \ S_{i_0} \not\subseteq \bigcup_{j=1}^{\Delta} S_{i_j} \right) \geq 1 - \left(\frac{e}{\Delta+1} \right)^{\Delta} \cdot e \cdot n^{-(\Delta/4)+1} > 0.$$

Therefore, there exists a selection of sets $S_1, S_2, ..., S_n$, for which no one of them is covered by a union of Δ others. □

Next we use this lemma for coloring. Each vertex $v \in V$ is assigned its own subset $F_{Id(v)}$ from a collection $\mathcal{J}$ of subsets of $[m]$, $m = 5 \lceil \Delta^2 \cdot \ln n \rceil$, whose existence is guaranteed by Lemma 3.21. Then each vertex v sends its set $F_{Id(v)}$ to all its neighbors. (In fact, it is enough just to send the index $Id(v)$, and the neighbors will compute $F_{Id(v)}$ locally.) Given its own set $F_{Id(v)}$, and the sets $F_{id(u_1)}, F_{id(u_2)}, ..., F_{id(u_h)}$ of all the $h \leq \Delta$ neighbors $u_1, u_2, ..., u_h$ of v, the vertex v finds an element

$$c \in F_{Id(u)} \setminus \left(\bigcup_{i=1}^{h} F_{Id(u_i)} \right).$$

Such an element exists because $F_{Id(u)} \not\subseteq \cup_{i=1}^{h} F_{Id(u_i)}$. The vertex v sets c to be its new color.

Next, we analyze this algorithm. Observe that it requires just one single round. Also, the coloring φ that it produces is an m-coloring with $m = O(\Delta^2 \cdot \log n)$.

Lemma 3.22 *φ is a legal coloring.*

Proof. Consider an edge $(v, u) \in E$. Then $\varphi(v) \in F_{Id(v)} \setminus F_{Id(u)}$ and $\varphi(u) \in F_{Id(u)}$. Hence $\varphi(v) \neq \varphi(u)$. □

Observe also that any legal coloring ψ could have been used instead of the Id numbers as an input coloring for this procedure. Generally, if the original number of colors n', then the resulting number of colors is $m = O(\Delta^2 \cdot \log n')$.

Theorem 3.23 *[55] The algorithm discussed above, given an n'-coloring of a graph $G = (V, E)$ with degree Δ, produces a $5 \lceil \Delta^2 \cdot \ln n' \rceil$-coloring of G within one single round.*

This theorem was significantly improved by Szegedy and Vishwanathan [74] who showed that an n'-coloring can be converted into $O(\Delta^2 \cdot \log \log n')$-coloring within one single round.

Note, however, that this algorithm can be invoked iteratively. It is easy to verify that within $\log^* n$ rounds the resulting coloring employs $O(\Delta^2 \cdot \log \Delta)$-coloring. Using another set system of Erdős et al. [27] (see below), one can further decrease the number of colors to $O(\Delta^2)$ within one additional round.

Corollary 3.24   *[55] An $O(\Delta^2)$-coloring of an n–vertex graph with maximum degree Δ can be computed within $\log^* n + O(1)$ rounds.*

We remark that the algorithm for computing set-systems which was described above is randomized. However, it can be easily derandomized (see [27, 55]) using an algebraic construction based on polynomials. (This construction is presented below.) The resulting algorithm has similar properties to the ones that were stated above. Using the algorithm of Szegedy and Vishwanathan [74], the running time in Corollary 3.24 can be improved to $\frac{1}{2}\log^* n + O(1)$. In view of the lower bounds of Linial [55] that we described in Section 4.2, this result is tight up to constant *in the additive term.*

Next, we describe how to compute $O(\Delta^2)$-coloring in $\log^* n + O(1)$ time using algebraic constructions. This algorithm is also based on [27, 55]. In [27] the authors devised constructions of Δ-cover-free set systems $\mathcal{F} = \{S^{(1)}, S^{(2)}, ..., S^{(n)}\}$, over a ground-set $[m]$ (i.e., $S^{(i)} \subseteq [m]$ for each $i \in [n]$). Specifically, Erdős et al. [27] showed that for any n and Δ, $n > \Delta$, one can build a Δ-cover-free family with $m = O(\Delta^2 \cdot \log n)$. The proof of this result by the probabilistic method was explained above. Next we describe an algebraic proof of a slightly weaker bound, specifically, $m = O(\Delta^2 \cdot \log^2 n)$.

Let X, $|X| = m$, be a ground-set, where $m = q^2$ for a prime q. It is convenient to view X as $X = GF(q) \times GF(q)$, where $GF(q)$ stands for a field of characteristic q. For a positive parameter d, let $\text{Poly}(d, q)$ denote the set of polynomials of degree d over $GF(q)$. For each polynomial $g() \in \text{Poly}(d, q)$, let $S_g = \{(a, g(a)) \mid a \in GF(q)\}$ be the set of all points on the graph of the polynomial $g()$. Let $\mathcal{F}_{d,q} = \{S_g \mid g() \in \text{Poly}(d, q)\}$. Observe that $|S_g| = q$, for every $g() \in \text{Poly}(d, q)$. Note that two such distinct sets may intersect in at most d elements. Hence to cover a fixed set S_g, one needs at least q/d other sets S_h from the family $\mathcal{F} = \mathcal{F}_{d,q}$.

Let $\Delta = \lceil q/d \rceil - 1 < q/d$. It follows that $\mathcal{F}$ is a Δ-cover-free family. Its cardinality is $|\mathcal{F}| = q^{d+1} = n$. By expressing q and d in terms of n, m and Δ, we obtain $m \cdot \log^2 m \leq 4(\Delta + 1)^2 \log^2 n$. Hence $m \leq 4(\Delta + 1)^2 \log^2 n$. (In fact, $m \leq 5(\Delta + 1)^2 \cdot \frac{\log^2 n}{\log^2(4(\Delta+1)^2 \log^2 n)}$, but we will not use this estimate.)

Another valuable setting of parameters is $d = 2$. Then we get $n = q^3$, $m = q^2$, $\Delta \geq \sqrt{m}/2 - 1$. Since $q = \sqrt{m}$, it follows that $m \leq 4(\Delta + 1)^2$. In other words, for $n \leq 8(\Delta + 1)^3$ one can have a groundset of size $m \leq 4(\Delta + 1)^2$. To summarize:

Theorem 3.25   *[27] For any positive integers n, Δ, $n > \Delta$, one can construct a Δ-cover-free family $\mathcal{F}$ with n sets over the groundset $[m]$, for some $m \leq 4(\Delta + 1)^2 \log^2 n$. Moreover, if $n \leq 8(\Delta + 1)^3$ then $m \leq 4(\Delta + 1)^2$.*

Note that for any $\Delta > 0$, and for any $n > \Delta$, (and not only a prime power), we can choose a prime q, $\lfloor (\Delta + 1) \log n \rfloor \leq q \leq 2\lfloor (\Delta + 1) \log n \rfloor$, and set $d = \lfloor \log n \rfloor$. (Such a prime q exists according to the Bertrand-Chebyshev postulate. See, e.g., Theorem 418 in [37].) Then the family

$\mathcal{F}_{d,q}$ is Δ-cover-free. Moreover $|\mathcal{F}_{d,q}| = q^{d+1} > n$. Thus we can select a subset of $\mathcal{F}_{d,q}$ of size n which is a Δ-cover-free family over a groundset $[m]$ of size $m = q^2 \leq 4(\Delta + 1)^2 \log^2 n$.

As was argued above, by applying the recoloring procedure which is based on these set-systems for $\log^* n + O(1)$ times, the initial n-coloring in which each vertex v is assigned $Id(v)$ as its color is converted into an $O(\Delta^2 \log^2 \Delta)$-coloring ψ for G. For a sufficiently large Δ, it holds that $O(\Delta^2 \log^2 \Delta) \leq 8(\Delta + 1)^3$. (If $\Delta = O(1)$ then $O(\Delta^2 \log^2 \Delta) = O(\Delta^2)$.) Hence we next use the second set system from Theorem 3.25 to convert this coloring into a $4(\Delta + 1)^2$-coloring of G. The overall running time is $\log^* n + O(1)$.

CHAPTER 4

Lower Bounds

This section is devoted to two lower bounds, both due to Linial [55]. The first one (Section 4.1) shows that coloring the balanced d-regular tree *unoriented* tree T_d with less than $\frac{1}{2}\sqrt{d}$ colors requires $\Omega\left(\frac{\log n}{\log d}\right)$ time. The second one (Section 4.2) shows that $O(1)$-coloring an *oriented* path requires at least $\frac{1}{2}\log^* n - O(1)$ time.

4.1 COLORING UNORIENTED TREES

We start with providing some intuition for the first result. There are known constructions [59] of d-regular graphs G_d with girth$(G) > \frac{\log n}{\log d}$ and chromatic number at least $\frac{1}{2}\sqrt{d}$. These constructions are based on Ramanujan graphs [59]. In fact, it is conjectured that the lower bound on the number of colors can be raised from $\frac{1}{2}\sqrt{d}$ to $\Omega\left(\frac{d}{\log d}\right)$ [59]. If this conjecture is true then it will follow that coloring a d-regular tree with $c \cdot \frac{d}{\log d}$ colors, for some fixed constant $c > 0$, requires $\Omega\left(\frac{\log n}{\log d}\right)$ time.

Observe that from the perspective of many vertices v, within less that $\frac{\log n}{\log d}$ rounds it cannot distinguish between being in G_d or T_d. (In fact, this is true if v is far away from tree leaves.) Hence if T_d can be legally α-colored, for some $\alpha < c \cdot \sqrt{d}$ colors for a sufficiently small constant $c > 0$, within $c \cdot \frac{\log n}{\log d}$ rounds, then G_d can be α-colored as well. (In this case the distributed algorithm for α-coloring T_d could be executed on G_d, which would produce a legal α-coloring of G_d.) But $\alpha < \chi(G_d)$, i.e., G_d cannot be α-colored, no matter how many rounds are used. Thus coloring T_d with $\alpha < c \cdot \sqrt{d}$ colors requires more than $c \cdot \frac{\log n}{\log d}$ rounds.

We will provide two proofs for this result. The first proof is simpler, and applies to both randomized and deterministic algorithms. The second one is more involved and applies only to deterministic algorithms. However, the second proof illustrates an important proof technique. This technique will also be used in Section 4.2.

4.1.1 THE FIRST PROOF

Consider first the problem of distributed coloring n-vertex graphs T_d and G_d, where the assignment of identifiers (henceforth, Id-assignment) is the following one. Every vertex v selects its Id uniformly at random from $[n^3]$. For short, we will refer to these problems as coloring *random* T_d and coloring *random* G_d. Suppose for contradiction that there exists a distributed algorithm $\mathcal{A}$ that requires $c \cdot \frac{\log n}{\log d}$ rounds or less, and colors random T_d legally with $c \cdot \sqrt{d}$ colors, with a positive probability. (The algorithm $\mathcal{A}$ may be either deterministic or randomized. In the former case the probability is taken over the choice of Ids, and in the latter case it is also taken over the coin tosses of the algorithm.)

Consider an execution $\mathcal{E}$ of $\mathcal{A}$ on the random G_d. Let $U \subseteq V(T_d)$ be a subset of vertices of T_d which are at distance greater than $c \cdot \frac{\log n}{\log d} + 1$ from their respective closest leaves. Observe that U is not empty, for a sufficiently small $c > 0$. Let $\text{view}(v, G_d, \mathcal{A})$ be the information accumulated by a vertex $v \in V(G_d)$ in an execution of $\mathcal{A}$ of random G_d after $c \cdot \frac{\log n}{\log d}$ rounds. Similarly, let $\text{view}(v', T_d, \mathcal{A})$ be the information accumulated by a vertex $v' \in U \subseteq V(T_d)$ in an execution of $\mathcal{A}$ on random T_d after the same number of rounds. Both these views are random variables, distributed precisely in the same way. Hence the distributions of the colors computed by $v \in V(G_d)$ and by $v' \in U \subseteq V(T_d)$ are the same as well. For the tree T_d the algorithm $\mathcal{A}$ employs $c \cdot \sqrt{d}$ colors, and so G_d will also be colored with the same number of colors. Moreover, with a positive probability, the coloring φ' produced by the algorithm is legal for T_d. In particular, with a positive probability, for every vertex $v' \in U$ and every neighbor w' of v' in T_d, $\varphi'(v') \neq \varphi'(w')$. Hence, with the same probability, for every vertex $v \in V(G_d)$, the coloring φ produced by the algorithm for random G_d satisfies for every neighbor w of v in G_d, $\varphi(v) \neq \varphi(w)$. Hence, with a positive probability, the coloring φ is a legal $(c \cdot \sqrt{d})$-coloring for G_d, but $\chi(G_d) > c \cdot \sqrt{d}$, contradiction.

Corollary 4.1 *There exists a constant $c > 0$, such that there is no algorithm for random T_d that employs $c \cdot \sqrt{d}$ colors, runs for $c \cdot \frac{\log n}{\log d}$ rounds or less and produces a legal coloring with a positive probability.*

Suppose now for contradiction that there exists some $(c \cdot \sqrt{d})$-coloring algorithm $\mathcal{B}$ for T_d that runs in $c \cdot \frac{\log n}{\log d}$ rounds and *for any assignment* of distinct Ids from the range $[n^3]$ to vertices of T_d with probability at least $1/2$ this algorithm produces a legal coloring. Invoke $\mathcal{B}$ on random T_d. If the Id-assignment that was selected randomly assigns all vertices distinct Ids, then with probability at least $1/2$ the algorithm $\mathcal{B}$ will produce a legal coloring. The random assignment satisfies this property with probability at least $1 - o(1)$, and so the algorithm $\mathcal{B}$ produces a legal coloring for random T_d with a positive probability at least $(1/2 - o(1))$. But this is a contradiction to Corollary 4.1.

Theorem 4.2 *There exists a constant $c > 0$ such that there is no algorithm that employs $c \cdot \sqrt{d}$ colors, runs for $c \cdot \frac{\log n}{\log d}$ rounds, and for any assignment of distinct Ids from the range $[n^3]$ to vertices of T_d provides a legal coloring with a constant probability.*

It is also easy to see that the range $[n^3]$ in Theorem 4.2 can be decreased to $[n]$ at the expense of decreasing the lower bound $c \cdot \frac{\log n}{\log d}$ by a factor of 3. (Instead of considering only n-vertex trees T_d one will have to allow balanced d-regular trees with $n^{1/3}$ vertices, and other $n - n^{1/3}$ vertices forming an isolated component.)

Theorem 4.2 implies that for any $\alpha \geq 3$, any algorithm that α-colors unoriented trees requires $\Omega(\frac{\log n}{\log \alpha})$ rounds. (Just consider a d-regular tree with $d = C \cdot \alpha^2$, for a sufficiently large constant C, and use Theorem 4.2.) Remarkably, this lower bound is tight. In Chapter 5 we will describe an algorithm that is based on forest-decomposition, which α-colors unoriented trees within $O(\frac{\log n}{\log \alpha})$ time!

There is also another important lower bound known. Specifically, Kuhn et al. [50, 52] showed that MM and MIS require $\Omega(\min\{\log \Delta, \sqrt{\log n}\})$ time. Moreover, for the MM problem this lower bound is shown for graphs G with girth$(G) = \Omega(\sqrt{\log n})$. (This is not the case for the MIS problem.) The indistinguishability argument which we described above implies that this lower bound for MM holds even for *unoriented trees*.

Theorem 4.3   *[11, 50, 52] The MM problem for unoriented n–vertex trees requires $\Omega(\sqrt{\log n})$ time. The lower bound applies both to deterministic and randomized algorithms.*

This lower bound is tight as well. Specifically a randomized algorithm that solves MM in $O(\sqrt{\log n})$ time in graphs of constant arboricity was devised in [11].

4.1.2   THE SECOND PROOF

In this section we provide an alternative proof for Theorem 4.2. (In fact, we will show a slightly weaker variant of it, in which we only allow deterministic algorithms.) Recall that for a graph G, a parameter $t \geq 0$, and a vertex v in G, we denote by $\hat{\Gamma}_t(v) = \{u \mid \text{dist}_G(u, v) \leq t\}$ the t-neighborhood of v. For any Id-assignment Φ from $[n]$ to $\hat{\Gamma}_t(v)$ we define a vertex $(\hat{\Gamma}_t(v), \Phi)$ in a graph $N_t(G)$, which we will now describe. The vertices of this graph will be pairs $(\hat{\Gamma}_t(v), \Phi)$, where v is a vertex of G, and Φ is an Id-assignment to vertices of $\hat{\Gamma}_t(v)$. Given two vertices $(\hat{\Gamma}_t(v), \Phi), (\hat{\Gamma}_t(u), \Psi)$ of $N_t(G)$, there is an edge between them in $N_t(G)$ iff all the following conditions hold:

1. Φ (respectively, Ψ) is an Id-assignment for $\hat{\Gamma}_t(v)$ (resp., $\hat{\Gamma}_t(u)$), for some neighboring vertices v, u in G.

2. There exists an Id-assignment Υ for the entire graph G, whose restriction to $\hat{\Gamma}_t(v)$ (respectively, $\hat{\Gamma}_t(u)$) is Φ (resp., Ψ).

Suppose that we are given a distributed algorithm Π that runs for t rounds and colors G in α colors. We can assume without loss of generality that the algorithm operates in two stages (in every single vertex v). In the first stage v collects all the information about $\hat{\Gamma}_t(v)$, i.e., the graph $G(\hat{\Gamma}_t(v))$ and the labels of its vertices. In the second stage v invokes some function f_Π on $\hat{\Gamma}_t(v)$ and the assignment Ψ of its vertices to compute the color $f_\Pi(v) = f_\Pi(\hat{\Gamma}_t(v), \Phi)$ of v.

It is easy to verify that any other algorithm can be simulated by an algorithm that operates in this way. Hence any deterministic algorithm Π that runs for t rounds can be fully characterized by the function f_Π as above from nodes $(\hat{\Gamma}_t(v), \Phi)$ of $N_t(G)$ to colors $[\alpha]$. Observe also that f_Π

is an α-coloring of the graph $N_t(G)$. Indeed if for neighboring pairs $(\hat{\Gamma}_t(v), \Phi), (\hat{\Gamma}_t(u), \Psi)$ the function f_Π assigns the same color, then there exists an Id-assignment Υ for the entire graph for which the algorithm Π returns the same color for both v and u. On the other hand, $(v, u) \in E$, contradiction to the assumption that Π produces a legal α-coloring for G for any input Id-assignment Υ for the vertices of G.

Corollary 4.4   *If there exists a deterministic algorithm Π that runs for t rounds and colors G in α (for every assignment of distinct Ids for its vertices), then $\chi(N_t(G)) \le \alpha$.*

It follows that there is no deterministic algorithm that colors G in $\chi(N_t(G)) - 1$ colors within t rounds. Interestingly, the opposite is correct as well.

Lemma 4.5   *For any graph G and positive integer t, there exists an algorithm that colors G using $\chi(N_t(G))$ colors within t rounds. (Here G is a graph given in advance. An algorithm that colors G is an algorithm that colors the graph for every possible assignment of distinct Ids to the vertices of G.)*

Proof. Let φ be a legal $\chi(N_t(G))$-coloring of the graph $N_t(G)$. Every vertex v is given $N_t(G)$ and φ. (This information can be "hard-wired" into memories of vertices before the computation starts.) In t rounds each vertex v collects the information about $\hat{\Gamma}_t(v)$, including the Ids of its vertices. Let Φ be the Id-assignment to $\hat{\Gamma}_t(v)$ that the vertex v learns. Then v computes the color $\varphi(\hat{\Gamma}_t(v), \Phi)$ of the node $(\hat{\Gamma}_t(v), \Phi)$ of $N_t(G)$, and returns it as its ultimate color. It is easy to verify that the resulting coloring is a legal $\chi(N_t(G))$-coloring for G. $\square$

For most graphs it is very hard to analyze $\chi(N_t(G))$. Some estimates are known only for very few graph families. Specifically, for unoriented d-regular n-vertex trees G it is known (see Section 4.1) that $\chi(N_t(G)) = \Omega(\sqrt{d})$ for $t < \frac{\log n}{\log d}$. Also, for an n-path P_n (and also for an n-cycle C_n) it is known that $\chi(N_t(P_n)) \ge \log^{(2t)} n$ (see Section 4.2). The latter implies that to color P_n with a constant number of colors one needs at least $\frac{1}{2} \log^* n - O(1)$ rounds.

Consider again the d-regular n-vertex graph G_d with $\text{girth}(G_d) > \frac{\log n}{\log d}$ and $\chi(G_d) \ge \frac{1}{2}\sqrt{d}$. (See Section 4.1.) For any t, $\chi(N_t(G_d)) \ge \chi(G_d) \ge \frac{1}{2}\sqrt{d}$. Set $t = \frac{1}{2} \cdot \frac{\log n}{\log d}$, and consider the d-regular unoriented tree T_d. We will next show that $\chi(N_t(T_d)) \ge \chi(N_t(G_d))$. It will follow that $\chi(N_t(T_d)) \ge \frac{1}{2}\sqrt{d}$, i.e., any t-round deterministic algorithm that colors T_d legally (for any choice of distinct Ids) must use at least $\frac{1}{2}\sqrt{d}$ colors.

Lemma 4.6 $N_t(G_d) \subseteq N_t(T_d)$.

Proof. Consider a vertex $(\hat{\Gamma}_t(v), \Phi)$ in $N_t(G_d)$, i.e., $v \in V(G_d)$ and Φ is an Id-assignment for vertices of $\hat{\Gamma}_t(v)$. One can pick an arbitrary vertex $v' \in U$ (i.e., a vertex in T_d at distance at least $\frac{1}{2} \cdot \frac{\log n}{\log d} + 1$ from its closest leaf), and assign its vertices identities according to Φ. Hence $(\hat{\Gamma}_t(v), \Phi)$ is a node in $N_t(T_d)$ as well. For an edge $((\hat{\Gamma}_t(v), \Phi), (\hat{\Gamma}_t(u), \Psi))$ in $N_t(G_d)$, there exist two neighboring vertices $(v, u) \in E(G_d)$ and an Id-assignment Υ whose restriction to $\hat{\Gamma}_t(v)$ (respectively, $\hat{\Gamma}_t(u)$) is Φ (resp., Ψ). Pick two neighboring vertices v', u' in U (in T_d), and assign Ids to vertices of $\hat{\Gamma}_t(v') \cup \hat{\Gamma}_t(u')$ according to Υ. It follows that nodes $(\hat{\Gamma}_t(v), \Phi)$ and $(\hat{\Gamma}_t(u), \Psi)$ are neighboring in $N_t(T_d)$ as well. $\square$

We conclude that $\chi(N_t(T_d)) \geq \chi(N_t(G_d)) \geq \frac{1}{2}\sqrt{d}$, for $t = \frac{1}{2} \cdot \frac{\log n}{\log d}$, proving the lower bound of Theorem 4.2.

4.2 COLORING THE n-PATH P_n

In this section we show that an $O(1)$-coloring of the n-vertex path P_n requires at least $\frac{1}{2} \log^* n - O(1)$ rounds for deterministic algorithms. This result is due to Linial [55]. Naor [65] extended this lower bound to randomized algorithms. Our presentation here is based on [55].

We will start with showing that $\chi(N_t(P_n)) \geq 3$ for $t \leq \frac{n-3}{2}$. As we saw in Section 4.1, this implies that no deterministic algorithm that runs for at most $\frac{n-3}{2}$ rounds can legally 2-color P_n. For a positive integer parameter s, let G_s be the graph whose vertices are s-tuples $(a_1, a_2, ..., a_s)$, $a_i \neq a_j$ for $i \neq j$, and for every $i \in [s]$, $a_i \in [n]$. There are edges $((a_1, a_2, ..., a_s), (a_2, a_3, ..., a_{s+1}))$ in G_s if $(a_1, a_2, ..., a_s)$, $(a_2, a_3, ..., a_{s+1})$ are vertices of G_s and $a_1 \neq a_{s+1}$.

Consider the graph $N_t(P_n)$, for some positive integer t. It contains the graph G_{2t+1}. Indeed, every node $(a_1, a, ..., a_{2s+1})$ in G_{2t+1} can be implemented as a t-neighborhood of a vertex v in the middle of the path $P_n = P$. (The identities $a_1, a_2, ..., a_t, a_{t+1}, a_{t+2}, ..., a_{2t+1}$ are then assigned to the vertices in the t-neighborhood of v. Specifically, v is assigned the Id that is equal to a_{t+1}. The vertex u at distance t from v that lies on the left side of v is assigned the Id a_1. The vertices on the subpath of P that connects u to v are assigned Ids $a_2, ..., a_t$. Symmetrically, the t vertices that follow v on P are assigned Ids $a_{t+2}, ..., a_{2t+1}$. Other vertices of P are assigned arbitrary Ids from $[n] \setminus \{a_1, ..., a_{2t+1}\}$. See Figure 4.1.)

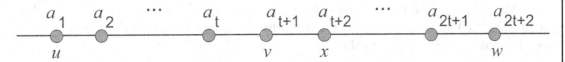

Figure 4.1: Implementing a node $(a_1, a_2, ..., a_{2t+1})$ of G_{2t+1} as a node of $N_t(P)$.

An edge $((a_1, ..., a_{2t+1}), (a_2, ..., a_{2t+1}, a_{2t+2}))$ of G_{2t+1} is implemented similarly as an edge of $N_t(P)$. One just needs to assign the vertex consequent to the one that received Id a_{2t+1}

the Id a_{2t+2}. (The vertex w in Figure 4.1.) Now let x be the neighbor of v that was assigned the label a_{t+2}. The nodes $(\hat{\Gamma}_t(v), \Phi)$ and $(\hat{\Gamma}_t(x), \Phi')$ are neighboring vertices in $N_t(P)$, where Φ is the assignment $(a_1, ..., a_{2t+1})$ to the $2t + 1$ vertices of P centered at v, and Φ' is the assignment $(a_2, ..., a_{2t+2})$ to the $2t + 1$ vertices of P centered at x. Hence G_{2t+1} is a subgraph of $N_t(P_n)$, and so $\chi(G_{2t+1}) \leq \chi(N_t(P_n))$.

We next argue that $\chi(G_{2t+1}) \geq 3$, and this will emply the desired bound $\chi(N_t(P_n)) \geq 3$. To complete the proof it is enough to show that G_{2t+1} contains an odd cycle, and thus it is not bipartite. It is easy to verify that the sequence of nodes $(1, 2, ..., 2t + 1), (2, 3, ..., 2t + 1, 2t + 2), (3, 4, ..., 2t + 2, 2t + 3), (4, 5, ..., 2t + 3, 1), (5, 6, ..., 2t + 3, 1, 2), ..., (2t + 3, 1, 2, ..., 2t)$ forms a cycle of length $(2t + 3)$ in G_{2t+1}, completing the proof. (See Figure 4.2.)

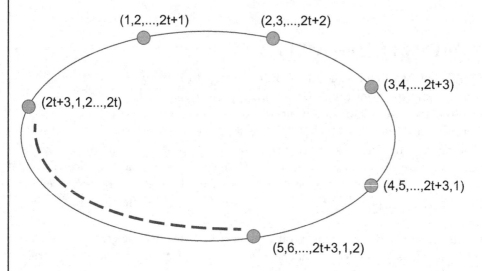

Figure 4.2: An odd cycle in G_{2t+1}.

Theorem 4.7   *For t, $1 \leq t \leq \frac{n-3}{2}$, it holds that $\chi(G_{2t+1}) \geq 3$. Hence P_n cannot be 2-colored by a deterministic algorithm in $\frac{n-3}{2}$ or less rounds.*

We will next strengthen the inequality $\chi(G_{2t+1}) \geq 3$, and show that $\chi(G_{2t+1}) \geq \log^{(2t)} n$. Since $\chi(N_t(P_n)) \geq \chi(G_{2t+1})$, this would imply that no deterministic algorithm that runs for t rounds can use less than $\log^{(2t)} n$ colors.

For a positive integer s, let G'_s be the subgraph of G_s induced by nodes $(a_1, a_2, ..., a_s)$ with $a_1 < a_2 < ... < a_s$. We will view G'_s as a *directed* graph: each edge $(a_1, a_2, ..., a_s), (a_2, a_3, ..., a_{s+1})$ will be oriented toward $(a_2, ..., a_{s+1})$. For a directed graph $H = (V, Q)$, The *directed line graph* $\vec{L}(H) = (Q, \mathcal{E})$ is given by $\mathcal{E} = \{(e = \langle u, v \rangle, e' = \langle v, w \rangle) \mid e, e' \in Q\}$. In the directed line graph $\vec{L}(G'_s)$ of G'_s an arc $\langle (a_1, ..., a_s), (a_2, ..., a_{s+1}) \rangle$ is connected to an arc $\langle(a_2, ..., a_s, a_{s+1}), (a_3, ..., a_{s+1}, a_{s+2})\rangle$. It follows that $\vec{L}(G'_s)$ is isomorphic to G'_{s+1}: we just map each arc $\langle(a_1, ..., a_s), (a_2, ..., a_{s+1})\rangle$ of G'_s to a node $(a_1, a_2, ..., a_{s+1})$ of G'_{s+1}.

Lemma 4.8   *For any directed graph $H = (V, Q)$, $\chi(\vec{L}(H)) \geq \log \chi(H)$.*

Proof. We will argue that

$$\chi(H) \leq 2^{\chi(\vec{L}(H))}. \tag{4.1}$$

Let φ be an x-coloring of $\vec{L}(H)$, for some $x \geq \chi(\vec{L}(H))$. We define a coloring ψ for H in the following way. For each index $i \in [x]$ and vertex $v \in V$ let

$$b_i(v) = \begin{cases} 1 & \text{if there exists an outgoing arc } \langle v, u \rangle \text{ with } \varphi(\langle v, u \rangle) = i \\ 0 & \text{otherwise} \end{cases}$$

Now $\psi(v) = \langle b_1(v), b_2(v), ..., b_x(v) \rangle$. Obviously $\psi(\cdot)$ is a 2^x-coloring. Next we argue the $\psi(\cdot)$ is a legal coloring. Consider an edge $e = \langle v, u \rangle \in Q$. Let $i = \varphi(e)$. Then there exists an outgoing edge of v φ-colored by i, but since $\varphi()$ is legal, there is no outgoing edge of u φ-colored by i. Hence $b_i(v) = 1 \neq b_i(u) = 0$, and so $\varphi(v) \neq \varphi(u)$. Hence ψ is a legal 2^x-coloring of H, proving (4.1). $\qquad \square$

Observe that G'_1 is just an n-clique K_n, with all edges $\langle i, j \rangle$, $i < j$, are oriented toward the endpoint with a greater index. Hence $\chi(G'_1) = n$. As a consequence (by Lemma 4.8), for any positive integer $s \geq 2$, $\chi(G'_s) \geq \log^{(s-1)} n$. In particular, for any positive integer $t \geq 1$, $\chi(G_{2t+1}) \geq \chi(G'_{2t+1}) \geq \log^{(2t)} n$. Since $G_{2t+1} \subseteq N_t(P_n)$, the next theorem follows.

Theorem 4.9   *No deterministic algorithm that runs for t rounds can color P_n with less than $\log^{(2t)} n$ colors.*

Set $t = \frac{\log^* n}{2} - 1$. Then $\log^{(2t)} n = \log^{(\log^* n - 2)} n > 4$. Hence no deterministic algorithm that runs in less than $\frac{\log^* n}{2} - 1$ rounds can 4-color P_n. More generally, we have:

Corollary 4.10   *$O(1)$-coloring P_n by a deterministic algorithm requires at least $\frac{\log^* n}{2} - O(1)$ rounds.*

As was mentioned above, this lower bound (due to [55]) was extended to randomized algorithms in [65].

CHAPTER 5

Forest-Decomposition Algorithms and Applications

Coloring forests can be performed extremely efficiently in the distributed setting, both in terms of running time and number of colors. Using the algorithms of Cole and Vishkin [18] or Goldberg, Plotkin and Shannon [31], one can compute 3-vertex-coloring of a forest in $O(\log^* n)$ time. However, coloring general graphs is a significantly more challenging task. The best currently known deterministic algorithms for general graphs for $(\Delta + 1)$-coloring require at least linear in Δ time, unless Δ is very large.[1] Nevertheless, for a wide range of graph families, it is possible to achieve much better results. If a graph can be decomposed into a reasonably small number of oriented forests, then both the running time and the size of the employed coloring palette can be reduced. Indeed, each of the forests in the decomposition can be colored quickly with 3 colors. However, using the decomposition to achieve a unified legal coloring of the entire input graph is more complicated. In this chapter we describe an algorithm that computes a forest-decomposition for graphs with bounded arboricity (see Section 2.3 for the definition of arboricity), and uses it for coloring them efficiently. The material in this chapter is based on [7]. See also Section 8.1, where we describe a simple forest-decomposition procedure due to Panconesi and Rizzi [68]. The latter procedure applies to graphs with bounded maximum degree Δ.

5.1 H-PARTITION

In this discussion we assume that all vertices know the arboricity a of the input graph and the number of vertices n before the algorithm starts. (See [7] for extensions to scenarios in which the arboricity or/and the number of vertices is unknown.) The algorithm starts with computing an H-*partition* of the graph (to be defined shortly). Then the H-partition is used for computing $O(a)$-forest-decomposition. Recall that the arboricity a is the minimum number of forests into which the edge-set of the input graph can be decomposed. For an integer parameter $A \geq 2a$, an H-*partition* is a vertex-partition into subsets $H_1, H_2, ..., H_\ell \subseteq V$, such that each vertex in H_i, $1 \leq i \leq \ell$, has at most A neighbors in $\bigcup_{j=i}^{\ell} H_j$. The parameter A is called the *degree* of the H-partition $H_1, H_2, ..., H_\ell$. The parameter ℓ is called the *size* of the H-partition. See Figure 5.1 in the end of this section for an illustration.

---

[1]For randomized algorithms the situation is better. Specifically, algorithms that run in $O(\log n)$ time, for all values of Δ, are known [1, 60, 61]. For deterministic algorithms one can compute a $(\Delta + 1)$-coloring in $2^{O(\sqrt{\log n})}$ time [69].

The procedure that computes an H-partition is called *Procedure Partition*. This procedure accepts as input the arboricity a of the graph, and an arbitrarily small positive real constant $\epsilon \leq 2$. The parameter ϵ determines the quality of the resulting H-partition. In other words, smaller values of ϵ result in H-partition with smaller degree, which, in turn, allows one to compute a forest-decomposition with fewer forests. However, selecting small values for ϵ affects the size of the H-partition, and, consequently, the running time is affected as well. Specifically, Procedure Partition computes an H-partition with degree at most $(2 + \epsilon) \cdot a$ and size $\ell = \lceil \frac{2}{\epsilon} \log n \rceil$ within ℓ rounds.

During the execution of Procedure Partition each vertex in V is either active or inactive. Initially, all the vertices are active. For every $i = 1, 2, ..., \ell$, in the ith round each active vertex with at most $(2 + \epsilon) \cdot a$ active neighbors joins the set H_i and becomes inactive. The pseudo-code of Procedure Partition is presented below.

Algorithm 1 Procedure Partition(a,ϵ): partitions the vertices into $\ell = \lceil \frac{2}{\epsilon} \log n \rceil$ sets such that every vertex $v \in H_i$, $i \in \{1, 2, ..., \ell\}$, has at most $(2 + \epsilon) \cdot a$ neighbors in $\bigcup_{j=i}^{\ell} H_j$.

Initially all vertices are active.

An algorithm for each vertex $v \in V$:

1: **for** round $i = 1, 2, ..., \ell$ **do**
2:    **if** v is active and has at most $(2 + \epsilon) \cdot a$ active neighbors **then**
3:       make v inactive
4:       add v to H_i
5:       send the messages 'inactive' and 'v joined H_i' to all the neighbors
6:    **end if**
7:    **for** each received 'inactive' message **do**
8:       mark the sender neighbor as inactive
9:    **end for**
10: **end for**

The next lemma shows that each vertex in the network becomes inactive during the execution, and joins one of the sets $H_1, H_2, ..., H_\ell$.

Lemma 5.1   *A graph $G = (V, E)$ with arboricity $a(G)$ has at least $\frac{\epsilon}{2+\epsilon} \cdot |V|$ vertices with degree $(2 + \epsilon) \cdot a$ or less.*

Proof. Suppose for contradiction that there are more than $\frac{2}{2+\epsilon} \cdot |V|$ vertices with degree greater than $(2 + \epsilon) \cdot a$. It follows that

$$2|E| = \sum_{v \in V} deg(v) > ((2 + \epsilon) \cdot a) \cdot |V| \cdot \frac{2}{2 + \epsilon} = 2 \cdot a \cdot |V| \geq 2 \cdot \frac{|E|}{|V| - 1} \cdot |V| > 2|E|.$$

This is a contradiction.   □

By the definition of arboricity, the subgraph induced by any subset of V of active vertices has arboricity at most a as well.

Lemma 5.2   *For any subgraph G' of G, the arboricity of G' is at most the arboricity of G.*

By Lemmas 5.1 and 5.2, in each round at least $(\frac{\epsilon}{2+\epsilon})$-fraction of the active vertices become inactive, and so after $\log_{(2+\epsilon)/2} n$ rounds all vertices become inactive. Since $\log_{(2+\epsilon)/2} n \leq \frac{2}{\epsilon} \log n$ for ϵ, $0 < \epsilon \leq 2$, we have proved the following lemma.

Lemma 5.3   *For a graph G with $a(G) = a$, and a parameter ϵ, $0 < \epsilon \leq 2$, Procedure Partition(a,ϵ) produces an H-partition $\mathcal{H} = \{H_1, H_2, ..., H_\ell\}$ of size $\ell \leq \left\lceil \log_{(2+\epsilon)/2} n \right\rceil \leq \left\lceil \frac{2}{\epsilon} \log n \right\rceil$.*

The next lemma shows that the H-partition $\mathcal{H}$ has a small degree.

Lemma 5.4   *The H-partition $\mathcal{H} = \{H_1, H_2, ..., H_\ell\}$, $\ell \leq \left\lceil \frac{2}{\epsilon} \log n \right\rceil$, has degree at most $A = (2 + \epsilon) \cdot a$.*

Proof. The vertex v was added to H_j in round number j. Every neighbor of v that belongs to one of the sets $H_j, H_{j+1}, ..., H_\ell$ was added to its set in round j or later. Therefore, at the end of round $j - 1$ all its neighbors in $H_j \cup H_{j+1} \cup ... \cup H_\ell$ were active. The vertex v has been added because the number of its active neighbors was at most $(2 + \epsilon) \cdot a$. Thus the number of the neighbors of v in $H_j \cup H_{j+1} \cup ... \cup H_\ell$ is at most $(2 + \epsilon) \cdot a$.   □

We summarize the properties of Procedure Partition in the following theorem.

Theorem 5.5   *For a graph G with arboricity $a(G) = a$, and a parameter ϵ, $0 < \epsilon \leq 2$, Procedure Partition(a, ϵ) computes an H-partition of size $\ell \leq \left\lceil \frac{2}{\epsilon} \log n \right\rceil$ with degree at most $(2 + \epsilon) \cdot a$. The running time of the procedure is $O(\log n)$.*

This procedure can be also used with a second parameter $q > 2$. (For convenience, this parameter is called ϵ when it is at most 2, and q when it is larger than 2.) Observe that Lemma 5.1 is applicable for all values of the second parameter. The number of rounds required to make all vertices inactive is at most $\log_{\frac{2+q}{2}} n = O(\frac{\log n}{\log q})$, and thus, for $q > 2$, set $\ell = \left\lfloor \log_{\frac{2+q}{2}} n \right\rfloor$. Consequently, the resulting H-partition has size $O(\frac{\log n}{\log q})$ as well. On the other hand, by Lemma 5.4, the degree of the H-partition is at most $(2 + q) \cdot a$.

Corollary 5.6   *For a graph G with arboricity $a(G) = a$, and a parameter q, $q > 2$, Procedure Partition(a,q) computes an H-partition of size $O(\frac{\log n}{\log q})$ with degree $A \leq (2 + q) \cdot a$. The running time of the procedure is $O(\frac{\log n}{\log q})$.*

An H-partition can be employed in order to compute a forest-decomposition as follows. Given an H-partition, one can employ it for computing an acyclic orientation of the input graph, whose out-degree is at most the out-degree of the H-partition. (More details are provided below.) Once an acyclic orientation is computed, each vertex becomes responsible only for its outgoing edges. In this way, for each edge e, exactly one of the endpoints of e is responsible for it. Next, each vertex assigns distinct labels $1, 2, \ldots$ to its outgoing edges. We will soon argue that all edges in the graph that receive the same label form a forest.

Now we turn to describe the procedure for computing forest-decomposition that is called *Procedure Forest-Decomposition*. Similarly to Procedure Partition, it accepts as input the parameters a and ϵ. In the first step it computes an H-partition with degree at most $(2 + \epsilon) \cdot a$. In the next step, it invokes a procedure called *Procedure Orientation*. Procedure Orientation orients the edges of the graph as follows. For each edge $e = (u, v)$, if the endpoints u, v are in different sets $H_i, H_j, i \neq j$, then the edge is oriented toward the endpoint in the set with a greater index. Otherwise, if $i = j$, the edge e is oriented toward the vertex with a greater Id among the two vertices u and v. The orientation μ produced by this step is acyclic. By Lemma 5.4, each vertex has μ-out-degree at most $(2 + \epsilon) \cdot a$.

Finally, in the last step Procedure Forest-Decomposition partitions the edge set of the graph into forests. Each vertex is in charge for its outgoing edges, and it assigns each outgoing edge a different label from the set $\{1, 2, \ldots, \lfloor (2 + \epsilon) \cdot a \rfloor\}$. This step will be henceforth referred to as the *labeling step*.

Algorithm 2 Forest-Decomposition(a, ϵ): partition the edge set into $\lfloor (2 + \epsilon) \cdot a \rfloor$ forests.

1: Invoke Procedure Partition(a, ϵ)   /* See Algorithm 1 */
2: $\mu :=$ Orientation()
3: Assign a distinct label to each μ-outgoing edge of v from the set $\{1, 2, \ldots, \lfloor (2 + \epsilon) \cdot a \rfloor\}$

The time complexity of Procedure Partition is $O(\log n)$, and the steps 2 and 3 of Procedure Forest-Decomposition, orienting and labeling the edges, require $O(1)$ rounds each. Hence the overall time complexity of the forest-decomposition algorithm is $O(\log n)$.

Definition 5.7   *Given an H-decomposition $\mathcal{H} = \{H_1, H_2, \ldots, H_\ell\}$ of a graph $G = (V, E)$, the H-index of a vertex $v \in V$ is the unique index $i \in [\ell] = \{1, 2, \ldots, \ell\}$ such that $v \in H_i$.*

Lemmas 5.8-5.10 constitute the proof of correctness of the algorithm for computing a forest-decomposition.

Lemma 5.8   *The orientation μ formed by Algorithm 2 is consistent.*

Proof. For an edge $e = (u, v)$, if u orients e toward v then either the H-index of v is greater than the H-index of u, or they have the same H-index but $ID(u) < ID(v)$. In both cases v orients e toward v as well. □

Lemma 5.9 *The orientation μ formed by the algorithm is acyclic.*

Proof. We show that there are no directed cycles with respect to μ. Let C be a cycle of G. Let v be a vertex in C such that the H-index i of v is the smallest index of a vertex in C, and such that $ID(v)$ is the smallest identity number in $H_i \cap C$. Let u, w denote the two neighbors of v in C. Obviously, both edges (v, u) and (v, w) are oriented outwards of v, and thus, the μ-out-degree of u in the cycle is 2. Hence C is not a directed cycle with respect to μ. Consequently, the orientation μ is acyclic. □

For each $i \in [\ell]$, consider the graph $G_i = G(H_i)$ induced by the set H_i. Lemma 5.4 implies that the maximum degree $\Delta(G_i)$ of a vertex in G_i is at most $(2 + \epsilon) \cdot a$. Moreover, a stronger statement follows:

Lemma 5.10 *Each vertex has μ–out-degree at most $(2 + \epsilon) \cdot a$.*

Proof. Let v be a vertex of G. Let j be the H-index of v. Each outgoing edge of v is connected to a vertex with an H-index that is greater than or equal to j. Hence by Lemma 5.4, v has at most $(2 + \epsilon) \cdot a$ outgoing edges. □

By Lemma 5.10, once the orientation μ is formed, each vertex can assign distinct labels to its outgoing edges from the range $1, 2, ..., \lfloor (2 + \epsilon) \cdot a \rfloor$. Denote $A = \lfloor (2 + \epsilon) \cdot a \rfloor$. The next lemma shows that the undirected graph induced by the set of edges labeled with the label i, for any $i \in [A]$, does not contain cycles.

Lemma 5.11 *For each label i, the set of edges labeled by i forms a forest.*

Proof. By Lemma 5.9, each cycle of G has a vertex with two outgoing edges in this cycle. Suppose for contradiction that there is a cycle C with all edges labeled by the same label i. There exists a vertex v in this cycle and two edges e_1, e_2 adjacent to v oriented outwards of v. Thus, the algorithm labeled the edges e_1, e_2 with different labels, contradiction. □

We summarize this section with the following corollary.

Corollary 5.12 *For a graph G with arboricity $a = a(G)$, and a parameter ϵ, $0 < \epsilon \leq 2$, Procedure Forest-Decomposition(a, ϵ) partitions the edge set of G into $A = \lfloor (2 + \epsilon) \cdot a \rfloor$ oriented forests in $O(\log n)$ rounds. Moreover, as a result of its execution each vertex v knows the label and the orientation of every edge (v, u) adjacent to v.*

Similarly to Procedure Partition, Procedure Forest-Decomposition can be invoked with second parameter $q > 2$. Lemmas 5.8–5.11 stay unchanged, and thus we obtain the following corollary.

Corollary 5.13   *For a graph G with $a(G) = a$, and a parameter q, $q > 2$, Procedure Forest-Decomposition(a, q) partitions the edge set of G into at most $(2 + q) \cdot a$ forests within time $O(\frac{\log n}{\log q})$.*

See Figure 5.1 for an illustration.

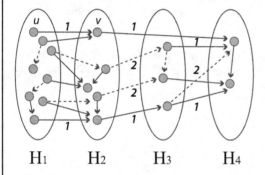

$$H_1 \qquad H_2 \qquad H_3 \qquad H_4$$

Figure 5.1: H-partition and Forest-Decomposition. (Some vertices and edges are omitted from the figure for clarity.) An outgoing edge from a vertex u to a vertex v labeled with a label i means that v is the parent of u in a tree of the ith forest F_i. Solid edges represent edges with the label '1'. Dashed edges represent edges with the label '2'.

5.2   AN $O(a)$-COLORING

A forest-decomposition allows us to compute a legal coloring of the entire graph very quickly. Since each vertex belongs to at most $A = O(a)$ forests, we can maintain a vector of size A for each vertex, for representing colors in different forests. The ith coordinate of the vertex represents the color that is assigned to the vertex in the ith forest. Next, we perform A *parallel* invocations of the CV algorithm for 3-coloring oriented forests. (See Section 3.4.) Invocation i, $i = 1, 2, ..., A$, computes a 3-coloring of the ith forest, and stores the result in the ith coordinate of the vector. Observe that such a vector can be seen as an integer number in the range $\{1, 2, ..., 3^A\}$. Observe also, that for each pair of neighbors u, v in the input graph, there exist a forest $F_i, i \in \{1, 2, ..., A\}$, in the decomposition, such that either u is the parent of v in the forest F_i or vice versa. In any case, the ith coordinate of the vector of v and that of the vector of u are different each from another. Thus, it is possible to compute a 3^A-coloring of a graph which is decomposed into A forests in

$O(\log^* n)$ time. The running time for computing a 3^A-coloring from scratch is $O(\log n)$. (Forest-decompositions can be computed in $O(\log n)$ time by Corollary 5.12. Observe that $A = O(a)$, and so this is a $3^{O(a)}$-coloring.)

We summarize this discussion by the following theorem.

Theorem 5.14   *A legal $3^{O(a)}$-coloring of an n-vertex graph $G = (V, E)$ with arboricity a can be computed deterministically within $O(\log n)$ time.*

Although the above algorithm is very simple and very fast, it produces an output with quite a large number of colors. Next, we discuss how to improve the number of colors to $O(a)$. (Recall that $a \leq \Delta$, and that for a wide range of graph families, a is significantly smaller than Δ.) This, however, comes at a price of increasing the running time. The improved algorithm is called Procedure *Arb-Color*. It colors the input graph G of arboricity $a = a(G)$ using $A + 1$ colors, where $A = \lfloor (2 + \epsilon) \cdot a \rfloor$, and ϵ is an arbitrarily small positive parameter. The running time of the algorithm is $O(a \cdot \log n)$.

The algorithm starts by executing Procedure Forest-Decomposition with the input parameter $a = a(G)$. This invocation returns an H-partition of G of size $\ell \leq \lceil \frac{2}{\epsilon} \log n \rceil$ and degree at most A. Then, for each index i, the graph $G_i = G(H_i)$ induced by the set H_i is colored using the KW algorithm for $(\Delta + 1)$-coloring (see Section 3.8). By Lemma 5.4, for all i, $i = 1, 2, ..., \ell$, the subgraph G_i satisfies $\Delta(G_i) \leq A$. Hence the algorithm colors each graph G_i with at most $A + 1$ colors. Denote by φ_i the coloring of G_i. Although each φ_i is a legal coloring, the resulting coloring of the entire input graph G is not necessarily legal. Thus, it needs to be converted into a legal $(A + 1)$-coloring of G. To this end the subgraphs $G_1, G_2, ..., G_\ell$ are gradually recolored. The recoloring starts from the last subraph G_ℓ, and proceeds backward, ending with the first subgraph G_1.

The recoloring is performed using a new orientation η of G, which is computed from the colorings $\varphi_1, \varphi_2, ..., \varphi_\ell$. The new orientation η is computed using a procedure called *Procedure New-Orientation* that works in the following way. For each edge (u, v) whose endpoints u and v belong to G_i and G_j respectively, for some $i < j$, the edge is oriented toward v. For each edge (u, v) whose both endpoints belong to the same G_i, for some $1 \leq i \leq \ell$, the edge is oriented toward the vertex with a greater φ_i-color. (Since φ_i is a legal coloring of G_i, it necessarily holds that $\varphi_i(u) \neq \varphi_i(v)$.) This completes the description of Procedure New-Orientation.

Observe that the procedure orients all the edges in the input graph, and that for edges e that cross between distinct subgraphs G_i and G_j, the orientations μ and η have assigned the same direction to e. (Recall that the orientation μ was computed within Procedure Forest-Decomposition. See Section 5.1.) However, inside subgraphs these orientations are different. Specifically, the length of the orientation η restricted to a subgraph G_i is at most the number of colors used by φ_i. (See Property 3.4.) This is in contrast to the orientation μ whose length within G_i may be arbitrarily large.

The new orientation η is used for constructing a new coloring φ of the input graph. The coloring is computed according to Property 3.3. Specifically, each vertex waits for all its parents *with respect to* η to select a color. Then it selects its own color to be different from the selections of all its parents. Since the length of η is $O(a \cdot \ell) = O(a \log n)$, and its out-degree is at most the degree of the H-partition, the new coloring φ is computed in $O(a \log n)$ time, and employs $A + 1$ colors. The coloring φ is the final coloring returned by the algorithm. This completes the description of Procedure Arb-Color. Its pseudocode is provided below.

Algorithm 3 Procedure Arb-Color(a,ϵ)

1: $A := \lfloor (2 + \epsilon) \cdot a \rfloor$
2: $\mathcal{H} = (H_1, H_2..., H_\ell) :=$ Forest-Decomposition(a,ϵ)
3: In parallel, color each graph G_i, $i = 1, 2, ..., \ell$, with $A + 1$ colors using the KW algorithm. Denote the resulting colorings φ_i, $i = 1, 2, ..., \ell$.
4: $\eta :=$ New-Orientation()
5: $\varphi :=$ Compute $(A + 1)$-coloring of G using η and Property 3.3

The correctness of the procedure follows from the above discussion. The running time of step 2 is $O(\log n)$. The running time of step 3 is $O(a \log a + \log^* n)$. The running time of step 5 is proportional to the length of the orientation η, which is $O(a \log n)$. The other steps require $O(1)$ time. Thus, the overall running time of Procedure Arb-Color is $O(a \log n)$.

Theorem 5.15 *For a graph G with arboricity $a = a(G)$, and a positive parameter ϵ, $0 < \epsilon \leq 2$, Procedure Arb-Color(a, ϵ) computes an $O(a)$ coloring of G in time $O(a \log n)$.*

We remark that invoking Procedure Arb-Color with $q > 2$ as second parameter results in inferior results than those given by Theorem 5.15. Specifically, it results in $O(q \cdot a)$-coloring in $O(q \cdot a \cdot \log n)$ time.

5.3 FASTER COLORING

On some occasions it is important that the number of colors that an algorithm employs is as small as possible. In other occasions the running time of the algorithm is crucial. Thus, sometimes one may want to compromise the running time for achieving a smaller number of colors, and sometimes the other way around. Thus, a tradeoff between the running time and the number of colors is often handy. Next, we describe an algorithm (from [7]) for computing $O(t \cdot a)$-coloring in $O(\frac{a}{t} \cdot \log n + a)$ time, for a parameter t, $1 \leq t \leq A + 1$. (Recall that $A = \lfloor (2 + \epsilon) \cdot a \rfloor$, for an arbitrarily small positive constant $\epsilon \leq 2$.) The algorithm is called *Procedure Tradeoff-Color*.

We start with describing a special case in which the procedure is invoked with the parameter $t = A + 1$. Later we describe the general case. The first steps of Procedure Tradeoff-Color are similar to those of Procedure Arb-Color (Algorithm 3). Specifically, steps 1–3 are exactly the same as in Procedure Arb-Color, and the only difference is that instead of steps 4-5 it invokes a procedure called *Recolor*.

Procedure Recolor accepts as input the H-partition $\mathcal{H} = \{H_1, H_2, ..., H_\ell\}$ of the graph G computed by Procedure Forest-Decomposition in step 2. Procedure Recolor proceeds iteratively, and creates a new coloring ψ. Vertices of the set H_ℓ retain their colors. For all other vertices $v \in V \setminus H_\ell$, $\psi(v)$ is initialized as NULL. In iteration i, $i = 1, 2, ..., \ell - 1$, vertices of the set $H_{\ell-i}$ are recolored. In the case of $t = A + 1$, each iteration requires exactly one round. All vertices of $H_{\ell-i}$ select a new color in parallel. A vertex v with $\varphi_{\ell-i}(v) = k$, where $1 \le k \le A + 1$, selects a new color from the range $\{(k - 1) \cdot (A + 1) + 1, (k - 1) \cdot (A + 1) + 2, ..., k \cdot (A + 1)\} = [(k - 1) \cdot (A + 1) + 1, \ k \cdot (A + 1)]$, which is not used by any neighbor of v in $\bigcup_{j=\ell-i}^{\ell} H_j$. (In other words, $\psi(v)$ is selected from the set $[(k - 1)(A + 1) + 1, k \cdot (A + 1)] \setminus \{\psi(w) \mid w \in \Gamma(v) \cap \bigcup_{j=\ell-i}^{\ell} H_j\}$. Note that in this variant of the algorithm, when the value of $\psi(v)$ is selected it holds that $\psi(v) = $ NULL for every $w \in H_{\ell-i}$.) Observe that there is at least one such color for any vertex v, because $deg(v, \bigcup_{j=\ell-i}^{\ell} H_j) \le A$, and so $|\{\psi(u) \mid u \in \bigcup_{j=\ell-i}^{\ell} H_j, \psi(u) \ne$ NULL$\}| \le A$ as well.

Consider, for example, iteration 1. In this iteration the vertices of $H_{\ell-1}$ select a new color. Specifically, all vertices v with $\varphi_{\ell-1}(v) = 1$ select a new color from the range $\{1, 2, ..., A + 1\}$. In parallel, the vertices v with $\varphi_{\ell-1}(v) = 2$ select a new color from the range $\{A + 2, A + 3, ..., 2(A + 1)\}$, and so on. Observe that for any pair of neighbors u, v that belong to the same $H_{\ell-i}$, $1 \le i < \ell$, their $\varphi_{\ell-i}$-colors are different, and that distinct $\varphi_{\ell-i}$-colors are associated with disjoint palettes (ranges). Hence u and v select distinct colors. Morover, any pair that belong to distinct H-sets select distinct colors as well. In this case, the vertex with a smaller H-index necessarily selects a new color which is distinct from the selection of its neighbor with a greater H-index.

Now we turn to the general case where $1 \le t \le A + 1$. Similarly to the previous case, Procedure Tradeoff-Color begins with executing steps 1-3 as in Procedure Arb-Color. Then it executes a general version of Procedure Recolor. (This version will be described shortly.) The pseudocode of Procedure Tradeoff-Color is provided below.

Algorithm 4 Procedure Tradeoff-Color(a, ϵ, t)

1: Execute steps 1-3 of Procedure Arb-Color
2: Recolor($t, \mathcal{H}$)

Procedure Recolor recolors roughly t color classes of $H_{\ell-i}$ in the same round. Specifically, Procedure Recolor groups the $(A + 1)$ color classes $C_1, C_2, ..., C_{A+1}$ of $H_{\ell-i}$ into $p = \lceil \frac{A+1}{t} \rceil$ disjoint subsets $S_1, S_2, ..., S_p$. Each subset S_j, $j = 1, 2, ..., p$, contains the color classes C_r with indices $r \in I_j = \{(j - 1)t + 1, (j - 1)t + 2, ..., \min\{j \cdot t, A + 1\}\}$, i.e., $S_j = \{C_r \mid r \in I_j\}$.

The ith iteration of Procedure Recolor continues for p rounds. In round j, $j = 1, 2, ..., p$, vertices of color classes C_r, $r \in I_j$, are recolored in parallel. To guarantee that no pair of neighboring vertices $u \in C_r$, $w \in C'_r$, $r \neq r'$, $r, r' \in I_j$, will select the same color, the color classes $\{C_r \mid r \in I_j\}$ are assigned disjoint palettes $\{P_r \mid r \in I_j\}$, $P_r = \{(A+1)(r-1-(j-1)t)+1,$ $(A+1)(r-1-(j-1)t)+2, ..., (A+1)(r-1-(j-1)t)+(A+1)\}$.

In other words, the color class $C_{(j-1)t+1}$ (i.e., $r = (j-1)t + 1$) is assigned the palette $P_{(j-1)t+1} = \{1, 2, ..., A+1\}$, the color class $C_{(j-1)t+2}$ is assigned the palette $P_{(j-1)t+2} = \{(A+1)+1, (A+1)+2, ..., 2(A+1)\}$, etc., for every $j = 1, 2, ..., p$.

Consider a vertex $v \in C_r$, $r \in I_j$. In round j of the ith iteration the vertex v selects a color from its palette P_r which is not taken by any neighbor in the set W of already recolored vertices. This completes the description of Procedure Recolor. Its pseudocode is provided below.

Algorithm 5 Procedure Recolor $(t, \mathcal{H} = (H_1, H_2, ..., H_\ell))$

1: $W := \emptyset$ /* the set of recolored vertices */
2: **for** $i := \ell - 1$ downto 1 **do**
3:      $k = ((\varphi_i(v) - 1) \bmod t)$
4:      **for** round $p := 1$ to $\left\lceil \frac{A+1}{t} \right\rceil$ **do**
5:          **for** each vertex v in H_i such that $(p-1) \cdot t < \varphi_i(v) \leq \min\{p \cdot t, A+1\}$ (in parallel) **do**
6:              recolor v with a color from the set:
                $\{k \cdot (A+1) + 1, k \cdot (A+1) + 2, ..., (k+1) \cdot (A+1)\} \setminus \{\psi(w) \mid w \in W \cap \Gamma(v)\}$
7:              $W := W \cup \{v\}$
8:          **end for**
9:      **end for**
10: **end for**

Each palette P_r contains $(A+1)$ colors. Consider a vertex v and the set W at the time when v is recolored (in step 6 of Algorithm 5). It holds that $\deg(v, W) \leq \deg(v, \bigcup_{j=\ell-i}^{\ell} H_j) \leq A$. Hence there necessarily exists a color for v in its palette, which is not used by its neighbors in W. Using an inductive argument on the number of iterations it can be shown that Procedure Tradeoff-Color produces a legal coloring.

For an upper bound on its running time, observe that Procedure Recolor runs for $O(\log n)$ iterations, and each iteration requires $\left\lceil \frac{A+1}{t} \right\rceil = O(\frac{a}{t})$ rounds. Hence the running time of Procedure Recolor is $O(\frac{a}{t} \log n)$. The running time of the step which computes a forest-decomposition is $O(\log n)$. Finally, invoking the KW algorithm (see Section 3.8, and step 3 of Procedure Arb-Color, Algorithm 3) requires $O(a \log a + \log^* n)$ rounds. Hence the overall running time of Procedure Tradeoff-Color is $O(\frac{a}{t} \cdot \log n + a \log a)$.

However, the improved running time of Procedure Tradeoff-Color (in comparison to the running time of Procedure Arb-Color—see Theorem 5.15) comes at a price. Specifically, since we used t disjoint palettes of size $A + 1$ each, the number of colors that were used is $t \cdot (A+1) = O(t \cdot a)$. We summarize the properties of Procedure Tradeoff-Color in the following theorem.

Theorem 5.16   *For a positive parameter t, $1 \leq t \leq A + 1$, Procedure Tradeoff-Color produces an $O(a \cdot t)$-coloring of the input graph in time $O(\frac{a}{t} \cdot \log n + a \log a)$.*

We remark that in Section 6 we will show that $(\Delta + 1)$-coloring for general graphs can be computed within $O(\Delta + \log^* n)$ time, rather than in $O(\Delta \cdot \log \Delta + \log^* n)$ time. This speeds up the algorithm of Theorem 5.16. Specifically, the improved running time is $O(\frac{a}{t} \cdot \log n + a)$.

Notice that by substituting $t = 1$ we obtain the $O(a)$-coloring algorithm (Procedure Arb-Color) which was described in Section 5.2. (See Theorem 5.15.)

Next, we describe a variant of Procedure Tradeoff-Color, that accepts as input $a = a(G)$, and a parameter q, $q > 2$. (In other words, the second parameter that the procedure accepts is now greater than 2, as opposed to $\epsilon \leq 2$.) This new variant computes an $O(a^2 \cdot q)$-coloring. In its first step it invokes Procedure Forest-Decomposition with the same pair of parameters a and q. By Corollary 5.13, this procedure partitions the edge set of G into at most $(2 + q) \cdot a$ forests, and it does so within time $O(\frac{\log n}{\log q})$. The other steps are very similar to those of the previous variant (when invoked with $t = A + 1$). The only difference is that the value of A is now $(2 + q) \cdot a$ and not $\lfloor (2 + \epsilon) \cdot a \rfloor$. By the same argument, this new variant computes an $O(a \cdot q \cdot t)$-coloring in $O\left(\frac{(2+q) \cdot a}{t} \cdot \frac{\log n}{\log q} + (2 + q) \cdot a \right)$ time, for any t, $1 \leq t \leq (2 + q) \cdot a = A$. In particular, by setting $t = a \cdot q$ we obtain an $O(a^2 \cdot q^2)$-coloring within $O(\frac{\log n}{\log q} + q \cdot a)$ time.

Finally, set $q' = q^2$. We get an $O(a^2 \cdot q')$-coloring within time $O(\frac{\log n}{\log q'} + a \cdot \sqrt{q'})$.

Corollary 5.17   *For an n-vertex graph G with arboricity a and a parameter $q > 2$, Procedure Tradeoff-Color invoked with parameters a and q computes an $O(a^2 \cdot q)$-coloring in time $O(\frac{\log n}{\log q} + a \cdot \sqrt{q})$.*

Consider an unoriented n-vertex tree T. Observe that its arboricity $a(T)$ is equal to 1. Set $q = \Delta^\epsilon$, for an arbitrarily small constant $\epsilon > 0$. Corollary 5.17 implies an $O(\Delta^\epsilon)$-coloring of T within $O(\frac{\log n}{\log \Delta})$ time. On the other hand, Linial [56] showed that an $o(\Delta^{1/2})$-coloring of an unoriented Δ-regular tree requires $\Omega(\frac{\log n}{\log \Delta})$ time (see Section 4.1). Therefore, remarkably, the running time of the $O(\Delta^\epsilon)$-coloring algorithm (provided by Corollary 5.17) for graphs with constant arboricity cannot be improved by more than a constant factor.

5.4   MIS ALGORITHMS

In this section we capitalize on the results of Section 5.3, and describe an algorithm that computes an MIS in graphs with bounded arboricity in sublogarithmic time. The algorithm employs the basic reduction from MIS to coloring. (See Section 3.2.)

First, observe that by Corollary 5.17, for any graph with arboricity $O((\log n)^{1/2-\epsilon})$, for a positive constant $\epsilon < \frac{1}{2}$, a legal $O(\frac{\log n}{\log \log n})$-coloring can be found in $O(\frac{\log n}{\log \log n})$ time. (To this end, set $q = (\log n)^\epsilon$.) Then the basic color reduction technique (see Section 3.2) that reduces the number of colors, one color per round, can be used to achieve $(\Delta + 1)$-coloring in additional $O(\frac{\log n}{\log \log n})$ rounds. We summarize this fact in the following corollary.

Corollary 5.18 *For a graph G with arboricity $a(G) = O((\log n)^{1/2-\epsilon})$, $0 < \epsilon < 1/2$, both $(\Delta + 1)$-coloring and $O(\frac{\log n}{\log \log n})$-coloring can be found in $O(\frac{\log n}{\log \log n})$ time.*

Corollary 5.18 can be used in conjunction with the basic reduction from MIS to coloring. (See Section 3.2.) Specifically, given an $O(\frac{\log n}{\log \log n})$-coloring, the reduction produces an MIS by handling one color class in each round. The overall running time is $O(\frac{\log n}{\log \log n})$. Consequently, we obtain an MIS algorithm for graphs with bounded arboricity that runs in sublogarithmic time.

Theorem 5.19 *Consider an n-vertex graph G with arboricity $a(G) = O((\log n)^{1/2-\epsilon})$, $0 < \epsilon < 1/2$. Procedure Tradeoff-Color combined with the standard reduction from an MIS to coloring, computes an MIS of G in time $O(\frac{\log n}{\log \log n})$.*

Whenever $a = \Omega(\sqrt{\log n})$ the same reduction can be used in conjunction with Lemma 5.16. The running time of the resulting algorithm for computing MIS becomes $O(\frac{a}{t} \cdot \log n + a \cdot t)$. This expression is optimized by setting $t = \sqrt{\log n}$.

Theorem 5.20 *Consider an n-vertex graph G with arboricity $a(G) = \Omega(\sqrt{\log n})$. Procedure Tradeoff-Color invoked with parameters a and $t = \sqrt{\log n}$, combined with the standard reduction from MIS to coloring, computes an MIS of G in time $O(a \cdot \sqrt{\log n})$.*

In particular, Theorem 5.20 implies that an MIS can be computed deterministically in polylogarithmic time on graphs with polylogarithmic arboricity. (This follows from Theorem 5.15 as well.)

In [7] it is shown that the algorithms presented in this section can be extended to scenarios in which the vertices do not know the value of the arboricity a or the number of vertices n at the beginning of the computation. The effect of the generalization on the running time of these algorithms is minor. The description of these extensions is outside the scope of this monograph. A far more general approach can be found in [44]. This approach allows one to transform algorithms that require some global knowledge into algorithms that do not require it, for a wide range of distributed algorithms.

CHAPTER 6

Defective Coloring

In this section we discuss computation of defective colorings (see also Section 2.4), and show how defective colorings can be transformed into legal ones. Specifically, we describe a $(\Delta + 1)$-coloring algorithm that requires $O(\Delta) + \log^* n$ time, which is based on defective coloring. The results of this section are due to [8, 48].

In this section and later we assume that all vertices know Δ and n before the beginning of execution. In the previous section we noted that many distributed algorithms can be extended to work without knowing in advance such parameters. In particular, it is shown in [44] that the legal $(\Delta + 1)$-coloring algorithms described in this section can be generalized to the scenario when Δ and n are not known in advance. The generalization affects the running time only by constant factors.

6.1 EMPLOYING DEFECTIVE COLORING FOR COMPUTING LEGAL COLORING

In a graph G colored by a defective coloring ψ a vertex may have a color identical to colors of some of its neighbors. Nevertheless, the number of neighbors with an identical color is bounded by the defect of ψ. This property allows one to employ defective colorings in order to compute legal colorings efficiently. Suppose that ψ is a d-defective p-coloring, for some integers d and p. Each vertex v in G has at most d neighbors colored with the color $\psi(v)$. Therefore, for $i = 1, 2, ..., p$, the subgraph $G_i \subseteq G$ induced by all vertices that are colored with color i, has maximum degree at most d. Hence, G_i can be colored with $(d + 1)$-colors, rather than $(\Delta + 1)$. Moreover, the running time of computing a $(d + 1)$-coloring of G_i depends on d as well. For example, one can use the KW algorithm (see Section 3.8) to compute a $(d + 1)$-coloring of G_i in $O(d \log d) + \log^* n$ time.

Suppose that we could compute a $\lfloor \Delta/p \rfloor$-defective p-coloring ψ of the graph G, for any p, $1 \le p \le \Delta$. In this case $d = \lfloor \Delta/p \rfloor$. Suppose also that the running time of this computation would be $f(n, \Delta)$, for some function f. Then we could color legally, in parallel, the subgraphs $G_1, G_2, ..., G_p$ induced by the color classes of ψ. We would use the color palette $\mathcal{P}_1 = \{1, 2, ..., d + 1\}$ for G_1, the color palette $\mathcal{P}_2 = \{d + 2, d + 3, ..., 2(d + 1)\}$ for G_2, and so on. Coloring all graphs G_i with the palettes $\mathcal{P}_i$ results in a legal $(\lfloor \Delta/p + 1 \rfloor \cdot p) = O(\Delta)$-coloring of G. (The coloring is legal because any pair of neighbors that belong to the same G_i are colored with distinct colors, as a result of invoking the KW algorithm on G_i. Any pair of vertices that belong to different subgraphs G_i and G_j are colored using disjoint palettes $\mathcal{P}_i$ and $\mathcal{P}_j$.)

Since the KW algorithm is used for coloring the subgraphs G_i, the overall running time would be $f(n, \Delta) + O(\Delta/p \cdot \log(\Delta/p)) + \log^* n$.

Thus, the ability to compute a $\lfloor \Delta/p \rfloor$-defective p-coloring efficiently, for sufficiently large p, would result in a legal $O(\Delta)$-coloring algorithm with sublinear in Δ running time. Unfortunately, computing such a defective coloring is a challenging open problem. (Though, in the sequential setting, a $\lfloor \Delta/p \rfloor$-defective p-coloring, can be computed for any input graph G, and any parameter p, using a simple greedy algorithm [58]. See Section 2.4.) On the other hand, a defective coloring with somewhat weaker parameters is sufficient for computing a $(\Delta + 1)$-coloring in $O(\Delta) + \log^* n$ time. Specifically, an $O(\Delta/p)$-defective p^2-coloring is appropriate for this goal, and it can be efficiently computed in the distributed setting. In this section we discuss how to use an $O(\Delta/p)$-defective p^2-coloring for computing a legal $(\Delta + 1)$-coloring. In the next section we describe how to compute an $O(\Delta/p)$-defective p^2-coloring from scratch.

We will be using the following theorem that states that an appropriate defective coloring can be computed efficiently. In the next section we discuss an algorithm that computes it, and prove its correctness.

Theorem 6.1 *Let p be a parameter such that $p \leq \Delta^\epsilon$, for an arbitrarily small constant $\epsilon > 0$. It is possible to compute an $O(\Delta/p)$-defective p^2-coloring within $O(\Delta^{3\epsilon}) + \log^* n$ deterministic time.*

Remark: This theorem is from [8]. A faster algorithm for computing an $O(\Delta/p)$-defective p^2-coloring for any p, $1 \leq p \leq \Delta$, was devised in [48]. The running time of that algorithm is $\log^* n + O(1)$.

We start with presenting a legal $(\Delta + 1)$-coloring algorithm that runs in $O(\Delta \log \log \Delta + \log^* n)$ time. This is already a significant improvement over the KW algorithm. This improved algorithm is called $\mathcal{A}_2$. (The KW algorithm will be denoted by $\mathcal{A}_1$.) The algorithm accepts as input a graph G. It starts with computing an $O(\Delta/p)$-defective p^2-coloring ψ of G, where $p = \lfloor \log \Delta \rfloor$. Recall that the color classes of ψ induce a partition into p^2 subgraphs $G_1, G_2, ..., G_{p^2}$, with maximum degree $O(\Delta/p) = O(\Delta/\log \Delta)$ each. Next, the algorithm $\mathcal{A}_2$ computes legal colorings of $G_1, G_2, ..., G_{p^2}$, in parallel. It does so by assigning disjoint palettes $\mathcal{P}_1, \mathcal{P}_2, ..., \mathcal{P}_{p^2}$ to the subgraphs, and employing the KW algorithm for computing an $O(\Delta/\log \Delta)$-coloring for each subgraph G_i, $i = 1, 2, ..., p^2$, in parallel. These colorings constitute a legal coloring of the entire graph using $O(\Delta/p \cdot p^2) = O(\Delta \log \Delta)$ colors. Finally, on its last step, the algorithm $\mathcal{A}_2$ reduces the number of colors from $O(\Delta \log \Delta)$ to $(\Delta + 1)$ using the KW iterative procedure. (Recall that the KW iterative procedure starts from a legal m-coloring, for some $m > \Delta$, and computes a legal $(\Delta + 1)$-coloring in $O(\Delta \log \frac{m}{\Delta})$ time. See Section 3.8.) See Algoritm 6 for the pseudocode of $\mathcal{A}_2$. The proof of correctness of the algorithm, and its running time analysis, are provided below.

Algorithm 6 $\mathcal{A}_2(G)$

1: $p := \lfloor \log \Delta \rfloor$
2: $\psi :=$ compute an $O(\Delta/p)$-defective p^2-coloring of G
3: Let $G_1, G_2, ..., G_{p^2}$ denote the subgraphs induced by the color classes of ψ
4: **for** $i = 1, 2, ..., p^2$, in parallel **do**
5:    $\varphi_i :=$ compute a legal $O(\Delta/p)$-coloring of G_i using the KW algorithm
6: **end for**
7: $\varphi :=$ compute a legal $O(\Delta \cdot p)$-coloring from $\varphi_1, \varphi_2, ..., \varphi_{p^2}$
8: $\varphi' :=$ invoke the KW iterative procedure on φ
9: return φ'

Theorem 6.2   *Algorithm $\mathcal{A}_2$ computes a legal $(\Delta + 1)$-coloring of G in $O(\Delta \log \log \Delta + \log^* n)$ time.*

Proof. First, we prove the correctness of the algorithm. Recall that all vertices know Δ before the execution starts. Let c be the constant hidden in the O-notation in the defect parameter in line 2 of the algorithm. The constant c is independent of the input graph, and thus can be provided to the vertices before the execution starts, as well. Therefore, in line 5 of the algorithm, for each vertex $v \in G_i, i = 1, 2, ..., p^2$, a color $\varphi_i(v)$ is computed such that $\varphi_i(v) \in \{(i-1) \cdot (c \cdot \lfloor \Delta/p \rfloor + 1) + 1, (i-1) \cdot (c \cdot \lfloor \Delta/p \rfloor + 1) + 2, ..., i \cdot (c \cdot \lfloor \Delta/p \rfloor + 1)\}$, and for each neighbor u of v in G_i, it holds that $\varphi_i(u) \neq \varphi_i(v)$. In line 7 a coloring φ of the entire graph is computed, by setting for each $v \in G_i, \varphi(v) := \varphi_i(v)$, for all $i = 1, 2, ..., p^2$. The coloring φ is legal since for any pair of neighbors u, v, they either belong to the same set G_i, which implies $\varphi(u) = \varphi_i(u) \neq \varphi_i(v) = \varphi(v)$, or belong to distinct sets G_i and $G_j, i \neq j$. In the latter case the ranges from which the colors $\varphi_i(u)$ and $\varphi_j(v)$ were selected are disjoint, and thus $\varphi(u) \neq \varphi(v)$ as well. Therefore, φ is a legal coloring that employs $((c \cdot \lfloor \Delta/p \rfloor + 1) \cdot p^2) = O(\Delta \cdot p) = O(\Delta \log \Delta)$ colors. In the last step this coloring is transformed into a legal $(\Delta + 1)$ coloring of G using the KW iterative procedure. This completes the correctness proof.

Next, we analyze the running time of the algorithm. By Theorem 6.1, line 2 requires $O(\Delta^{3 \cdot \epsilon} + \log^* n)$ time. Line 5 invokes the KW algorithm on graphs with maximum degree $O(\Delta/p) = O(\Delta/\log \Delta)$. This requires $O(\Delta/\log \Delta \cdot \log(\Delta/\log \Delta) + \log^* n) = O(\Delta + \log^* n)$ time. Line 7 is performed locally without any communication. Line 8 invokes the KW iterative procedure on a graph with an initial m-coloring, where $m = O(\Delta \log \Delta)$. The running time of this invocation is $O(\Delta \cdot \log(\frac{m}{\Delta})) = O(\Delta \log \log \Delta)$. Hence, the overall running time is $O(\Delta \log \log \Delta + \log^* n)$. $\square$

Next, we build a series of algorithms $\mathcal{A}_3, \mathcal{A}_4, \mathcal{A}_5, ...$ that compute $(\Delta + 1)$-coloring. Each algorithm $\mathcal{A}_k, k = 3, 4, 5, ...$, improves upon the algorithm $\mathcal{A}_{k-1}$. Specifically, for any constant integer $k > 2$, the running time of $\mathcal{A}_k$ is $O(\Delta \log^{(k)} \Delta + \log^* n)$. The structure of an algorithm $\mathcal{A}_k$ is very similar to that of $\mathcal{A}_2$. The main difference is that instead of using the KW algorithm in line 5, it invokes the algorithm $\mathcal{A}_{k-1}$. In addition, the values of some parameters are changed appropriately. See the pseudocode of an algorithm $\mathcal{A}_k$ below. Its analysis is provided in the next theorem.

Algorithm 7 $\mathcal{A}_k(G)$

1: $p := \left\lfloor \log^{(k-1)} \Delta \right\rfloor$
2: $\psi :=$ compute an $O(\Delta/p)$-defective p^2-coloring of G
3: Let $G_1, G_2, ..., G_{p^2}$ denote the subgraphs induced by the color classes of ψ
4: **for** $i = 1, 2, ..., p^2$, in parallel **do**
5: $\quad \varphi_i :=$ compute a legal $O(\Delta/p)$-coloring of G_i using the algorithm $\mathcal{A}_{k-1}$
6: **end for**
7: $\varphi :=$ compute a legal $O(\Delta \cdot p)$-coloring from $\varphi_1, \varphi_2, ..., \varphi_{p^2}$
8: $\varphi' :=$ invoke the KW iterative procedure on φ
9: return φ'

Theorem 6.3 *For any constant integer $k \geq 2$, the algorithm $\mathcal{A}_k$ computes a legal $(\Delta + 1)$-coloring of G in $O(\Delta \log^{(k)} \Delta + \log^* n)$ time.*

Proof. We prove the theorem by induction on k. The base case ($k = 2$) follows directly from Theorem 6.2. For the induction step, assume that an algorithm $\mathcal{A}_{k-1}$ computes a $(\Delta + 1)$-coloring in $O(\Delta \log^{(k-1)} \Delta + \log^* n)$ time. Next, we analyze the algorithm $\mathcal{A}_k$. The proof of correctness for $\mathcal{A}_k$ is very similar to the proof of Theorem 6.2. Thus, we present here only the running time analysis. Line 2 of Algorithm $\mathcal{A}_k$ requires $O(\Delta^{3\epsilon} + \log^* n)$ time, by Theorem 6.1. By the induction hypothesis, line 5 of $\mathcal{A}_k$ requires $O(\Delta/p \cdot \log^{(k-1)}(\Delta/p) + \log^* n) = O(\Delta + \log^* n)$ time. (Recall that $p = \left\lfloor \log^{(k-1)} \Delta \right\rfloor$.) Line 8 of $\mathcal{A}_k$ invokes the KW iterative procedure on an m-colored graph with $m = O(\Delta \cdot p) = O(\Delta \cdot \log^{(k-1)} \Delta)$. The running time of this invocation is $O(\Delta \cdot \log(\frac{m}{\Delta})) = O(\Delta \log^{(k)} \Delta)$. Therefore, the overall running time of the algorithm $\mathcal{A}_k$ is $O(\Delta \log^{(k)} \Delta + \log^* n)$. $\square$

The series of algorithms $\mathcal{A}_2, \mathcal{A}_3, \mathcal{A}_4, ..., \mathcal{A}_k$ can be extended to superconstant values of k. In particular, for $k = \lceil \log^* \Delta \rceil$, the algorithm $\mathcal{A}_k$ requires $O(\Delta + \log^* \Delta \log^* n)$ time. By a more sophisticated algorithm, this can be improved to $O(\Delta) + \log^* n$. Since this algorithm is somewhat technically involved, we will not present it here. (The details can be found in [8].) Instead, we describe an algorithm due to [48] that achieves the same running time, but employs a different technique. However, it is still based on computation of defective colorings. It requires computing a (Δ/c)-defective $O(c^2)$-coloring, for a constant c. Observe that it is possible to achieve such a coloring using Theorem 6.1, within $o(\Delta) + \log^* n$ time. To this end, one needs to select p to be larger than the constant hidden in the O-notation of the defect parameter $O(\Delta/p)$ in Theorem 6.1. We summarize this in the next theorem.

Theorem 6.4   *For any constant integer $c > 0$, a (Δ/c)-defective $O(c^2)$-coloring can be computed in $o(\Delta) + \log^* n$ time.*

The additive term of $\log^* n$ in the running time given in Theorem 6.4 corresponds to an initial stage of the algorithm for computing defective coloring. This stage computes a legal $O(\Delta^2)$-coloring. In the consequent stages of the algorithm it is used to compute a (Δ/c)-defective $O(c^2)$-coloring in $o(\Delta)$-time. Therefore, if a legal $O(\Delta^2)$-coloring is provided a priori, computing the defective coloring as above requires $o(\Delta)$ time (rather than $o(\Delta) + \log^* n$ time).

Using Theorem 6.4 a legal $(\Delta + 1)$-coloring algorithm that runs in $O(\Delta) + \log^* n$ time is obtained in the following way. The algorithm accepts as input the graph G. First, it computes a $(\Delta/2)$-defective $O(1)$-coloring ψ of G. Then it recursively computes legal $(\Delta/2 + 1)$-colorings of the $O(1)$ graphs induced by the color classes of ψ. Next, these colorings are merged into a unified legal $O(\Delta)$-coloring of G. Finally, the number of colors is reduced to $(\Delta + 1)$. This completes the description of the algorithm. Its pseudocode is provided below. In the pseudocode, $\tilde{\Delta}$ denotes the maximum degree in the input graph G. $\Delta' = \Delta(G')$ denotes (an upper bound on) the maximum degree of the graph G' in which the procedure is invoked. (G' is a subgraph of G. In the first invocation $G' = G$ and $\Delta' = \tilde{\Delta}$). Next, we prove the correctness of the algorithm and analyze its running time.

Theorem 6.5   *Procedure Delta-Col invoked on an input graph G with maximum degree Δ computes a legal $(\Delta + 1)$-coloring of G in $O(\Delta) + \log^* n$ time.*

Proof. We start with proving the correctness of the algorithm. The proof is by induction on Δ. For the base case ($\Delta = 1$), the algorithm computes a legal $(\Delta + 1)$-coloring of G in line 2 of the algorithm. For the induction step, assume that the algorithm is correct for any $\Delta' < \Delta$. We prove the correctness for graphs with $\Delta(G) = \Delta = \tilde{\Delta}$. The algorithm computes a d-defective c-coloring of G in line 5. It induces a partition of G into c subgraphs $G_1, G_2, ..., G_c$, each with maximum degree at most $d = \Delta/2$. Then, Procedure Delta-Col is invoked recursively on these subgraphs in line 8. By the induction hypothesis, it computes legal $(\Delta/2 + 1)$-colorings $\varphi_1, \varphi_2, ..., \varphi_c$, for $G_1, G_2, ..., G_c$, respectively. Consequently, these colorings can be transformed into a legal $(c \cdot (\Delta/2 + 1))$-coloring of G, in line 10 of the algorithm. Then, the number of colors is reduced to $(\Delta + 1)$ using the KW iterative procedure, in line 11. This completes the correctness proof.

Algorithm 8 Procedure Delta-Col(G')

1: **if** ($\Delta' < \tilde{\Delta}/\log\tilde{\Delta}$) **then**
2:     φ' := compute a legal ($\Delta' + 1$)-coloring using the KW iterative procedure
3: **else**
4:     $d := \lfloor \Delta'/2 \rfloor$
5:     ψ := compute a d-defective c-coloring using Theorem 6.4
       /* $c = O(1)$ is a universal constant */
6:     **for all** colors $i \in [c]$ in parallel **do**
7:         denote by G_i the subgraph induced by all vertices with ψ-color i
8:         Delta-Col(G_i)   /* recursive call */
9:     **end for**
10:    φ := compute a legal $c \cdot (d + 1)$-coloring from $\varphi_1, \varphi_2, ..., \varphi_c$
11:    φ' := invoke the KW iterative procedure with input coloring φ
12: **end if**
13: return φ'

Next, we analyze the running time of the algorithm. First, we note that computing a d-defective c-coloring requires $o(\Delta) + \log^* n$ only in the first time the computation is performed. (See Theorem 6.4, and the discussion that follows it.) In the next computations of defective colorings, the running time becomes $o(\Delta)$. This is possible since during the first computation an $O(\tilde{\Delta}^2)$-coloring ψ of the input graph is computed in $\log^* n + O(1)$ time. Given the $O(\tilde{\Delta}^2)$-coloring ψ of the input graph we compute an $O(\Delta'^2)$-coloring ψ' of a subgraph G' in $O(1)$ time via the algorithm of Linial [56]. Specifically, Δ' satisfies $\Delta' \geq \tilde{\Delta}/\log\tilde{\Delta}$. Hence ψ can be viewed also as an $O(\Delta'^2 \log^2 \Delta')$-coloring of G'. Such a coloring can be converted into an $O(\Delta'^2)$-coloring of G' within $O(1)$ rounds. (See Chapter 3.10.) Therefore, the factor of $\log^* n + O(1)$ appears only in the initial invocation. Thus, the running time of the algorithm is $f(n, \Delta) = \log^* n + O(1) + T(\Delta)$, where $T(\Delta)$ is a recursive function. By lines 5, 8, and 11 of the algorithm, we conclude that $T(\Delta) = o(\Delta) + T(\Delta/2) + O(\Delta) = T(\Delta/2) + O(\Delta)$, if $\Delta \geq \tilde{\Delta}/\log\tilde{\Delta}$. Otherwise, by lines 1-2 it is easy to verify that $T(\Delta) = O(\Delta\log\Delta) = O(\tilde{\Delta})$. The recursive equation $T(\Delta) = T(\Delta/2) + O(\Delta)$ solves to $T(\tilde{\Delta}) = O(\tilde{\Delta})$.   □

Theorem 6.5 in conjunction with Theorem 6.1 can be used to devise a tradeoff between the running time and the number of colors in a straightforward way. Specifically, for any $p \leq \Delta^{1/4}$, a legal $O(\Delta \cdot p)$-coloring can be computed in $O(\Delta/p) + \log^* n$ time. To this end, compute an $O(\Delta/p)$-defective p^2-coloring φ', in time $O(\Delta^{3\epsilon}) + \log^* n = O(\Delta^{3/4}) + \log^* n$. Then compute a legal $O(\Delta/p)$-coloring of each subgraph induced by a color class of φ'. These computations can be performed for all color classes of φ' in parallel, and using disjoint color palettes. This step requires $O(\Delta/p) + \log^* n$ time. As a result a legal $O(\Delta \cdot p)$-coloring is obtained. The overall running time is $O(\Delta/p + \log^* n)$. We remark that using a more sophisticated procedure one can obtain a tradeoff for the entire range $1 \leq p \leq \Delta$. (See [8, 48].) We summarize this in the next theorem.

Theorem 6.6   *For any p, $1 \leq p \leq \Delta$, a legal $O(\Delta \cdot p)$-coloring can be computed in $O(\Delta/p + \log^* n)$ time.*

6.2   DEFECTIVE COLORING ALGORITHMS

In the previous section we demonstrated how a legal coloring can be computed by combining defective colorings. In this section we describe algorithms for computing defective colorings from scratch. Combining the algorithms from the previous section with the algorithms from this section results in an efficient algorithm for computing legal colorings from scratch.

In Section 6.2.1 we present a tool, called Procedure Refine, which transforms one defective coloring φ into another defective coloring φ'. The latter coloring has a slightly larger defect than φ has, but it typically uses much fewer colors. In Section 6.2.2 Procedure Refine is used to devise an algorithm for constructing defective colorings from scratch.

6.2.1   PROCEDURE REFINE

Many algorithms for computing a legal $(\Delta + 1)$-coloring employ the following standard technique. Whenever a vertex is required to select a color it selects a color that is different from the colors of all its neighbors. Its neighbors select their colors in different rounds. On the other hand, if one is interested in a defective coloring, a vertex can select a color that is used by some of its neighbors. Moreover, some neighbors can perform the selection in the same round. Consequently, the computation can potentially be significantly more efficient than that of a $(\Delta + 1)$-coloring.

We start with presenting a procedure, called *Refine*, that accepts as input a graph with an m-defective γ-coloring φ, and a parameter p, $1 \leq p \leq \Delta$, for some integers m, γ, and p, and computes an $(m + \lfloor \Delta/p \rfloor)$-defective p^2-coloring in time $O(\gamma)$. The procedure employs acyclic partial orientations. (See Section 3.3 for definitions concerning acyclic partial orientations.)

While acyclic orientations are useful for computing legal colorings, acyclic partial orientations are useful for computing defective ones. Specifically, Procedure Refine computes such an orientation, and then uses it for computing a defective coloring. In order to compute the partial orientation, it orients each edge (u, v) for which $\varphi(u) \neq \varphi(v)$ toward the endpoint with the smaller φ-color. All other edges remain undirected. (These are the edges that connect vertices with the same φ-color.) Denote the resulting orientation by η. Since not all edges have to be oriented, the length of an acyclic partial orientation may be significantly smaller than the length of any possible complete orientation of the input graph. (The length of an orientation is defined in Definitions 3.1–3.5.) Consequently, if it is possible to employ a partial orientation instead of a complete one, then the coloring computation can be performed much faster.

Once an acyclic partial orientation is obtained, in the way that was described above, Procedure Refine employs it to computes a new defective coloring φ'. It proceeds in two stages. In the first stage each vertex v computes a new color $\psi(v)$ from the range $[p] = \{1, 2, ..., p\}$ in the following way. Once v receives the color $\psi(u)$ from each of its parents u, it sets $\psi(v)$ to be the color from $[p]$ that is used by the minimal number of its parents, breaking ties arbitrarily. In other words, v selects a color i, such that for every $j = 1, 2, ..., p$, it holds that

$$\left|\{u \text{ is a parent of } v : \psi(u) = i\}\right| \leq \left|\{u \text{ is a parent of } v : \psi(u) = j\}\right|.$$

In particular, if there is a color in the range $[p]$ that is not used by any parent, then it is selected. Then v sends its selection $\psi(v)$ to all its neighbors. In the second stage the orientation is reversed, and each vertex v computes a new color $\Psi(v)$ from the range $[p]$ in a similar way. Specifically, it waits for all its parents to select a Ψ-color, and then selects a color which is used by the minimal number of parents. Denote the reversed orientation by $\bar{\eta}$. (Observe that the parents of v in the orientation $\bar{\eta}$ are the children of v in the orientation η.) Then v sends its selection $\Psi(v)$ to all its neighbors.

Once the vertex v has computed both colors $\psi(v)$ and $\Psi(v)$, it sets its final color $\varphi'(v) = (\Psi(v) - 1) \cdot p + \psi(v)$. Intuitively, the color $\varphi'(v)$ can be seen as a pair $(\Psi(v), \psi(v))$. This completes the description of Procedure Refine. Next, we show that the procedure is correct.

Lemma 6.7   *The coloring φ' produced by Procedure Refine is an $(m + \lfloor \Delta/p \rfloor)$-defective p^2-coloring.*

Proof. First, observe that for each vertex v, it holds that $1 \leq \psi(v), \Psi(v) \leq p$, and thus, $1 \leq \varphi'(v) \leq p^2$. It is left to show that for each vertex v, the number of neighbors u of v with $\varphi'(u) = \varphi'(v)$ is at most $(m + \lfloor \Delta/p \rfloor)$. Recall that procedure Refine accepts a defective coloring φ as input. For a vertex $v \in V$, denote by $\mathcal{S}(v)$ the set of neighbors of v with a smaller φ-color. Denote by $\mathcal{G}(v)$ the set of neighbors of v with a greater φ-color. Notice that $\mathcal{S}(v)$ and $\mathcal{G}(v)$ correspond to the parents and the children of v, respectively, in the orientation η. Each vertex v has at most m neighbors z such that $\varphi(v) = \varphi(z)$. By the pigeonhole principle, the number of neighbors u of v with $\varphi(u) < \varphi(v)$ and $\psi(u) = \psi(v)$ is at most $\lfloor |\mathcal{S}(v)|/p \rfloor$, since v selected $\psi(v)$ to be the color from $[p]$ that is used by the minimal number of its neighbors from $\mathcal{S}(v)$. Similarly, the number of neighbors w of v with $\varphi(w) > \varphi(v)$ and $\Psi(w) = \Psi(v)$ is at most $\lfloor |\mathcal{G}(v)|/p \rfloor$. Observe that for any neighbor u of v, if $\varphi'(u) = \varphi'(v)$ then $\psi(u) = \psi(v)$ and $\Psi(u) = \Psi(v)$. Consequently, the number of neighbors u with $\varphi'(u) = \varphi'(v)$ is at most $(m + \lfloor |\mathcal{S}(v)|/p \rfloor + \lfloor |\mathcal{G}(v)|/p \rfloor) \leq (m + \lfloor \deg(v)/p \rfloor) \leq (m + \lfloor \Delta/p \rfloor)$. $\square$

The two stages of Procedure Refine can be executed in parallel. Thus, Refine can be executed within γ rounds. This is argued formally in the next lemma.

Lemma 6.8   *The time complexity of Procedure Refine is γ.*

Proof. We prove by induction on i that after i rounds, $i = 1, 2, ..., \gamma$, each vertex with $\varphi(v) \leq i$ has selected its color $\psi(v)$. For the base case, consider all the vertices v with $\varphi(v) = 1$. There are no vertices u with $\varphi(u) < 1$, and thus, each vertex v with $\varphi(v) = 1$ selects the color $\psi(v)$ in the first round. Now, for $i \geq 2$, assume that after $(i - 1)$ rounds, each vertex with $\varphi(v) \leq (i - 1)$ has selected its color $\psi(v)$. Then, by the induction hypothesis, in round i, for a vertex v with $\varphi(v) = i$, all the neighbors u of v satisfying $\varphi(u) < \varphi(v) = i$ have selected their color $\psi(u)$ in round $(i - 1)$ or earlier. Hence, if v has not selected the color $\psi(v)$ before round i, it necessarily selects it in round i. Therefore, after γ rounds all the vertices in the graph have selected the color $\psi(v)$ and the first stage is completed. Similarly, the second stage is completed after another γ rounds. The computation of $\varphi'(v)$ from $\psi(v)$ and $\Psi(v)$ is performed immediately after the second stage is finished, and it requires no additional communication. Finally, note that the two stages can be executed in parallel. Thus, the running time is γ. □

For a graph $G = (V, E)$ whose vertices are provided with an m-defective k-coloring, for some parameters m and k, we say that G is *m-defective k-colored*.

We summarize this section with the following corollary.

Corollary 6.9 *For positive integers γ, m, and p, suppose that Procedure Refine is invoked on a graph G with maximum degree Δ. Suppose also that G is m-defective γ-colored. Then the procedure produces an $(m + \lfloor \Delta/p \rfloor)$-defective p^2-coloring of G within at most γ rounds.*

6.2.2   PROCEDURE DEFECTIVE-COLOR

In this section we describe an algorithm called *Procedure Defective-Color*. The algorithm accepts as input a graph $G = (V, E)$, and two integer parameters p, q such that $1 \leq p \leq \Delta$, $p^2 < q$, and $q < c' \cdot \Delta^2$, for some positive constant $c' > 0$. It computes an $O(\frac{\log \Delta}{\log(q/p^2)} \cdot \Delta/p)$-defective p^2-coloring of G in time $O(\log^* n + \frac{\log \Delta}{\log(q/p^2)} \cdot q)$ from scratch. In particular, if we set $q = \Delta^\epsilon \cdot p^2$ for an arbitrarily small positive constant ϵ, we get an $O(\Delta/p)$-defective p^2-coloring algorithm with running time $O(\log^* n + \Delta^\epsilon \cdot p^2)$. The algorithm starts by computing a legal coloring with a very large number of colors. Next, the algorithm proceeds in phases. In each phase the number of colors is reduced by a factor of q/p^2. However, this increases the defect parameter of the coloring by an additive term of $\lfloor \Delta/p \rfloor$. Selecting appropriate parameters for p and q enables us to keep the defect parameter and the running time in check.

Next, we describe the algorithm in detail. The algorithm starts by computing an $O(\Delta^2)$-coloring of the input graph. This coloring φ can be computed in $\log^* n + O(1)$ time from scratch using the algorithm of Linial [56]. Let c, $c > 0$, be a constant such that $c \cdot (\Delta^2)$ is an upper bound on the number of colors employed. Let $h = \lfloor c \cdot \Delta^2/q \rfloor$. (The constant c' mentioned in the beginning of the section is sufficiently small to ensure that $h \geq 1$.) Each vertex v with $1 \leq \varphi(v) \leq h \cdot q$ joins the set V_j with $j = \lceil \varphi(v)/q \rceil$. Vertices v that satisfy $h \cdot q < \varphi(v) \leq c \cdot \Delta^2$ join the set V_h. In other words, the index j of the set V_j to which the vertex v joins is determined by $j = \min\{\lceil \varphi(v)/q \rceil, h\}$. Observe that for every index j, $1 \leq j \leq h-1$, the set V_j is colored with exactly q colors, and V_h is colored with q' colors with $q \leq q' \leq 2q$. By definition, for each j, $1 \leq j \leq h-1$, V_j is 0-defective q-colored (i.e., the defect is $m = 0$ and the number of colors is $k = q$), and V_h is 0-defective q'-colored ($m = 0$, $k = q'$). For each j, $1 \leq j \leq h$, denote this coloring of V_j by ψ_j. Then, for each graph $G(V_j)$ induced by the vertex set V_j, Procedure *Refine* is invoked on $G(V_j)$ with the parameter p, in parallel for $j = 1, 2, .., h$. As a result of these invocations, each graph $G(V_j)$ is now $\lfloor \Delta/p \rfloor$-defective p^2-colored. Let φ'_j denote this coloring. Next, each vertex v selects a new color $\varphi''(v)$ by setting $\varphi''(v) = \varphi'_j(v) + (j-1) \cdot p^2$, where j is the index such that $v \in V_j$. The number of colors used by the new coloring φ'' is at most $h \cdot p^2 \leq c \cdot (\Delta^2) \cdot p^2/q$. It follows that the coloring φ'' is a $\lfloor \Delta/p \rfloor$-defective $(c \cdot (\Delta^2) \cdot p^2/q)$-coloring of G.

This process is repeated iteratively. On each iteration the vertex set is partitioned into disjoint subsets V_j, such that in each subset the vertices are colored by at most q different colors, except one subset in which the vertices are colored by at most $2q$ colors. Then, in parallel, the coloring of each subset is converted into a p^2-coloring. Consequently, in each iteration the number of colors is reduced by a factor of at least q/p^2. (Except for the last iteration in which the number of colors is larger than p^2 but smaller than $2q$, and it is reduced to p^2.) However, for a vertex v, the number of neighbors of v that are colored by the same color as v, that is, the defect $def_\varphi(v)$ of v, may grow by an additive term of $\lfloor \Delta/p \rfloor$ in each iteration. The process terminates when the entire graph G is colored by at most p^2 colors. (After $\log_{q/p^2}(c \cdot \Delta^2)$ iterations all vertices know that G is colored by at most p^2 colors.) In each iteration an upper bound γ on the number of currently employed colors is computed. In the last iteration, if $\gamma < q$ then all the vertices join the same set V_1, and consequently $V_1 = V$, and Procedure Refine is invoked on the entire graph G. See Figure 6.1 for an illustration. The pseudo-code of the algorithm is provided below.

In what follows we prove the correctness of Procedure Defective-Color. We start with proving the following invariant regarding the variable γ. Let γ_i denote the value of γ at the end of the ith iteration. For technical convenience, we define γ_0 to be the value of γ at the beginning of the first iteration.

Lemma 6.10   *For $i = 0, 1, 2, ...$, after the ith iteration, the number of colors employed by φ is at most γ_i.*

Proof. The proof is by induction on i.
Base ($i = 0$): In the first step of Procedure Defective-Color, the graph G is colored using $(c \cdot \Delta^2)$ colors. Therefore, after 0 iterations, the number of colors employed by φ is at most $\gamma_0 = c \cdot \Delta^2$.
Induction step: By the induction hypothesis, after iteration $(i-1)$, the number of colors employed by φ is at most γ_{i-1}. In iteration i the vertex set V of G is partitioned into $h = \max\{\lfloor \gamma_{i-1}/q \rfloor, 1\}$ disjoint subsets V_j, $j = 1, 2, ..., h$. Each of these subsets except V_h is colored with at most q colors. The set V_h is colored with at most $2q$ colors. Procedure Refine produces a new coloring in each set V_j such that the number of colors used in the set V_j is at most p^2, for

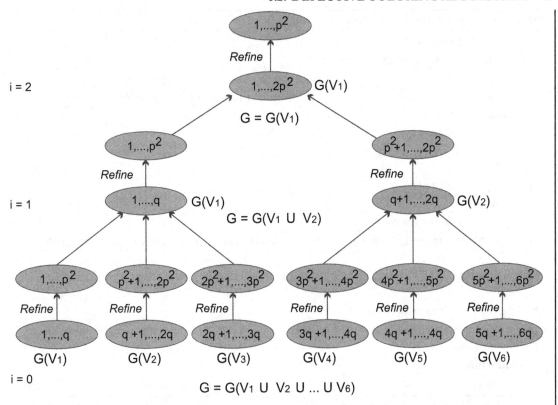

Figure 6.1: An execution of Procedure Defective-Color with the parameters p and q, such that $q = 3p^2$, on an initially $(6q)$-colored graph G. Each oval represents a subgraph. The range inside the oval represents the color palette employed by the subgraph. For j, $1 \leq j \leq 6$, the set V_j changes after each iteration, and contains all vertices that are currently colored using the palette $\{(j - 1) \cdot q + 1, (j - 1) \cdot q + 2, ..., j \cdot q\}$.

$j = 1, 2, ..., h$. Consequently, the number of colors used by φ at the end of iteration i is at most $(\max\{\lfloor \gamma_{i-1}/q \rfloor, 1\}) \cdot p^2 = \gamma_i$. (See steps 8, 13, and 14 of Algorithm 9.) $\square$

By step 14 of Algorithm 9, $\gamma_{i+1} \leq \max\{\gamma_i \cdot p^2/q, \ p^2\}$, for $i = 0, 1, 2, ...$, and $\gamma_0 = c \cdot \Delta^2$. Therefore,

$$\gamma_i \leq \max\{c \cdot \Delta^2 \cdot (p^2/q)^i, \ p^2\}. \tag{6.1}$$

Next, we analyze the defect of the coloring produced by Procedure Defective-Color.

Theorem 6.11   *Procedure Defective-Color invoked with the parameters p, q, computes an $O(\frac{\log \Delta}{\log(q/p^2)} \cdot \Delta/p)$-defective p^2-coloring.*

Algorithm 9 Procedure Defective-Color(p, q)

Algorithm for each vertex $v \in V$

1: $\varphi :=$ color G with $(c \cdot \Delta^2)$ colors
2: $\gamma := c \cdot \Delta^2$ /* the current number of colors */
3: $i = 0$ /* the index of the current iteration */
4: **while** $\gamma > p^2$ **do**
5:    **if** $\gamma < q$ **then**
6:       $j := 1$
7:    **else**
8:       $j := \min\{\lceil \varphi(v)/q \rceil, \lfloor \gamma/q \rfloor\}$
9:    **end if**
10:   set V_j to be the set of v
11:   $\psi_j(v) := \varphi(v) - (j - 1) \cdot q$ /* $\psi_j(\cdot)$ is an $(i \cdot \lfloor \Delta/p \rfloor)$-defective $(2q)$-coloring of $G(V_j)$ */
12:   $\varphi_j' :=$ Refine$(G(V_j), \psi_j, p)$ /* $\varphi_j'(\cdot)$ is an $((i + 1)\lfloor \Delta/p \rfloor)$-defective p^2-coloring of $G(V_j)$ */
13:   $\varphi(v) := \varphi''(v) := \varphi_j'(v) + (j - 1) \cdot p^2$
14:   $\gamma := (\max\{\lfloor \gamma/q \rfloor, 1\}) \cdot p^2$ /* $\varphi(\cdot)$ is an $((i + 1)\lfloor \Delta/p \rfloor)$-defective γ-coloring of G */
15:   $i := i + 1$
16: **end while**
17: **return** φ

Proof. We prove by induction on i that after i iterations $\varphi(\cdot)$ is an $(i \cdot \Delta/p)$-defective $(\max\{c \cdot \Delta^2 \cdot (p^2/q)^i, \ p^2\})$-coloring of G.

Base $(i = 0)$: Observe that a 0-defective $(c \cdot \Delta^2)$-coloring is computed in the first step of the algorithm. Therefore, before the beginning of the first iteration, φ is a 0-defective $(c \cdot \Delta^2)$-coloring of G.

Induction step: Let φ be the coloring produced after $i - 1$ iterations. By the induction hypothesis, φ is an $((i - 1) \cdot \Delta/p)$-defective $(\max\{c \cdot \Delta^2 \cdot (p^2/q)^{i-1}, \ p^2\})$-coloring of G. In iteration i, the vertex set V of G is partitioned into $h = \max\{\lfloor \gamma_{i-1}/q \rfloor, 1\}$ disjoint subsets V_j. If there is only one subset $V_1 = V$, then $G(V_1) = G$ is colored with at most $2q$ colors. Otherwise, each induced graph $G(V_j)$, $1 \leq j < h$, is colored by q different colors. The induced graph $G(V_h)$ is colored by at most $2q$ colors. Therefore, for each j, $1 \leq j \leq h$, the coloring ψ_j computed in step 11 of the ith iteration is an $((i - 1) \cdot \Delta/p)$-defective $(2q)$-coloring of $G(V_j)$. In step 12, Procedure Refine is invoked on $G(V_j)$ with p as input. As a result, an $((i - 1) \cdot \Delta/p + \Delta/p)$-defective p^2-coloring φ_j' of $G(V_j)$ is produced. In other words φ_j' is an $(i \cdot \Delta/p)$-defective p^2-coloring of $G(V_j)$, i.e., $def(\varphi_j') \leq i \cdot \Delta/p$. To finish the proof, we next argue that $def(\varphi'')$ is at most $i \cdot \Delta/p$ too. (The coloring φ'' is defined in line 13 of Algorithm 9.)

Consider a vertex v, and a neighbor u of v. First, suppose that $v \in V_j$, $u \in V_\ell$, and $j \neq \ell$. Suppose without loss of generality that $j < e$. Then

$$\varphi''(v) - \varphi''(u) = (\varphi'_j(v) - \varphi'_\ell(u)) + (j - \ell) \cdot p^2 \geq \varphi'_j(v) - \varphi'_\ell(u) + p^2.$$

Since $\varphi'_j(v) - \varphi'_\ell(u) \geq -p^2 + 1$, it follows that $\varphi''(v) \neq \varphi''(u)$.
Second, consider a neighbor $w \in V_j$ of v. If $\varphi'_j(v) \neq \varphi'_j(w)$ then also

$$\varphi''(v) = \varphi'_j(v) + (j - 1) \cdot p^2 \neq \varphi''(w) = \varphi'_j(w) + (j - 1) \cdot p^2.$$

Since $def(\varphi'_j) \leq i \cdot \Delta/p$, there are at most $(i \cdot \Delta/p)$ neighbors $w \in V_j$ of v such that $\varphi'_j(w) = \varphi'_j(v)$. Consequently, the coloring $\varphi = \varphi''$ that is produced in line 13 of the ith iteration is an $(i \cdot \Delta/p)$-defective $(\max\{c \cdot \Delta^2 \cdot (p^2/q)^i, \ p^2\})$-coloring of G. This completes the inductive proof. By (6.1) after $\frac{\log(c \cdot \Delta^2)}{\log(q/p^2)}$ iterations, φ is a $(\frac{\log(c \cdot \Delta^2)}{\log(q/p^2)} \cdot \Delta/p)$-defective p^2-coloring of G. $\qquad\square$

Procedure Defective-Color starts with computing an $O(\Delta^2)$-coloring. The algorithm of Linial [56] computes a $(c \cdot \Delta^2)$-coloring in time $\log^* n + O(1)$. The number of iterations performed by Procedure Defective-Color is at most $\log_{q/p^2}(c \cdot \Delta^2) = \frac{\log(c \cdot \Delta^2)}{\log(q/p^2)}$. Each iteration invokes Procedure Refine that requires $O(q)$ time, and performs some additional computation that requires $O(1)$ time. The running time of Procedure Defective-Color is given below.

Theorem 6.12 *Procedure Defective-Color invoked with parameters p,q, runs in $T(n) + O(q \cdot \frac{\log \Delta}{\log(q/p^2)})$ time, where $T(n)$ is the time required for computing $O(\Delta^2)$-coloring. If Linial's algorithm is used for $O(\Delta^2)$-coloring, the running time of Procedure Defective-Color is $O(q \cdot \frac{\log \Delta}{\log(q/p^2)}) + \log^* n$. It produces an $O(\frac{\log \Delta}{\log(q/p^2)} \cdot \Delta/p)$-defective p^2-coloring.*

Observe that by substituting $p = \Delta^\epsilon$, $q = \Delta^{3\epsilon}$, for a sufficiently small constant $\epsilon > 0$, into Theorem 6.12, we obtain Theorems 6.1 and 6.4. Those theorems, in turn, imply Theorems 6.5 and 6.6, i.e., that $(\Delta + 1)$-coloring can be computed in $O(\Delta) + \log^* n$ deterministic time, and that an $O(\Delta \cdot p)$-coloring can be computed in $O(\Delta/p + \log^* n)$ deterministic time, for any $1 \leq p \leq \Delta$. Moreover, an $O(\Delta^2)$-coloring can, in fact, be computed in $\frac{1}{2} \log^* n + O(1)$ time [74]. Using the algorithm of [74] instead of Linial's Algorithm [55] within the above algorithm produces a $(\Delta + 1)$-coloring in $O(\Delta) + \frac{1}{2} \log^* n$ time.

CHAPTER 7

Arbdefective Coloring

In his seminal paper [55] in 1987 Linial devised an $O(\Delta^2)$-coloring algorithm that runs in $\log^* n + O(1)$ time. (See Section 3.10 in the current monograph.) He also raised a major open question which triggered a lot of research in the area of distributed symmetry breaking. His question was whether in deterministic polylogarithmic time one can come up with a coloring algorithm with significantly fewer than Δ^2 colors. This section is based on the paper [9] by the authors of this monograph. This paper showed that $\Delta^{1+o(1)}$-coloring can be computed in deterministic polylogarithmic time (specifically, in $O(f(\Delta) \cdot \log \Delta \cdot \log n)$ time, where $f(\Delta) = \omega(1)$ is an arbitrarily slowly growing function). This result answered Linial's question in the affirmative. The main technical tool introduced in [9] on our way to this result was the notion of *arbdefective coloring*. In this section we describe algorithms for computing arbdefective colorings, and show how they can be used for producing legal colorings.

7.1 SMALL ARBORICITY DECOMPOSITION

In this section we discuss a generalization of defective coloring which is called *arbdefective coloring*. A b-arbdefective k-coloring is a coloring of the vertices with k colors, such that each color class induces a subgraph with *arboricity* at most b. Arbdefective coloring partitions the input graph into subgraphs of bounded arboriciy, but the maximum degree of these subgraphs may be unbounded. Nevertheless, one can still efficiently compute legal colorings of such subgraphs using the algorithms described in Section 5. The challenging task is to compute appropriate partitions of bounded-arboricity subgraphs. This seems to be a more difficult task than computing defective coloring. We start with describing an algorithm for computing an $O(a^{2/3})$-arbdefective $O(a^{1/3})$-coloring. (Later we discuss algorithms that apply to a wider range of parameters.) This algorithm employs some of the procedures described in previous sections. In particular, it employs Procedure Defective-Color that computes $O(\Delta/p)$-defective p^2-coloring. But in contrast to the coloring produced by this procedure, the product of the parameters of the arbdefective coloring is $O(a^{2/3} \cdot a^{1/3}) = O(a)$. In other words, the product of the parameters of the arbdefective coloring is *linear* in a, while the product of parameters of the defective coloring is *superlinear* in Δ. This makes arbdefective colorings very useful for efficient computation of legal colorings. In fact, it turns out that by using arbdefective colorings one can compute a legal coloring much more efficiently than by using defective ones.

 The algorithm for computing an $O(a^{2/3})$-arbdefective $O(a^{1/3})$-coloring accepts as input a graph G. The first stage of the algorithm computes an acyclic partial orientation with certain helpful properties. Specifically, the orientation is sufficiently short, and has bounded deficit. This stage is called *Procedure Partial-Orientation*. (See Algorithm 10 for its pseudocode. The argument t is set as $a^{1/3}$.) Procedure Partial-Orientation starts with computing an H-partition $\mathcal{H} = H_1, H_2, ..., H_\ell$ of G, $\ell = O(\log n)$, with degree $A = O(a)$. Recall that each subgraph $G(H_i)$, $i \in \{1, 2, .., \ell\}$, has maximum degree at most A. (See Lemma 5.4.) Next, for $i = 1, 2, ..., \ell$ in parallel, it computes an $O(a^{2/3})$-defective $O(a^{2/3})$-coloring ψ_i of $G(H_i)$. (To this end, it invokes Procedure Defective-Color on $G(H_i)$ with the parameters $p = a^{1/3}$, $q = a^{2/3+\epsilon}$, for an arbitrarily small positive constant ϵ. See Theorem 6.12.)

The colorings ψ_i are used to compute an acyclic partial orientation μ of the input graph as follows. Each edge that connects endpoints from distinct H-sets is oriented toward the endpoint with greater H-index. Each edge that connects endpoints from the same H-set, but with distinct colors, is oriented toward the endpoint with the greater color. The rest of the edges, that connect endpoints from the same set and with the same color, remain unoriented. This completes the description of Procedure Partial-Orientation.

Algorithm 10 Procedure Partial-Orientation(G, t)

1: $H_1, H_2, ..., H_\ell :=$ an H-partition of G.
2: **for** $i = 1, 2, ..., \ell$ in parallel **do**
3:      compute an $\lfloor a/t \rfloor$-defective $O(t^2)$-coloring ψ_i of $G(H_i)$.
4: **end for**
5: **for** each edge $e = (u, v)$ in E in parallel **do**
6:      **if** u and v belong to different H-sets **then**
7:          orient e toward the endpoint with greater H-index.
8:      **else**
9:          /* $u, v \in H_i$ for some i, $1 \le i \le \ell$ */
10:         **if** u and v have different colors **then**
11:             orient e toward the endpoint with greater ψ_i-color.
12:         **end if**
13:     **end if**
14: **end for**

The orientation produced by invoking the procedure on the input graph G, and the parameter $t = \lfloor a^{1/3} \rfloor$, has out-degree $O(a)$ (by Lemma 5.4) and length $O(a^{2/3} \cdot \log n)$ (as we shortly prove). In addition, it has another helpful property. The number of unoriented edges connected to each vertex, that is, the maximum *deficit* is bounded. (See Definition 3.5 (3).) Since each vertex $v \in V$ has at most $O(a^{2/3})$ neighbors in the same H-set H_i with the same ψ_i-color, the deficit of the orientation μ which was obtained from the colorings ψ_i by Algorithm 10 is $O(a^{2/3})$.

Next, we analyze the length of μ. To prove that the length of μ is $O(a^{2/3} \log n)$ consider the graph G' which is obtained by removing all unoriented edges from G. For an index $i \in \{1, 2, ..., \ell\}$, for each vertex $v \in H_i$, consider the ordered pair $\langle \psi_i(v), i \rangle$ as the color of v in G'.

Then G' is colored legally using $O(a^{2/3} \log n)$ colors. Denote this coloring by ρ. Observe that μ is an induced orientation of the coloring ρ. Thus, by Property 3.4, the length of μ is $O(a^{2/3} \log n)$. For future reference we summarize the properties of μ below.

Corollary 7.1   *The acyclic partial orientation μ which was produced by Algorithm 10 invoked with $t = \lfloor a^{1/3} \rfloor$ has out-degree $A = O(a)$, length $\ell = O(t^2 \cdot \log n) = O(a^{2/3} \log n)$, and deficit $d = O(a/t) = O(a^{2/3})$.*

Once a partial orientation μ has been computed, it is used for computing an $O(a^{2/3})$-arbdefective $O(a^{1/3})$-coloring φ. To this end each vertex v selects its color $\varphi(v)$ once all its parents have done so. It selects a color from the range $\{1, 2, ..., \lfloor a^{1/3} \rfloor\}$, which is used by the minimum number of parents. This completes the description of the algorithm. Its pseudocode is provided below. (The parameters t and k are set to $t = k = \lfloor a^{1/3} \rfloor$.) Next we prove its correctness.

Algorithm 11 Procedure Arbdefective-Coloring(G, k, t)

1: μ = Partial-Orientation(G, t)
2: **once** all the parents u of v with respect to μ have selected a color $\varphi(u)$ **do**
   v selects a color $\varphi(v)$ from the palette $\{1, 2, ..., k\}$ which is used by the minimum number of parents of v

---

Lemma 7.2   *The coloring φ produced by the above algorithm invoked with the parameters $k = \lfloor a^{1/3} \rfloor$ and $t = \lfloor a^{1/3} \rfloor$ is an $O(a^{2/3})$-arbdefective $O(a^{1/3})$-coloring.*

Proof. The number of colors used by φ is at most $k = t = O(a^{1/3})$. For any $i \in \{1, 2, ..., t\}$, consider the subgraph G_i of G induced by all vertices v with $\varphi(v) = i$. We need to prove that $a(G_i) = O(a^{2/3})$, for all $i = \{1, 2, ..., t\}$. To this end we first note that for each vertex $v \in V$, the number of parents of v in G (under the orientation μ) that have the same φ-color as that of v is at most $O(a^{2/3})$. Indeed, the out-degree of μ is $A = O(a)$, and each vertex v selects a color $\varphi(v) = i \in \{1, 2, ..., t\}$ that is used by the minimum number of parents. Therefore, by pigeonhole principle, v has at most $O(A/t) = O(a^{2/3})$ parents (under μ) in G with the same φ-color as that of v.

Observe that $v \in V(G_i)$. Although v has $O(a^{2/3})$ parents under μ in G, note that μ is a partial orientation. Therefore, it may leave some edges incident on v in G_i unoriented. Next we show that these edges can also be oriented while preserving an upper bound of $O(a^{2/3})$ on the maximum out-degree.

Consider the orientation μ restricted to the subgraph G_i. The number of parents under μ in G_i of a vertex $v \in G_i$ is $O(a^{2/3})$. Denote be E'_i the set of edges of G_i that are oriented by μ, and by E''_i the set of edges of G_i which are not oriented. Consider the graph $G'_i = (V, E'_i)$. The orientation μ restricted to G'_i is an acyclic complete orientation with out-degree $O(a^{2/3})$. In other words, each vertex in G_i' has $O(a^{2/3})$ parents under μ. Therefore, the arboricity of G_i' is $O(a^{2/3})$. On the other hand, the graph $G_i'' = (V, E_i'')$ consists of all unoriented edges of G_i with respect to the restriction of the orientation μ to G_i. Therefore, each unoriented edge of G_i is also unoriented in G. Recall that μ has deficit $d = O(a^{2/3})$. Therefore, each vertex in G belongs to at most d unoriented edges. Consequently, each vertex in G_i belongs to at most d unoriented edges of G_i as well. Therefore, the maximum degree of G_i'', which includes only unoriented edges, is also at most d. Consequently, $a(G_i'') \leq \Delta(G_i'') \leq d = O(a^{2/3})$. Therefore, the arboricity of $G_i' \cup G_i''$ is $O(a^{2/3}) \cdot 2 = O(a^{2/3})$. Since $E(G_i) = E_i' \cup E_i''$, it follows that $a(G_i) = O(a^{2/3})$.   □

Lemma 7.3   *An $O(a^{2/3})$-arbdefective $O(a^{1/3})$-coloring of a graph G with arboricity a can be computed within $O(a^{2/3+\epsilon} \cdot \log n)$ time, for an arbitrarily small positive constant ϵ.*

Proof. The first stage of Algorithm 11 involves invoking Procedure Partial-Orientation, which, in turn, invokes Procedure Partition and Procedure Defective-Color. Procedure Partition requires $O(\log n)$ time. (See Theorem 5.5.) Procedure Defective-Color invoked with $q = a^{2/3+\epsilon}$, $p = a^{1/3}$, requires $O(q \cdot \frac{\log a}{\log q/p^2} + \log^* n) = O(a^{2/3+\epsilon} + \log^* n)$ time. (See Theorem 6.12.) The second stage employs the partial orientation μ that was computed in the first stage, for computing the coloring φ. The running time depends linearly on the length of the orientation. Therefore, the running time of the second stage is $O(a^{2/3} \log n)$. Hence, the overall running time is $O(a^{2/3+\epsilon} \cdot \log n)$.   □

Once an $O(a^{2/3})$-arbdefective $O(a^{1/3})$-coloring φ is computed, it can be used for obtaining a legal coloring. Specifically, φ partitions the input graph G into subgraphs $G_1, G_2, ..., G_t$, each of arboricity $O(a^{2/3})$. Therefore, for $1 \leq i \leq t$ in parallel, G_i can be colored with $O(a^{2/3})$-colors within $O(a^{2/3} \log n)$ time, by Corollary 5.15. By using $t = O(a^{1/3})$ unique palettes of size $O(a^{2/3})$ each for $G_1, G_2, ..., G_t$, a legal $O(a)$-coloring of the input graph G is obtained. To summarize, an $O(a)$-coloring can be computed from scratch within $O(a^{2/3+\epsilon} \cdot \log n)$ time, for an arbitrarily small positive constant. Note that this is already a significant improvement over the bound $O(a \cdot \log n)$. (See Theorem 5.15.)

7.2   EFFICIENT COLORING ALGORITHMS

In this section we dicuss how to improve further the running time of the algorithm that computes a legal $O(a)$-coloring. Before we describe the improved algorithm, we analyze the performance of Procedure Arbdefective-Coloring in the general scenario of accepting any positive parameters k, t, rather then fixing $k = t = \lfloor a^{1/3} \rfloor$. (See Algorithm 11.) As a first step, we generalize Corollary 7.1.

Lemma 7.4   *Let ϵ be an arbitrarily small positive constant. Procedure Partial-Orientation invoked on a graph G and an integer parameter $t > 0$ produces an acyclic orientation μ of out-degree*

$\lfloor(2 + \epsilon) \cdot a\rfloor$, *length $O(t^2 \cdot \log n)$, and deficit at most $\lfloor a/t\rfloor$. The running time of the procedure is* $O(\log n)$.

Proof. The out-degree of the orientation μ is at most $A = \lfloor(2 + \epsilon) \cdot a\rfloor$, by Lemma 5.4. Next, we analyze the length of the orientation μ. Consider a directed path (oriented consistently with respect to μ) in a subgraph $G(H_i)$, $1 \le i \le \ell$. The length of this path is at most the number of colors used in the defective coloring ψ_i of $G(H_i)$, which is $O(t^2)$. Now consider a directed path P in the graph G with respect to the orientation μ. The path may contain up to $O(\log n)$ edges that cross between different H-sets. Between any pair of such edges in the path, there are up to $O(t^2)$ consequent edges whose endpoints belong to the same H-set. Hence, the length of a directed path P in G is $O(t^2 \log n)$. (See Figure 7.1.) For analyzing the deficit, observe that for every vertex $v \in H_i$, for some i, $1 \le i \le \ell$, the number of edges which are not oriented by μ and incident to v is at most the defect of the coloring φ_i of H_i. Indeed, the only edges incident to v that are left unoriented by the procedure are edges (v, u) with $v, u \in H_i$ and $\varphi_i(u) = \varphi_i(v)$. Therefore the deficit of μ is at most $\lfloor a/t\rfloor$.

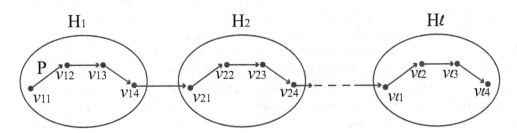

Figure 7.1: A directed path $P = (v_{11}, v_{12}, ..., v_{\ell 4})$ with respect to the orientation produced by Algorithm 10. In this example each H_i is colored with 4 colors. For all $i \in \{1, 2, ..., \ell\}$, $j \in \{1, 2, 3, 4\}$, v_{ij} is colored by j. P contains at most $\ell - 1 = O(\log n)$ edges that cross between different H_i's.

Next, we analyze the running time of the procedure. Procedure Partial-Orientation starts with computing an H-partition. This step requires $O(\log n)$ time. For the step that computes an $\lfloor a/t\rfloor$-defective $O(t^2)$-coloring of a graph $G(H_i)$ that has maximum degree $A = O(a)$, we use an algorithm by Kuhn. (Theorem 4.9 in [48].) This algorithm requires $O(\log^* n)$ time. Alternatively, if t is reasonably small (i.e., $t < \log^{1/2-\eta} n$, for some small constant $\eta > 0$), one can also use the algorithm from Theorem 6.12 with $p = t$, $q = t^{2+\eta}$. The running time of this step is $O(t^{2+\eta} + \log^* n) = o(\log n)$. Other steps require $O(1)$ time.

We remark that without using the algorithm of [48], the running time of the procedure becomes $O(t^{2+\eta} + \log n)$ (instead of $O(\log n)$). This is also sufficient for deriving main results of this section. $\qquad\square$

Corollary 7.5   *Procedure Arbdefective-Coloring invoked on a graph G and two positive integer parameters k and t computes an* $\lfloor a/t + (2+\epsilon) \cdot a/k \rfloor$-*arbdefective k-coloring in time* $O(t^2 \log n)$.

Proof. By Lemma 7.4, the orientation μ which is returned in step 1 of Procedure Arbdefective-Coloring is a partial orientation with length $\ell = O(t^2 \cdot \log n)$, out-degree $m = \lfloor (2+\epsilon) \cdot a \rfloor$, and deficit $\tau \leq \lfloor a/t \rfloor$. Consider the coloring φ returned by step 2 of the procedure. The arboricity of a subgraph induced by a color class i, $1 \leq i \leq k$, of φ is at most $\lfloor m/k \rfloor + \tau$. (Notice that μ is acyclic, and each vertex has at most $\lfloor m/k \rfloor$ parents with its color, and at most τ unoriented edges incident on it. Now the arboricity bound follows similarly to the proof of Lemma 7.2.) Hence, the arbdefective coloring φ has arbdefect at most $\lfloor \tau + \lfloor m/k \rfloor \rfloor = \left\lfloor \lfloor a/t \rfloor + \frac{\lfloor (2+\epsilon) \cdot a \rfloor}{k} \right\rfloor \leq \lfloor a/t + (2+\epsilon) \cdot a/k \rfloor$. Step 2 requires $O(\ell) = O(t^2 \cdot \log n)$ time. The invocation of Procedure Partial-Orientation requires, by Theorem 7.4, $O(\log n)$ time. Hence the overall running time of Procedure Arbdefective-Coloring is $O(t^2 \cdot \log n) + O(\log n) = O(t^2 \cdot \log n)$. $\square$

Now we are ready to describe the improved algorithm for $O(a)$-coloring. The main idea of the improved algorithm is invoking Procedure Arbdefective-Coloring several times. Since Procedure Arbdefective-Coloring produces subgraphs of smaller arboricity than that of the input graph, it can be invoked again on the subgraphs, producing a refined decomposition, in which each subgraph has even smaller arboricity. For example, invoking the procedure on a graph G with the parameters $k = t = \lceil a^{1/6} \rceil$, results in an $O(a^{5/6})$-arbdefective $O(a^{1/6})$-coloring. Invoking the Procedure Arbdefective-Coloring with the same parameters again on all the $O(a^{1/6})$ subgraphs induced by the initial arbdefective coloring results in an $O(a^{2/3})$-arbdefective $O(a^{1/6})$-coloring of each subgraph. If distinct palettes are used for each subgraph, the entire graph is now colored with an $O(a^{2/3})$-arbdefective $O(a^{1/3})$-coloring. The running time of this computation is $O(t^2 \cdot \log n) = O(a^{1/3} \log n)$. This computation is much faster than a single invocation of Procedure Arbdefective-Coloring with the parameters $k = t = \lceil a^{1/3} \rceil$, even though the latter invocation yields the same (up to constant factors) results. However, to obtain a legal coloring of the original graph G, each subgraph still has to be colored legally. Given an $O(a^{2/3})$-arbdefective $O(a^{1/3})$-coloring π, we can convert it into a legal $O(a)$-coloring within additional $O(a^{2/3} \log n)$ time. (This is accomplished by $O(a^{2/3})$-coloring each of the $O(a^{1/3})$ subgraphs induced by color classes of π.) To speed up this computation, the arboricity of all subgraphs has to be decreased. Therefore, we need to invoke Procedure Arbdefective-Coloring more times to achieve an $o(a^{2/3})$-arbdefective coloring. Indeed, applying Procedure Arbdefective-Coloring with $k = t = \lceil a^{1/6} \rceil$ on each of the $O(a^{1/3})$ subgraphs produces an $O(\sqrt{a})$-arbdefective $O(\sqrt{a})$-coloring of the entire input graph. This, in turn, directly gives rise to an $O(a)$-coloring within $O(\sqrt{a} \cdot \log n)$ time.

We employ this idea in the following algorithm called *Procedure Legal-Coloring*. The procedure receives as input a graph G and a positive integer parameter p. Procedure Legal-Coloring proceeds in phases. In the first phase Procedure Arbdefective-Coloring is invoked on the input graph G with the parameters $k := p$ and $t := p$. Consequently, a decomposition into p subgraphs is produced, in which each subgraph has arboricity $O(a/p)$. In each of the consequent phases Procedure Arbdefective-Coloring is invoked in parallel on all subgraphs in the decomposition that was created in the previous phase. As a result, a refinement of the decomposition is produced, i.e., each subgraph is partitioned into p subgraphs of smaller arboricity. Consequently, after each phase, the number of subgraphs in G grows by a factor of p, but the arboricity of each subgraph decreases by a factor of $\Theta(p)$. Hence, the product of the number of subgraphs and the arboricity of subgraphs remains $O(a)$ after each phase. (As long as the number of phases is constant.) Once the arboricities of all subgraphs become small enough, Lemma 5.15 is used for a fast parallel coloring of all the subgraphs, resulting in a unified legal $O(a)$-coloring of the input graph.

Algorithm 12 Procedure Legal-Coloring(G, p)

1: $G_1 := G$
2: $\alpha := a(G_1)$ /* $a(G)$ is assumed to be known to all vertices */
3: $\mathcal{G} := \{G_1\}$ /* The set of subgraphs */
4: **while** $\alpha > p$ **do**
5:   $\hat{\mathcal{G}} := \emptyset$ /* Temporary variable for storing refinements of the set $\mathcal{G}$ */
6:   **for** each $G_i \in \mathcal{G}$ in parallel **do**
7:     $G'_1, G'_2, ..., G'_p$:= Arbdefective-Coloring$(G_i, k := p, t := p)$
       /* G'_j is the subgraph of G_i induced by all the vertices that are assigned the color j by the arbdefective coloring */
8:     **for** $j := 1, 2, ..., p$ in parallel **do**
9:       $z := (i - 1) \cdot p + j$ /* Computing a unique index for each subgraph */
10:      $\hat{G}_z := G'_j$
11:      $\hat{\mathcal{G}} := \hat{\mathcal{G}} \cup \{\hat{G}_z\}$
12:    **end for**
13:   **end for**
14:   $\mathcal{G} := \hat{\mathcal{G}}$
15:   $\alpha := \lfloor \alpha/p + (2 + \epsilon) \cdot \alpha/p \rfloor$
      /* The new upper bound for the arboricity of each of the subgraphs */
16: **end while**
17: $A := \lfloor (2 + \epsilon)\alpha \rfloor + 1$
18: **for** each $G_i \in \mathcal{G}$ in parallel **do**
19:   color G_i legally using the palette $\{(i - 1) \cdot A + 1, (i - 1) \cdot A + 2, ..., i \cdot A\}$
      /* Using Lemma 5.15 */
20: **end for**

Let η be an arbitrarily small positive constant. We show that invoking Procedure Legal-Coloring on G with the input parameter $p := \lfloor a^{\eta/2} \rfloor$ results in an $O(a)$-coloring in $O(a^\eta \log n)$ time. The following lemma constitutes the proof of correctness of the algorithm.

We assume without loss of generality that the arboricity a is sufficiently large to guarantee that $p \geq 16$. (Otherwise, it holds that $a \leq 17^{2/\eta}$, i.e., the arboricity is bounded by a constant. In this case, by Lemma 5.15, one can directly compute an $O(1)$-coloring in $O(\log n)$ time).

Let α_i and $\mathcal{G}_i$ denote the values of the variables α and $\mathcal{G}$, respectively, in the end of iteration i of the while-loop of Algorithm 12 (lines 4-16).

Lemma 7.6   **(1)** *(Invariant for line 16 of Algorithm 12) In the end of iteration i of the while-loop, $i = 1, 2, ...$, each graph in the collection $\mathcal{G}_i$ has arboricity at most α_i.*
(2) *The while-loop runs for a constant number of iterations. (Assuming that $p = \lfloor a^{\eta/2} \rfloor$.) Specifically, the number of iterations is at most $4/\eta$.*
(3) *For $i = 1,2,...$, after i iterations, it holds that $\alpha_i \cdot |\mathcal{G}_i| \leq (3 + \epsilon)^i \cdot a$.*

Proof. **The proof of (1):** The proof is by induction on the number of iterations. For the base case, observe that after the first iteration, $\mathcal{G}$ contains at most p subgraphs produced by Procedure Arbdefective-Coloring. The arboricity of each subgraph is at most $\lfloor a/t + (2 + \epsilon) \cdot a/k \rfloor = \lfloor a/p + (2 + \epsilon) \cdot a/p \rfloor = \alpha_1$.

For the inductive step, consider an iteration i, $i \geq 2$. By the induction hypothesis, each subgraph in $\mathcal{G}_{i-1}$ has arboricity at most α_{i-1}. During iteration i, Procedure Arbdefective-Coloring is invoked on all subgraphs in $\mathcal{G}_{i-1}$. Consequently, $\mathcal{G}_i$ contains new subgraphs, each with arboricity at most $\lfloor \alpha_{i-1}/p + (2 + \epsilon) \cdot \alpha_{i-1}/p \rfloor$, which is exactly the value α_i of α in the end of iteration i. (See line 15 of Algorithm 12.)

The proof of (2): The variable α is initialized as a. In each iteration the variable α is decreased by a factor of at least $b = p/(3 + \epsilon)$. Hence, the number of iterations is at most $\log_b a$. Recall that $p = \lfloor a^{\eta/2} \rfloor$. For any $0 < \epsilon < 1/2$, and a sufficiently large a, it holds that

$$\log_b a = \frac{\log a}{\log(p/(3 + \epsilon))} \leq \frac{\log a}{\log(\frac{1}{4}a^{\eta/2})} = \frac{2/\eta \cdot \log a^{\eta/2}}{\log a^{\eta/2} - 2} \leq 4/\eta.$$

The proof of (3): The correctness of this assertion follows directly from the fact that in each iteration the number $|\mathcal{G}|$ of subgraphs grows by a factor of p, and the arboricity of each subgraph decreases by a factor of at least $p/(3 + \epsilon)$. $\square$

The next theorem follows from Lemma 7.6.

Theorem 7.7   *Invoking Procedure Legal-Coloring on a graph G with arboricity a with the parameter $p = \lfloor a^{\eta/2} \rfloor$ for a positive constant $\eta < 1$, computes a legal $O(a)$-coloring of G within $O(a^\eta \cdot \log n)$ time.*

Proof. We first prove that the coloring is legal. Observe that the selection of unique indices in line 9 guarantees that any two distinct subgraphs that were added to the same set $\hat{\mathcal{G}}$ are colored using distinct palettes. In addition, in each iteration each vertex belongs to exactly one subgraph in $\mathcal{G}$. Consequently, once the while-loop terminates, each vertex v belongs to exactly one subgraph in $\mathcal{G}$. Let $G_i \in \mathcal{G}$ be the subgraph that contains v. Let α' denote the value of α on line 17 of Algorithm 12, i.e., right after the while-loop. As we have seen, the arboricity of G_i is at most α'. Hence, G_i is colored legally using a unique palette containing $A = \lfloor (2 + \epsilon)\alpha' + 1 \rfloor$ colors. Consequently, the color of v is different from the colors of all its neighbors, not only in G_i, but in the entire graph G.

Now we analyze the number of colors in the coloring. By Lemma 7.6, the number of colors employed is $(\lfloor (2 + \epsilon)\alpha' \rfloor + 1) \cdot |\mathcal{G}| \le (3 + \epsilon)^c \cdot a$, for some explicit constant c. (For a sufficiently large a, the appropriate constant is $c = 4/\eta + 1$.) Hence, the number of employed colors is $O(a)$.

Next, we analyze the running time of Procedure Legal-Coloring. By Lemma 7.6(2), during the execution of Procedure Legal-Coloring, the Procedure Arbdefective-Coloring is invoked for a constant number of times. Note also that each time it is invoked with the same values of the parameters $t = k = p = \lfloor a^{\eta/2} \rfloor$. Hence, by Corollary 7.5, executing the while-loop requires $O(t^2 \log n) = O(a^\eta \log n)$ time. By Lemma 5.15, the additional time required for coloring all the subgraphs in step 19 of Algorithm 12 is $O(p \log n) = O(a^{\eta/2} \log n)$. (By the termination condition of the while-loop (line 4), once the algorithm reaches line 19, it holds that $\alpha \le p$.) Therefore, the total running time is $O(a^\eta \log n)$. $\square$

Theorem 7.7 implies that for the family of graphs with polylogarithmic (in n) arboricity, an $O(a)$-coloring can be computed in time $O((\log n)^{1+\eta'})$, for an arbitrarily small positive constant η'. In the case of graphs with superlogarithmic arboricity, even better results than those that are given in Theorem 7.7 can be achieved. In this case one can execute Procedure Legal-Coloring with the parameter $p = \left\lfloor \frac{a^{\eta'}}{\log n} \right\rfloor$. Since a is superlogarithmic in n, and $\eta' > 0$ is a constant, it holds that $p > a^{\eta'/2}$, for a sufficiently large n. Therefore, Procedure Legal-Coloring executes its loop for a constant number of times. Consequently, the number of colors employed is still $O(a)$. The running time is the sum of running time of Procedure Arbdefective-Color and the running time of computing legal colorings of graphs of arboricity at most p, which is $O(\frac{a^{2\eta'}}{\log^2 n} \cdot \log n + \frac{a^{\eta'}}{\log n} \cdot \log n) = O(a^{2\eta'})$. If we set $\eta' = \eta/2$, the running time becomes $O(a^\eta)$. We summarize this result in the following corollary.

Corollary 7.8 *Let η be an arbitrarily small constant. For any graph G, a legal $O(a)$-coloring of G can be computed in time $O(a^\eta + (\log n)^{1+\eta})$.*

Next, we demonstrate that one can trade the number of colors for time. Specifically, we show that if one is allowed to use slightly more than $O(a)$ colors, the running time can be bounded by $polylog(n)$, *for all values of arboricity* a. To this end we select the parameter p to be polylogarithmic in a. With this value of p the running time $O(p \log n)$ of the coloring step in line 19 of Algorithm 12 becomes polylogarithmic. Moreover, setting the parameters t and k to be polylogarithmic in a results in a polylogarithmic running time of Procedure Arbdefective-Coloring. (By Corollary 7.5 the running time of a single invocation of Procedure Arbdefective-Coloring is $O(t^2 \cdot \log n)$.) The number of iterations of the while-loop is $O(\log_p a)$. Consequently, the total running time is also polylogarithmic. However, the number of iterations becomes superconstant. Hence the number of colors grows beyond $O(a)$. The specific parameters we select are $p = k = t = f(a)^{1/2}$, for an arbitrarily slow-growing function $f(a) = \omega(1)$. The results of invoking Procedure Legal-Coloring with these parameters are given below.

Theorem 7.9   *Invoking Procedure Legal-Coloring with the parameter* $p = f(a)^{1/2}$, $f(a) = \omega(1)$ *as above, requires* $O(f(a) \log a \log n)$ *time. The resulting coloring employs* $a^{1+o(1)}$ *colors.*

Proof. Set $b = p/(3 + \epsilon)$. The number of iterations is at most $\log_b a = O(\frac{\log a}{\log f(a)})$. Each iteration requires $O(p^2 \log n) = O(f(a) \log n)$ time. Hence the running time of Procedure Legal-Coloring is

$$\log_b a \cdot O(f(a) \log n) = O(\frac{f(a)}{\log f(a)} \log a \log n).$$

By Lemma 7.6(3), the total number of employed colors is at most

$$a \cdot (3 + \epsilon)^{O(\log a/ \log f(a))} = a^{1+O(1/ \log f(a))} = a^{1+o(1)}.$$

$\square$

More generally, as evident from the above analysis, the running time of Algorithm 12 is $O(p^2 \log_p a \log n)$, and the number of colors used is $2^{O(\log_p a)} \cdot a$. Another noticeable point on the tradeoff curve is on the opposite end of the spectrum, i.e., $p = C$, for some sufficiently large constant C. (The constant need to be larger than 16. See the discussion preceding Lemma 7.6.) Here the tradeoff gives rise to $a^{1+C' \cdot (1/ \log C)}$-coloring in $O(\log a \log n)$ time, for some fixed constant C'. (The constant C' does not depend on C, and thus, $\log C$ can be made arbitrarily larger than C'.)

Corollary 7.10   *For an arbitrarily small constant* $\eta > 0$, *Procedure Legal-Coloring invoked with* $p = 2^{O(1/\eta)}$ *produces an* $O(a^{1+\eta})$-*coloring in* $O(\log a \log n)$ *deterministic time.*

Corollary 7.10 also implies that any graph G for which there exists a constant $\nu > 0$ such that $a \leq \Delta^{1-\nu}$ can be colored with $o(\Delta)$ colors in $O(\log a \log n)$ time. This goal is achieved by computing an $O(a^{1+\nu})$-coloring of the input graph G. Since $a^{1+\nu} \leq \Delta^{1-\nu^2}$, this is an $o(\Delta)$-coloring of G. Therefore, Corollary 7.10 gives rise to a deterministic polylogarithmic $(\Delta + 1)$-coloring algorithm for a very wide family of graphs. This fact is summarized in the following corollary.

Corollary 7.11 *For the family of graphs with arboricity $a \leq \Delta^{1-\nu}$, for an arbitrarily small constant ν, one can compute $(\Delta + 1)$-coloring within $O(\log a \log n)$ deterministic time.*

Also, since $a \leq \Delta$, Corollary 7.10 implies that an $O(\Delta^{1+\eta})$-coloring can be computed in $O(\log \Delta \log n)$ deterministic time, for an arbitrarily small constant $\eta > 0$. Similarly, Theorem 7.9 implies that $\Delta^{1+o(1)}$-coloring can be computed in $O(f(\Delta) \log \Delta \log n)$ time, for an arbitrarily slowly growing function $f = \omega(1)$. These results from [9] answer in the affirmative an open question of Linial [55]. (See the discussion in the beginning of this section.)

CHAPTER 8

Edge-Coloring and Maximal Matching

In this section we explore colorings of the *edge-set* of a graph. Since an edge-coloring of a graph G can be computed using a vertex coloring of the line-graph $L(G)$, all algorithms described in the previous sections for vertex-coloring can be used for computing edge-colorings as well. However, line graphs have some special properties that are absent in general graphs. These properties allow for more efficient computation of vertex-coloring of line graphs, which, in turn, gives rise to efficient edge-coloring algorithms on *general graphs*. These algorithms are the subject of the current chapter. The algorithms in Section 8.1 are due to Panconesi and Rizzi [68]. The algorithms in Section 8.2 are from [10].

8.1 EDGE-COLORING AND MAXIMAL MATCHING USING FOREST-DECOMPOSITION

We start with describing a $(2\Delta - 1)$-edge-coloring distributed algorithm for oriented trees (due to [68]). Next it will be used as a building block for computing edge-colorings of general graphs. The algorithm for oriented trees is called *Procedure Tree-Edge-Color*. It accepts as input an oriented tree $T = (V, E)$. Each vertex $v \in V$ holds a list l_v of colors that are forbidden for edges adjacent on v. Initially, $l_v = \emptyset$ for all $v \in V$. The procedure starts with computing a *3-vertex-coloring* of T using the algorithm of Cole and Vishkin [18]. Then it proceeds in three phases. In phase i, $i = 1, 2, 3$, all vertices $v \in V$ colored by i, in parallel, assign colors φ to edges (v, w) incident on them which connect them with their *children* w. A color for an edge (v, w) is selected from the pallete $[2\Delta - 1] \setminus (l_v \cup l_w)$. The colors are selected such that for each pair of children w, w' of v, $\varphi(v, w) \neq \varphi(v, w')$. Then all vertices $v \in V$ update their lists l_v to contain the colors of all edges incident on v that have already been colored. This completes the description of the algorithm. Its pseudocode is provided below.

Lemma 8.1 *Procedure Tree-Edge-Color computes a legal $(2\Delta - 1)$-edge-coloring of an oriented tree T.*

Proof. First we show that each edge $e = (v, w) \in E$ is assigned a color from $[2\Delta - 1]$ during an execution of the algorithm. Suppose without loss of generality that v is the parent of w. In round

---

Algorithm 13 Procedure Tree-Edge-Color(T)

An algorithm for each vertex $v \in V$:

1: $\psi := $ 3-vertex-coloring of T
2: **for** $i := 1, 2, 3$ **do**
3:    **if** $\psi(v) = i$ **then**
4:       **for** each child w of v **do**
5:          /* Iterations are performed sequentially, but within a single round (locally) */
6:          $\varphi(v, w) := $ a color from $[2\Delta - 1] \setminus (l_v \cup l_w)$
7:          $l_v = l_v \cup \{\varphi(v, w)\}$
8:       **end for**
9:       **for** each child w of v, in parallel **do**
10:         send $\varphi(v, w)$ to w
11:       **end for**
12:    **end if**
13:    **if** v receives a color $\varphi(u, v)$ from its parent u **then**
14:       $l_v = l_v \cup \{\varphi(u, v)\}$
15:    **end if**
16:    send l_v to all neighbors
17: **end for**

$i = \psi(v) \in [3]$ the edge e is assigned a color. Notice that the palette $[2\Delta - 1] \setminus (l_v \cup l_w)$ is not empty, since l_v and l_w contain the colors assigned to edges incident on v and w, respectively. Thus $|l_v| \leq \Delta - 1$ and $|l_w| \leq \Delta - 1$. (Because at the time of selection of the color of (v, w), each of the vertices v and w have at most $\Delta - 1$ colored edges incident on them.) Therefore, $|[2\Delta - 1] \setminus (l_v \cup l_w)| \geq 1$, and so there exists an available color for e.

Next, we show that the coloring is legal. Let $e = (v, w)$, $e' = (v, u)$ be a pair of edges that share a common vertex v. If v is the parent of w and u, then e and e' are assigned distinct colors during an execution of the loop in lines 4-8. Otherwise, either v is the child of w, or v is the child of u. Suppose without loss of generality that the latter is the case. Then w is the child of v. Consequently, e and e' are assigned colors in distinct phases. (Because $\psi(u) \neq \psi(v)$, u is the parent of v, and v is the parent of w.) Suppose without loss of generality that the color of e' is selected in a later phase. Then $\varphi(e')$ is selected from the palette $[2\Delta - 1] \setminus (l_v \cup l_u)$, where $\varphi(e) \in l_v$. Therefore, $\varphi(e') \neq \varphi(e)$. $\square$

Lemma 8.2 *The running time of Procedure Tree-Edge-Color is* $\log^* n + O(1)$.

Proof. The first step that computes 3-vertex-coloring requires $\log^* n + O(1)$ time. Next, we show that each of the three phases of the algorithm (lines 2 - 17) can be performed within a constant number of rounds. In the beginning of a phase i, each vertex v knows the sets l_w of all its neighbors w that were computed in previous phases. These sets do not change during the execution of the loop (lines 4 - 8), because $\psi(w) \neq i$ for all neighbor w of v. Therefore, the loop can be performed locally. Hence, the entire phase can be implemented within a single round. Thus, the overall running time is $\log^* n + O(1)$.   □

Procedure Tree-Edge-Color can be extended to work on an oriented forest in a straight-farward way. Simply invoke procedure Tree-Edge-Color in all the trees of the forest in parallel. Obviously, the resulting coloring is a legal $(2\Delta - 1)$-edge coloring of the forest, since edges from different forests do not share common vertices. The running time of the algorithm on forests remain $\log^* n + O(1)$. We call the extended algorithm *Procedure Forest-Edge-Color*.

Procedure Tree-Edge-Color can be also extended to compute a maximal matching (hence-forth, MM). Like Procedure Tree-Edge-Color, the modified procedure, called Tree-MM, also starts with computing a 3-vertex-coloring ψ of T. Then it proceeds in 3 phases, and in phase $i = 1, 2, 3$ the vertices v with $\psi(v) = i$ are active. In phase i, $i \in [3]$, vertices v with $\psi(v) = i$ decide the status of their descending edges (v, u). (We say that the edge (v, u) is *descending* if v is the parent of u.) Like in Procedure Tree-Edge-Color, this is done locally sequentially by v. Specifically, if v is unmatched then it picks an arbitrary unmatched child u of v (if exists), and inserts the edge (v, u) into the matching. Then v and u infrom their neighbors that they became matched. The analysis of Procedure Tree-MM is analogous to that of Procedure Tree-Edge-Color. The running time of both procedures is $\log^* n + O(1)$. It also extends to oriented forests, and computes MM in them in $\log^* n + O(1)$ time. This extended routine will be referred to as *Procedure Forest-MM*.

Next, we show how to extend these algorithms further, to work on general graphs. This extension, however, comes at a price of increasing the running time. The algorithm for general graphs is called *Procedure Simple-Edge-Color*. It accepts as input a graph G. First, it computes a Δ-forest-decomposition of G. To this end it orients the edges toward endpoints with greater Ids. Then each vertex assigns distinct labels from the set $[\Delta]$ to its outgoing edges. For $i = 1, 2, ..., \Delta$, all edges that were assigned the label i form a forest F_i. Next, Procedure Simple-Edge-Color proceeds in Δ phases. In each phase $i = 1, 2, ..., \Delta$, it computes an edge-coloring of the forest F_i in a way that avoids conflicts with previously colored forests. In other words, in the beginning of phase i, for each vertex $v \in V$, the list of forbidden colors l_v contains the colors of all edges incident on v that have been colored before phase i. Thus, once a color for an edge is selected, it is not only distinct from the colors of ajacent edges in the same forest, but also from the adjacent edges in other forests that have been already colored. This completes the description of the algorithm. Its pseudocode is provided below. (We remark that 3-vertex coloring of all forests can be performed in parallel before the beginning of executing the Δ phases of edge-coloring forests. In this way the step of computing 3-vertex-coloring in each phase (line 1 of Algorithm 13) actually will not require any computation, since the coloring has been already computed earlier. See lines 2-4 of Algorithm 14.)

Algorithm 14 Procedure Simple-Edge-Color(G)

An algorithm for each vertex $v \in V$:

1: $\{F_1, F_2, ..., F_\Delta\} := \Delta$-forest-decomposition
2: **for** $i := 1, 2, ..., \Delta$, in parallel **do**
3:    $\psi_i := 3$-vertex-coloring of F_i
4: **end for**
5: $l_v := \emptyset$
6: **for** $i := 1, 2, ..., \Delta$ **do**
7:    Forest-Edge-Color(F_i)
8:    $l_v := \{\varphi(v, u) \mid u \in \Gamma(v), \ (v, u) \text{ is colored}\}$
9: **end for**

Lemma 8.3   *For any graph $G = (V, E)$, Procedure Simple-Edge-Color computes a legal $(2\Delta - 1)$-edge-coloring of G.*

Proof. Similarly to the proof of Lemma 8.1, before a color for an edge $(u, v) \in E$ is selected, it holds that $|l_u| \leq \Delta - 1$ and $|l_v| \leq \Delta - 1$. Thus there always exists an available color for (u, v) from $[2\Delta - 1] \setminus (l_u \cup l_v)$. Next we show that the coloring is legal. Let $e = (v, w), e' = (v, u)$ be a pair of edges in E that share a common vertex v. If $e, e' \in F_i$, for some $i \in [\Delta]$, then $\varphi(e) \neq \varphi(e')$ by the correctness of Procedure Tree-Edge-Color. (We remark that Procedure Tree-Edge-Color is correct even if in the beginning of its execution some lists l_x satisfy $l_x \neq \emptyset$, as long as there are always available colors for edges $(x, y) \in E$ from $[2\Delta - 1] \setminus (l_x \cup l_y)$.) If $e \in F_i, e' \in F_j$ for some $i < j$ then the color of e' is selected in a later phase than that of e. Consequently, at the time of selection of the color of $e' = (v, u)$ it holds that $\varphi(e) = \varphi(v, w) \in l_v$. Therefore, the selected color of e' satisfies $\varphi(e') \in [2\Delta - 1] \setminus (l_v \cup l_u)$, and thus, $\varphi(e') \neq \varphi(e)$. The remaining case $i > j$ is symmetrical. $\qquad\square$

Lemma 8.4   *The running time of Procedure Simple-Edge-Color is $O(\Delta) + \log^* n$.*

Proof. Computing Δ-forest-decomposition in line 1 requires $O(1)$ time. Computing 3-vertex-coloring for Δ forests in parallel in lines 2-4 requires $\log^* n + O(1)$ time. Each of the Δ phases in lines 6-9 requires $O(1)$ time. Therefore, the overall running time is $O(\Delta) + \log^* n$. $\qquad\square$

The next theorem summarizes the analysis of Procedure Simple-Edge-Color.

Theorem 8.5   *A $(2\Delta - 1)$-edge-coloring of general graphs can be computed in $O(\Delta) + \log^* n$ time.*

Procedure Forest-MM can be extended in an analogous way to produce an MM for a general graph in time $O(\Delta) + \log^* n$.

Next consider the $(2\Delta - 1)$-edge-coloring and the MM problems in graphs of bounded arboricity (at most a). One can use an algorithm similar to Procedure Simple-Edge-Color, except that instead of computing a Δ-forest-decomposition in line 1 of Algorithm 14 we compute a forest-decomposition into $A \le a \cdot q$ forests, for some parameter $q > 2$. The rest of the algorithm is identical to Algorithm 14, but Δ has to be replaced by A in lines 2 and 6. The modified algorithm will be called *Procedure Arb-Edge-Color*.

The same analysis as in Lemmas 8.3 and 8.4 shows that Procedure Arb-Edge-Color produces a $(2\Delta - 1)$-edge-coloring within $O(A) + \log^* n$ time, in addition to the time required to compute the forest-decomposition. The latter is, by Lemma 5.13, $O(\frac{\log n}{\log q})$. Hence the overall running time is $O(a \cdot q + \frac{\log n}{\log q})$. For graphs with arboricity $a \le \log^{1-\epsilon} n$, for some constant $\epsilon > 0$, we can set $q = \log^{\epsilon/2} n$, and obtain running time $O(\frac{\log n}{\log \log n})$. Also, evidently, the running time of this algorithm is polylogarithmic in n as long as the arboricity is polylogarithmic in n. (By setting $q = 3$ one gets here time $O(a + \log n)$.) Moreover, similarly to Procedure Simple-Edge-Color, Procedure Arb-Defective-Color can also be easily extended to compute a MM within the same time.

Theorem 8.6 *[7] For graphs with arboricity $a \le \log^{1-\epsilon} n$, for some constant $\epsilon > 0$, it is possible to compute $(2\Delta - 1)$-coloring and MM in $O(\frac{\log n}{\log \log n})$ deterministic time. Moreover, they can be always computed in time $O(a + \log n)$.*

8.2 EDGE-COLORING USING BOUNDED NEIGHBORHOOD INDEPENDENCE

A graph with *bounded neighborhood independence* c is a graph in which every 1-neighborhood of a vertex contains at most c independent vertices, for some integer parameter $c > 0$. In other words, for each vertex $v \in V$, the size of any independent set $I \subseteq \Gamma(v)$ is at most c. Consider, for example, the line graph $L(G)$ of a graph $G = (V, E)$. A vertex v in $L(G)$ corresponds to an edge $e_v \in G$. An independent set of vertices $I \in \Gamma(v)$ corresponds to a set of edges $J_I \subseteq E$, such that each $e \in J_I$ share a common endpoint with e_v, but each pair of edges $e, e' \in J_I$ do not intersect. Therefore, $|J_I| \le 2$, and consequently, $|I| \le 2$. Thus, any line graph $L(G)$ has neighborhood independence bounded by 2. In this section we show that graphs with bounded neighborhood independence can be vertex-colored much faster than by using algorithms for general graphs described in previous sections. In particular, these results apply to vertex-coloring of line graphs, which, in turn, gives rise to efficient edge-coloring algorithms for general graphs. The results in this section are from [10].

As a first step we show that graphs with bounded neighborhood independence and bounded arboricity must also have bounded degree. This fact allows one to compute defective colorings of graphs with bounded neighborhood independence more efficiently than in general graphs.

Specifically, for general graphs it is currently known only how to compute efficiently $O(\Delta/p)$-defective p^2-coloring (see Section 6.2) and $O(a/p)$-arbdefective $O(p)$-coloring (see Chapter 7). On the other hand, for graphs with bounded neighborhood independence, $O(\Delta/p)$-defective $O(p)$-coloring can be computed very efficiently for reasonably small values of $p \geq 1$. Efficient defective coloring with these parameters (notice that the product of the defect and the number of colors is linear in Δ) gives rise to efficient algorithms for legal $O(\Delta)$-vertex-coloring of graphs with bounded neighborhood independence.

Lemma 8.7 *A graph $G = (V, E)$ with arboricity bounded by a and neighborhood independence bounded by c, for some integer parameters $a, c > 0$, has maximum degree at most $2a \cdot c$.*

Proof. First, notice that G can be vertex-colored legally using $2a$ colors, because $\chi(G) \leq \deg(G) + 1 \leq 2a(G) = 2a$. (See Section 2.3.2, Lemma 2.30). Let $v \in V$ be a vertex such that $\deg(v) = \Delta(G)$. The subgraph $G(\Gamma(v))$ can be colored with $2a$ colors as well. Let φ be such a coloring. By the pigeonhole principle, there exists a color k, $1 \leq k \leq 2a$, such that $|\{u \in \Gamma(v) \mid \varphi(u) = k\}| \geq \frac{\deg(v)}{2a}$. On the other hand, all vertices colored by the same color form an independent set. The size of the independent set $\{u \in \Gamma(v) \mid \varphi(u) = k\}$ is at most c. Therefore, $c \geq \frac{\deg(v)}{2a} = \frac{\Delta}{2a}$. Hence, $\Delta(G) \leq 2a \cdot c$. $\square$

By Lemma 8.7, an $O(\Delta/p)$-arbdefective $O(p)$-coloring of a graph with neighborhood independence bounded by c is also an $O((2\Delta/p) \cdot c)$-defective $O(p)$-coloring of the graph. Therefore, for obtaining defective colorings of such graphs, it is sufficient to compute an appropriate arbdefective coloring. Next, we describe an efficient algorithm for computing an $O(\Delta/p)$-arbdefective $O(p)$-coloring. This algorithm is called *Procedure Arbdefective-Coloring-Bounded*. It is very similar to Procedure Arbdefective-Coloring. (See Section 7.1, Algorithm 11.) The only difference is that in the beginning of the partial-orientation phase the partition $\mathcal{H}$ consists only of a single graph $H_1 = G$, i.e., the entire input graph. The pseudocode of the procedure is provided in Algorithm 16 below. It employs Algorithm 15 as a sub-routine.

Algorithm 15 Procedure Partial-Orientation-Bounded(G, t)

1: compute a $\lfloor \Delta/t \rfloor$-defective $O(t^2)$-coloring ψ of G.
2: **for** each edge $e = (u, v)$ in E in parallel **do**
3:     **if** u and v have different ψ-colors **then**
4:         orient e toward the endpoint with a greater ψ-color.
5:     **end if**
6: **end for**

Procedure Partial-Orientation-Bounded computes an orientation μ with deficit $\lfloor \Delta/t \rfloor$ and length $O(t^2)$. Thus, Procedure Arbdefective-Coloring-Bounded computes a $(\Delta/t + \Delta/k)$-arbdefective k-coloring. The running time of step 1 of Procedure Partial-Orientation-Bounded

---

Algorithm 16 Procedure Arbdefective-Coloring-Bounded(G, k, t)

1: μ = Partial-Orientation-Bounded(G, t)
2: **once** all the parents u of v with respect to μ have selected a color $\varphi(u)$ **do**
   v selects a color $\varphi(v)$ from the palette $\{1, 2, ..., k\}$ which is used by the minimum number of parents of v

---

is $\log^* n + O(1)$, by using the algorithm of Kuhn [48]. The other steps of the procedure require constant time. Thus, the running time of step 1 of Algorithm 16 is $\log^* n + O(1)$. Step 2 of Algorithm 16 requires time proportional to the length of μ, which is $O(t^2)$. We summarize the properties of the algorithm in the next theorem.

Theorem 8.8   *For positive integer parameters t, k, satisfying $0 < t, k < \Delta$, an $(\Delta/t + \Delta/k)$-arbdefective k-coloring of an input graph G can be computed in $O(t^2) + \log^* n$ time.*

We remark that Theorem 8.8 holds for general graphs, and not only on graphs with bounded neighborhood independence. However, for graphs with bounded neighborhood independence, Theorem 8.8 in conjunction with Lemma 8.7 imply that *defective* colorings of such graphs with appropriate parameters can be computed efficiently.

Corollary 8.9   *Let G be a graph with neighborhood independence bounded by c, for some integer $c > 0$. For positive integer parameters t, k, satisfying $0 < t, k < \Delta$, a $(2 \cdot (\Delta/t + \Delta/k) \cdot c)$-defective k-coloring of the graph G can be computed in $O(t^2) + \log^* n$ time.*

Proof. Let φ be an $(\Delta/t + \Delta/k)$-arbdefective k-coloring of G computed by procedure Arbdefective-Coloring-Bounded. The arboricity of a subgraph G_i induced by a color class i of φ, for $1 \le i \le k$, is at most $(\Delta/t + \Delta/k)$. Thus by Lemma 8.7, the maximum degree of G_i is $2 \cdot (\Delta/t + \Delta/k) \cdot c$. Thus, φ is a $(2 \cdot (\Delta/t + \Delta/k) \cdot c)$-defective k-coloring.   □

For graphs in which the neighborhood independence is bounded by a constant, the above corollary implies an $O(\Delta/p)$-defective p-coloring, for an integer $0 < p < \Delta$. (To this end, set $t = k = p$.) Such a coloring can be used to achieve a legal $O(\Delta)$-vertex-coloring of such graphs faster than in $O(\Delta + \log^* n)$ time. Specifically, compute an $O(\Delta^{2/3})$-defective $\Delta^{1/3}$-coloring ψ in $O(\Delta^{2/3} + \log^* n)$ time. Then compute a legal $O(\Delta^{2/3})$-coloring φ of each subgraph induced be a color class of ψ, using distinct palettes. This requires $O(\Delta^{2/3} + \log^* n)$ time as well. Overall, a legal $O(\Delta)$-coloring of the entire input graphs is obtained in $O(\Delta^{2/3} + \log^* n)$ time. This approach can be improved if the computation of defective colorings is performed several times recursively, similarly to the approach in Section 7.2. In other words, we need to compute defective colorings on subgraphs induced by color classes of a coloring ψ returned by Procedure Arbdefective-Coloring-Bounded. To this end, we show that the family of graphs with bounded neighborhood independence is closed under taking vertex-induced subgraphs.

Lemma 8.10   *Let $G = (V, E)$ be a graph with neighborhood independence bounded by c. For any $V' \subseteq V$, the neighborhood independence of the induced subgraph $G' = G(V')$ is at most c as well.*

Proof. For a vertex $u \in V'$, $\Gamma_{G'}(u)$ is the neighborhood of u in G', and $\Gamma_G(u)$ is the neighborhood of u in G. Suppose for contradiction that there exists a vertex $u \in V'$ such that there is an independent set $W \subseteq \Gamma_{G'}(u)$ with cardinality $|W| > c$. For a pair of vertices $v, w \in W$, it holds that $(v, w) \notin E$. (Because $v, w \in V'$ and $v, w \in V$. Therefore if $(v, w) \in E$, then (v, w) must be present in any induced subgraph that contains the vertices u, w. But the vertices v and w are not connected in $G(V')$, thus they are not connected in G as well.) In addition, $\Gamma_{G'}(u) \subseteq \Gamma_G(u)$. Therefore, $W \subseteq \Gamma_G(u)$ is an independent set with more than c vertices, and it is contained in the neighborhood $\Gamma_G(u)$ of the vertex u. This is a contradiction.   □

The improved algorithm for computing vertex-colorings of graphs with bounded neighborhood independence is called *Procedure Legal-Coloring-Bounded*. It accepts as input a graph G with neighborhood independence bounded by c, a parameter d which is an upper bounded on $\Delta(G)$, and a parameter $p > 4 \cdot c$. If $d \leq p$ then a $(d + 1)$-coloring is directly computed on G in $O(d) + \log^* n$ time using Algorithm 8 from Section 6. Otherwise, an $O(c \cdot d/p)$-defective p-coloring ψ of G is computed. The p color classes of ψ induce the subgraphs $G_1, G_2, ..., G_p$, each with maximum degree $O(c \cdot d/p)$. Next, Procedure Legal-Coloring-Bounded is invoked recursively on $G_1, G_2, ..., G_p$ in parallel. These invocations produce legal q-colorings of $G_1, G_2, ..., G_p$. (We will analyze the value of q later.) Then these colorings are merged into a unified $O(q \cdot p)$-coloring of the input graph G. This completes the description of the algorithm. Its pseudocode is provided below.

Algorithm 17 Procedure Legal-Color-Bounded(G, d, p)

1: **if** $d \leq p$ **then**
2:      $\varphi :=$ a $(d + 1)$-coloring of G
3:      return φ
4: **else**
5:      $\psi :=$ Arbdefective-Coloring-Bounded$(G, k := p, t := p)$
6:      denote by G_i the graph induced by color class i of ψ, $i \in \{1, 2, ..., p\}$
7:      **for** $i = 1, 2, ..., p$, in parallel **do**
8:          $\varphi_i :=$ Legal-Color-Bounded$(G_i, \lfloor 4 \cdot c \cdot d/p \rfloor, p)$
9:          $\varphi(v) := (\varphi_i(v) - 1) \cdot p + i$
10:     **end for**
11:     return φ
12: **end if**

Lemma 8.11 *Suppose that Procedure Legal-Color-Bounded is invoked on a graph G with bounded neighborhood independence c, and the parameters $d = \Delta = \Delta(G)$ and $p > 4 \cdot c$. Then the procedure produces a legal $((4c)^{\log_{p/4c} \Delta} \Delta)$-vertex coloring in $O((p^2 + \log^* n) \cdot \log_{p/4c} \Delta)$ time.*

Proof. First we prove that the procedure invoked with the above parameters produces the required coloring. The proof is by induction on the recursion depth.

Base: If $d \leq p$ then the procedure computes in line 2 a legal $(\Delta + 1)$-coloring of G.

Step: If $d > p$ then the procedure computes a $\lfloor 4 \cdot c \cdot d/p \rfloor$-defective p-coloring ψ of G in line 5. (See Corollary 8.9.) Denote $d' = \lfloor 4 \cdot c \cdot d/p \rfloor$. By induction hypothesis, each of the subgraphs $G_1, G_2, ..., G_p$ is colored legally with at most $((4c)^{\log_{p/4c} d'} d')$ colors in line 8. Next, in line 9 these colorings are transformed into a legal coloring with at most $((4c)^{\log_{p/4c} d'} d') \cdot p \leq ((4c)^{\log_{p/4c} d'} 4 \cdot c \cdot d/p) \cdot p \leq (4c)^{\log_{p/4c} d'+1} \cdot d \leq (4c)^{\log_{p/4c}(d' \cdot p/4c)} \cdot d \leq (4c)^{\log_{p/4c} d} \cdot d$.

Next, we analyze the running time of the procedure. Observe that in each recursive invocation, the bound on the maximum degree of the subgraph on which the procedure is invoked is decreased by a factor of at least $p/4c > 1$. Consequently, the depth of the recursion tree is at most $\log_{p/4c} \Delta$. The running time of the procedure is given by $T(d) = T(4 \cdot c \cdot d/p) + O(p^2) + \log^* n$.

This recursive formula solves to $T(\Delta) = O((p^2 + \log^* n) \cdot \log_{p/4c} \Delta)$. □

Consider a graph G with neighborhood independence bounded by $c = O(1)$. By setting $p = \Delta^\epsilon$ in Lemma 8.11, for an arbitrarily small constant $\epsilon > 0$, we obtain a legal $O(\Delta)$-vertex-coloring of G in $O(\Delta^{2\epsilon} + \log^* n)$ time. Alternatively, by setting $p = (\log \Delta)^\epsilon$, we obtain a legal $\Delta^{1+o(1)}$-vertex-coloring in $O((\log \Delta)^{1+2\epsilon} + \log^* n \cdot \frac{\log \Delta}{\log \log \Delta})$ time. Finally, by setting $p = c'$ for a large constant $c' \gg c$, we obtain a legal $O(\Delta^{1+\epsilon})$-vertex-coloring in $O(\log^* n \cdot \log \Delta)$ time. These results (due to [10]) are summarized in the following theorem.

Theorem 8.12 *Consider a graph G with neighborhood independence bounded by $c = O(1)$. Let $\epsilon > 0$ be an arbitrarily small constant.*
(1) An $O(\Delta)$-vertex-coloring of G can be computed in $O(\Delta^\epsilon + \log^* n)$ time.
(2) A $\Delta^{1+o(1)}$-vertex-coloring of G can be computed in $O((\log \Delta)^{1+\epsilon} + \log^* n \cdot \frac{\log \Delta}{\log \log \Delta})$ time.
(3) An $O(\Delta^{1+\epsilon})$-vertex-coloring of G can be computed in $O(\log^* n \cdot \log \Delta)$ time.

We conclude this section by arguing that the techniques described above can be used to devise very efficient edge-coloring algorithms for *general* graphs. These algorithms are based on the observation that line graphs have neighborhood independence bounded by 2. (See the discussion in the beginning of this section).

Recall that for any graph G and positive integer k, a legal k-coloring of *vertices* of $L(G)$ is a legal k-coloring of *edges* of G, and vice versa. Recall also that the maximum degree $\Delta(L(G))$ of the line graph $L(G)$ satisfies $\Delta(L(G)) \leq 2(\Delta - 1)$, where $\Delta = \Delta(G)$. Consequently, if we are given a line graph $L(G)$ of a graph G with $\Delta(G) = \Delta$, one can compute an $O(\Delta(L(G))) =$

$O(\Delta)$-vertex-coloring of $L(G)$ in $O(\Delta^\epsilon + \log^* n)$ time, for any constant $\epsilon > 0$. Similarly, one can also compute $\Delta^{1+o(1)}$-vertex-coloring (respectively, $O(\Delta^{1+\epsilon})$-vertex-coloring) of $L(G)$ in $O((\log \Delta)^{1+\epsilon} + \log^* n \cdot \frac{\log \Delta}{\log \log \Delta})$ (resp., $O(\log^* n \cdot \log \Delta)$) time. These vertex colorings give rise directly to edge coloring of G with the same number of colors.

On the other hand, in the distributed edge-coloring problem we are given as input the graph G, rather than its line graph $L(G)$. Nevertheless, one can simulate the distributed computation of an algorithm on $L(G)$ using the network $G = (V, E)$. To this end each vertex of $L(G)$ is simulated by one endpoint of an appropriate edge in G. Consequently, a message sent over an edge of $L(G)$ will be sent over at most two edges in the simulation on G.

Lemma 8.13 *Any algorithm with running time T for the line graph $L(G)$ of the input graph G can be simulated by G, and requires at most $2T + O(1)$ time.*

Proof. For each edge $e \in E$, one of the endpoints of e simulates a vertex in $L(G)$ that corresponds to e. (Note that each vertex in G may simulate many vertices of $L(G)$.) Specifically, for each edge $e = (u, v) \in E$, such that $Id(u) < Id(v)$, the vertex that corresponds to e in $L(G)$ is simulated by u. We denote the vertex in $L(G)$ that corresponds to e by v_e. The Id of v_e is set as the ordered pair $\langle Id(u), Id(v) \rangle$. This guarantees unique Ids for vertices in $L(G)$. Sending a message from a vertex w in $L(G)$ to its neighbor w' is simulated as follows. If the vertices that simulate w and w' are neighbors in G, the message is sent directly. Otherwise, the distance between the simulating vertices is 2. The vertices w and w' correspond to edges e and e' in E that share a common endpoint v'. In this case the message is sent from the vertex that simulates w to v', and from v' to the vertex that simulates w'. Hence any algorithm for the line graph can be simulated on the original graph, increasing the running time by a factor of at most 2. The additive term of $O(1)$ in the running time above reflects the time spent for computing unique Ids for vertices of $L(G)$. $\square$

Since $L(G)$ has neighborhood independence bounded by 2, we can apply Lemma 8.13 in conjunction with Theorem 8.12, and obtain the following theorem.

Theorem 8.14 *Consider a graph $G = (V, E)$, and let $\epsilon > 0$ be an arbitrarily small constant.*
(1) An $O(\Delta)$-edge-coloring of G can be computed in $O(\Delta^\epsilon + \log^* n)$ time.
(2) A $\Delta^{1+o(1)}$-edge-coloring of G can be computed in $O((\log \Delta)^{1+\epsilon} + \log^* n \cdot \frac{\log \Delta}{\log \log \Delta})$ time.
(3) An $O(\Delta^{1+\epsilon})$-edge-coloring of G can be computed in $O(\log^* n \cdot \log \Delta)$ time.

CHAPTER 9

Network Decompositions

In this chapter we describe an important general technique for solving distributed symmetry breaking problems, called the *network decomposition technique*. Algorithms that are based on this technique consist of two stages. In the first stage a *network decomposition* is constructed, and in the second stage this decomposition is used to solve a problem at hand.

A *network decomposition* of a graph $G = (V, E)$ with positive integer parameters α and β is a partition of G into clusters of radius at most α, which satisfies an additional property. Given a partition $\mathcal{P} = \{C_1, C_2, ..., C_q\}$ of the graph $G = (V, E)$, $\bigcup_{C \in \mathcal{P}} C = V, C_i \cap C_j = \emptyset$ for $i \neq j$, the supergraph $\mathcal{G} = (\mathcal{P}, \mathcal{E})$ induced by $\mathcal{P}$ is given by $\mathcal{E} = \{(C, C') \mid C, C' \in \mathcal{P}, \exists (v, v') \in E, v \in C, v' \in C'\}$. In a network decomposition $\mathcal{P}$ with parameters α and β, the chromatic number $\chi(\mathcal{G})$ of the supergraph $\mathcal{G}$ is required to be at most β. In a *strong* (repectively, *weak*) network decomposition the strong (resp., weak) diameter of each cluster C, given by $\mathrm{Diam}(C) = \max\{\mathrm{dist}_{G(C)}(v, v') \mid v, v' \in C\}$ (resp., $\mathrm{Diam}(C) = \max\{\mathrm{dist}_G(v, v') \mid v, v' \in C\}$) is required to be at most α. In addition, each cluster $C \in \mathcal{P}$ has a designated vertex x_c, called the *center* of C.

The network decomposition technique was invented by Awerbuch et al. [5]. They developed a deterministic algorithm for constructing a strong network decomposition with the parameters $\alpha = \beta = 2^{O(\sqrt{\log n \log \log n})}$ that requires $2^{O(\sqrt{\log n \log \log n})}$ time. Panconesi and Srinivasan [69] improved upon this and devised a deterministic algorithm for constructing strong network decompositions with $\alpha = \beta = 2^{O(\sqrt{\log n})}$ that requires $2^{O(\sqrt{\log n})}$ time. Linial and Saks [57] came up with a randomized algorithm for building weak network decompositions with $\alpha = \beta = O(\log n)$, with running time $O(\log^2 n)$. Barenboim [6] recently devised a randomized $O(1)$-time algorithm for constructing strong network decompositions with $\alpha = O(1)$ and $\beta = n^{1/2+\epsilon}$, for an arbitrarily small constant $\epsilon > 0$.

The algorithms of [5, 69] gave rise to deterministic algorithms for MIS and $(\Delta + 1)$-coloring that require $2^{O(\sqrt{\log n})}$ time. Remarkably, these algorithms are the current state-of-the-art *deterministic* algorithms for these problems. (For the MM problem, Hanckowiak et al. [35] showed that one can outperform an algorithm based on network decompositions by a different approach.) The algorithm of Linial and Saks [57] gives rise to a randomized MIS, $(\Delta + 1)$-coloring and MM algorithms that require $O(\log^2 n)$ time. As we will see in Chapter 10, one can do much better for these problems when randomization is allowed using a different approach (which is not based on network decompositions).

This chapter is based on the paper of Awerbuch et al. [5]. In Section 9.1 we show how network decompositions can be used for solving distributed symmetry breaking problems. In

Sections 9.2 and 9.3 we describe deterministic algorithms for computing network decompositions with $\alpha = \beta = 2^{O(\sqrt{\log n \log \log n})}$.

9.1 APPLICATIONS OF NETWORK DECOMPOSITIONS

Suppose that we are given a (strong or weak) network decomposition $\mathcal{P} = (C_1, C_2, ..., C_q)$, with parameters α and β. Suppose also that each center x_i of a cluster C_i, for $i \in [q]$, is provided with a color $\varphi(C_i) = \varphi_i \in [\beta]$, so that φ is a legal β-coloring for the supergraph $\mathcal{G} = (\mathcal{P}, \mathcal{E})$ induced by the decomposition $\mathcal{P}$. Next we show that this decomposition can be used to compute an MIS of G within $O(\alpha \cdot \beta)$ time.

For all clusters C with $\varphi(C) = 1$, the center $x = x_C$ of each cluster C collects in parallel the data about the graph $G(C)$ induced by C into x. In addition, x learns the states of all vertices in $\Gamma(C) = \{u \mid u \in \Gamma(v), v \in C\}$, i.e., for each $u \in \Gamma(C)$, the center x learns if u belongs to the MIS U that was constructed so far, or not. (The set U is initialized as an empty set.) Once x knows the topology of $G(C)$ and the states of vertices in $\Gamma(C)$, it computes locally the subset $C' \subseteq C$ of vertices that are not adjacent to a vertex from U. Then x computes locally an MIS for $G(C')$, and adds this MIS to the set U both locally, and by informing all vertices in C. This is done in parallel by all clusters C with $\varphi(C) = 1$. This completes the first phase of the algorithm. Then the same computation is done in parallel for clusters of color 2 (phase 2), and then for clusters of color 3, etc. Overall there are β phases, each of which lasts for $O(\alpha)$ rounds. Hence the total running time of this computation is $O(\alpha \cdot \beta)$.

For each $i = 1, 2, ..., \beta$, let $Z_i = \bigcup\{C \in \mathcal{P} \mid \varphi(C) = i\}$, and $\hat{Z}_i = \bigcup_{j=1}^{i} Z_i$.

Lemma 9.1 *For $i = 1, 2, ..., \beta$, after i phases of the algorithm, the set $U = U_i$ is an MIS for $\hat{Z}_i$.*

Proof. The proof is by induction on i.
Base: For any pair C, C' of clusters φ-colored by 1, $\mathrm{dist}_G(C, C') \geq 2$. Also, in the beginning of phase 1 the set $U = U_0$ is empty. Hence the algorithm computes an MIS I_C for each cluster C with $\varphi(C) = 1$, and $U_1 = \bigcup\{I_C \mid \varphi(C) = 1\}$. Since $\hat{Z}_1 = Z_1 = \bigcup\{C \mid \varphi(C) = 1\}$, it follows that U_1 is an MIS for Z_1.
Step: For some $i < \beta$, we assume that U_i is an MIS for $\hat{Z}_i$. For every cluster C with $\varphi(C) = i + 1$, let $C' = \mathrm{kernel}(C) \subseteq C$ be its subset of vertices which have no neighbors in U_i. Now let $Z'_{i+1} = \bigcup\{\mathrm{kernel}(C) \mid \varphi(C) = i + 1\}$. Observe that for every pair of clusters $C, \hat{C}$ with $\varphi(C) = \varphi(\hat{C}) = i + 1$, it holds that $\mathrm{dist}_G(C, \hat{C}) \geq 2$, and so $\mathrm{dist}_G(\mathrm{kernel}(C), \mathrm{kernel}(\hat{C})) \geq 2$ as well. The algorithm computes an MIS I_C for $\mathrm{kernel}(C)$, for each C with $\varphi(C) = i + 1$. Hence $\bigcup\{I_C \mid \varphi(C) = i + 1\}$ is an MIS for Z'_{i+1}. Also, U_i is an MIS for $\hat{Z}_i \cup (Z_{i+1} \setminus Z'_{i+1}) = \hat{Z}_{i+1} \setminus Z'_{i+1}$. Hence $U_{i+1} = U_i \cup \bigcup\{I_C \mid \varphi(C) = i + 1\}$ is an MIS for $(\hat{Z}_{i+1} \setminus Z'_{i+1}) \bigcup Z'_{i+1} = \hat{Z}_{i+1}$. $\square$

Observe that a similar algorithm can solve also the $(\Delta + 1)$-coloring problem.

Corollary 9.2   *[5] Given a network decomposition with parameters α and β, the MIS and the $(\Delta + 1)$-coloring problems can be solved in $O(\alpha \cdot \beta)$ deterministic time.*

9.2   RULING SETS AND FORESTS

In this section we describe a procedure for computing a *ruling set*. Ruling sets (to be defined in the sequel) are used in the deterministic construction of network decompositions due to [5], which we will present in Section 9.3.

Definition 9.3   *For a graph $G = (V, E)$, a subset $W \subseteq V$ of vertices, and a pair of positive integers λ and ρ, a set $I \subseteq W$ is said to be a (λ, ρ)-ruling set for W in G if*
(1) for every pair of distinct vertices $v, v' \in I$, it holds that $dist_G(v, v') \geq \lambda$, and
(2) for every vertex $u \in W \setminus I$, there exists a "ruling" vertex $v \in I$, such that $dist(v, u) \leq \rho$.

Observe that an MIS for W is a $(2, 1)$-ruling set for W.

Next we present a procedure for constructing $(c, c \cdot \lceil \log n \rceil)$-ruling sets, for an arbitrary parameter $c \geq 1$, which requires $O(\log n)$ time. The procedure is called *Procedure Ruling-Set*. The construction is due to Goldberg et al. [31]. The procedure starts with partitioning all vertices of W into two disjoint sets $W_0 \cup W_1 = W$, where W_0 (respectively, W_1) is the subset of vertices of W with even (resp., odd) Ids. Then the procedure is invoked recursively in parallel on W_0 and W_1. This computation returns $(c, c \cdot \lceil \log n/2 \rceil)$-ruling sets I_0 and I_1, for W_0 and W_1 respectively. Now the unified ruling set I for W is constructed in the following way. All vertices of I_0 join I. Also, all vertices $z \in I_1$ that are at distance at most c in G from some vertex of I_0 are knocked out. All other vertices z from I_1 join I. This completes the computation of I. In other words $I \leftarrow I_0 \cup \{z \in I_1 \mid dist_G(I_0, z) > c\}$.

To complete the description of this procedure we only need to specify the termination condition of the recursion. We do this next. When vertices of W join W_0 or W_1, the least significant bit of their Ids is truncated. So if the Ids of verices in W contain $\lceil \log n \rceil$ bits, then Ids of vertices in W_0 and W_1 contain $\lceil \log n/2 \rceil = \lceil \log n \rceil - 1$ bits. When we are left with a set W with single-bit Ids, the ruling set I for it is computed in the following way. At this time $|W| \leq 2$. Then the vertex in W with Id 0, if exists, joins I. Next, the vertex with Id 1 in W, if exists, joins I if there is no other vertex in I at distance at most c from it in G. This completes the description of Procedure Ruling-Set.

Lemma 9.4   *Procedure Ruling-Set invoked on $W \subseteq V$ with a parameter c returns a $(c, c \cdot \lceil \log n \rceil)$-ruling set in $O(\log n)$ time.*

Proof. The proof is by induction on the number of bits in Ids of vertices in W.

Base (1 bit): The set I computed by the algorithm is a (c, c)-ruling set for W.

Step (i + 1 bits): By induction hypothesis, I_0 (respectively, I_1) is a $(c, c \cdot i)$-ruling set for W_0 (resp., W_1). Recall that $I = I_0 \cup \{z \in I_1 \mid \text{dist}_G(I_0, z) > c\}$. Obviously, for every $v, v' \in I$, it holds that $\text{dist}_G(v, v') > c$. Consider some $u \in W$. If $u \in W_0$ then, by the induction hypothesis, there exists a vertex $v_0 \in I_0$ such that $\text{dist}_G(v_0, u) \leq c \cdot i$. Otherwise, $u \in W_1$. Then, by the induction hypothesis, there exists $v_1 \in I_1$ such that $\text{dist}_G(v_1, u) \leq c \cdot i$. If $v_1 \in I$ then we are done. Otherwise, there exists $v_0 \in I_0$ such that $\text{dist}_G(v_0, v_1) \leq c$, and so $\text{dist}_G(v_0, u) \leq c \cdot (i + 1)$.

This proves that I is a $(c, c \cdot \lceil \log n \rceil)$-ruling set. For the running time analysis note that each level of the recursion requires $O(c)$ time, and there are $\lceil \log n \rceil$ levels.   □

A notion of *ruling forests* is closely related to that of ruling sets.

Definition 9.5   *For a graph $G = (V, E)$, a subset $W \subseteq V$ of vertices, and a pair of positive integer parameters λ and ρ, a (λ, ρ)-ruling forest $\mathcal{F} = \{(T_1, r_1), (T_2, r_2), ..., (T_q, r_q)\}$, for some integer q, is a collection of vertex-disjoint rooted trees whose roots form a (λ, ρ)-ruling set for W in G. Moreover, for every $u \in W$ there exists a root r_i of a tree $(T_i, r_i) \in \mathcal{F}$, such that $\text{dist}_{T_i}(r_i, u) \leq \rho$.*

Given a (λ, ρ)-ruling set I for W it is easy to construct a (λ, ρ)-ruling forest $\mathcal{F}$ for W. Specifically, we conduct a breadth-first-search (henceforth, BFS) to distance ρ from each vertex $v \in I$ in parallel. If a vertex x is discovered in parallel by two BFSs originated in v and v', $v, v' \in I$, then x joins one of these BFS trees arbitrarily. Once a vertex x joins a BFS tree rooted at a vertex $v \in I$, it never switches loyalty, i.e., it stays in the tree of v' forever. It is easy to verify that the resulting collection of the BFS trees rooted at vertices of I is a (λ, ρ)-ruling forest for U. Its computation requires $O(\rho)$ time. We will henceforth refer to this computation as *Procedure Ruling-Forest*. It accepts as input a positive integer parameter c and a set $W \subseteq V$. It first computes a $(c, c \cdot \lceil \log n \rceil)$-ruling set I for W by invoking Procedure Ruling-Set, and then converts it into a ruling forest in the way described above.

Corollary 9.6   *Procedure Ruling-Forest invoked on $W \subseteq V$ with a parameter c returns a $(c, c \cdot \lceil \log n \rceil)$-ruling forest $\mathcal{F}$ for W.*

9.3   CONSTRUCTING NETWORK DECOMPOSITIONS

In this section we describe an algorithm (due to [5]) for constructing network decompositions. It uses Procedure Ruling-Forest described in Section 9.2 as a blackbox. Let k be a positive integer parameter. In a graph $G = (V, E)$, let $Z = Z_0$ be a set of vertices with degrees at least $n^{1/k}$. We construct a $(3, 3 \cdot \lceil \log n \rceil)$-ruling forest $\mathcal{F} = \mathcal{F}_0$ for $Z = Z_0$ by invoking Procedure Ruling-Forest with parameters $W = Z$ and $c = 3$. (The parameter c will be set as $c = 3$ in all invocations of Procedure Ruling-Forest.) Denote $U = V \setminus V(F) = U_0$. For every $u \in U_0$, it holds that $\deg(U) < n^{1/k}$. For each of these vertices $u \in U_0$, we form a singleton cluster $\{u\}$, and add it to the initially empty partition $\mathcal{P}$. We denote by $\mathcal{P}'$ the partition that will be ultimately built by the algorithm. Some of the neighbors of u may later be merged into the same cluster. However, the degree of the cluster $\{u\}$ in the subgraph $\mathcal{G}$ induced by the resulting partition $\mathcal{P}'$ (which is currently under construction) will still be less than $n^{1/k}$. Each of the trees $(T, r) \in \mathcal{F}$ becomes a *1-level cluster* $C = C(T, r)$ centered at r. The singleton clusters $\{u\}$ for $u \in V$ are *0-level clusters*.

Write $\hat{V}_0 = \{\{v\}\} \mid v \in V\}$ and $\hat{V}_1 = \{C = C(T, r) \mid (T, r) \in \mathcal{F}_0\}$. Denote also $\hat{U}_0 = \{\{u\}\| u \in U_0\}$, and let $\hat{G}_0$ be the supergraph induced by the partition $\hat{V}_0$ of G into singleton clusters. Analogously, let $\hat{G}_1$ be the supergraph induced by the set $\hat{V}_1$ of clusters. Specifically, the edge set $\hat{E}_1$ of $\hat{G}_1$ is given by $\hat{E}_1 = \{(C, C') \mid C, C' \in \hat{V}_1, \exists (v, v') \in E, v \in C, v' \in C'\}$. Let $\hat{Z}_1$ be the set of clusters of $\hat{V}_1$ with degree at least $n^{1/k}$ in $\hat{G}_1$. Let $\hat{U}_1 = \hat{V}_1 \setminus \hat{Z}_1$ be the clusters of degree less than $n^{1/k}$ in $\hat{G}_1$. The clusters of $\hat{U}_1$ are now added to $\mathcal{P}$. The edges between clusters of $\hat{U}_0$ and $\hat{U}_1$ are oriented toward clusters of $\hat{U}_1$. More generally, the algorithm will now construct a sequence of sets $\hat{U}_0, \hat{U}_1, \dots$. The edges between clusters of $\hat{U}_i$ and $\hat{U}_j$ for $i < j$ are oriented toward clusters of $\hat{U}_j$. The edges between clusters of $\hat{U}_i$, for some $i = 0, 1, 2, \dots$, are oriented arbitrarily. Denote by μ the orientation of the supergraph $\mathcal{G}$ that we have just defined.

Observe that similarly to the clusters of $\hat{U}_0$, for each cluster $C \in \hat{U}_1$, its out-degree under the orientation μ is less than $n^{1/k}$. Indeed, its degree in $\hat{G}_1$ is less than $n^{1/k}$, and its out-degree under μ in $\mathcal{P}'$ will not be greater than that. (Because some clusters of $\hat{G}_1$ may get merged into a single cluster of $\mathcal{P}'$, but no clusters of $\hat{G}_1$ will be splitted.)

Next, the algorithm invokes Procedure Ruling-Forest to compute a $(3, 3 \cdot \lceil \log n \rceil)$-ruling forest $\mathcal{F}_1$ for $\hat{Z}_1$. Each tree $(T, r) \in \mathcal{F}_1$ (observe that r is a cluster of $\hat{V}_1$ and T is a tree in $\hat{G}_1$, i.e., each node of T is a cluster of $\hat{V}_1$) is now merged into a 2-level cluster C. Specifically, C is a union of all 1-level clusters that belong to the tree T. These 2-level clusters form the vertex set $\hat{V}_2$ of the supergraph $\hat{G}_2$, and the algorithm proceeds with clustering them according to the same rule. Specifically, for each $i = 0, 1, 2, \dots$, we are given a set $\hat{V}_i$ of i-level clusters, and a supergraph $\hat{G}_i$ induced by it. The clusters of $\hat{V}_i$ of degree less than $n^{1/k}$ in $\hat{G}_i$ are added to $\mathcal{P}$. (The set of these clusters is called $\hat{U}_i$.) The Procedure Ruling-Forest is invoked in the graph $\hat{G}_i$ with the set $\hat{Z}_i = \hat{V}_i \setminus \hat{U}_i$ to form a $(3, 3 \cdot \lceil \log n \rceil)$-ruling forest $\hat{\mathcal{F}}_i$. Each tree of $\hat{\mathcal{F}}_i$ becomes a cluster of level $i + 1$.

This continues for k phases. After k phases we have a partition $\mathcal{P} = \hat{U}_0 \cup \hat{U}_2 \cup \dots \cup \hat{U}_{k-2}$, and the set of $(k - 1)$-level clusters $\hat{V}_{k-1}$. We will promptly show that $|\hat{V}_{k-1}| \leq n^{1/k}$. The clusters of $\hat{V}_{k-1}$ are now added to the partition $\mathcal{P}$ to form the ultimate partition $\mathcal{P}'$ which the algorithm returns. We write $\hat{U}_{k-1} = \hat{V}_{k-1}$ and $\mathcal{P} = \mathcal{P}' = \bigcup_{i=0}^{k-1} \hat{U}_i$. This completes the description of the algorithm. As was argued above, under the orientation μ which was defined above, assuming $|\hat{V}_{k-1}| \leq n^{1/k}$, the out-degree of any cluster $C \in \mathcal{P}'$ in the supergraph $\mathcal{G}$ is at most $n^{1/k}$.

In the next lemma we argue that $|\hat{V}_{k-1}| \leq n^{1/k}$.

Lemma 9.7   *For $i = 0, 1, \dots, k - 1$, it holds that $|\hat{V}_i| \leq n^{1-i/k}$.*

Proof. We prove by induction on i that for every cluster $C \in \hat{V}_i$, it holds that $|C| \geq n^{i/k}$.

Base: $\hat{V}_0 = \{\{v\} \mid v \in V\}$, and so each $C = \{v\} \in \hat{V}_0$ has size $1 = n^{0/k}$.

Step: For a non-negative integer $i < k - 1$, suppose that for every cluster $C \in \hat{V}_i$, it holds that $C \geq n^{i/k}$. $\hat{Z}_i$ is the subset of i-level clusters with degree at least $n^{1/k}$ in $\hat{G}_i$, and $\mathcal{F}_i$ is a $(3, 3 \cdot \lceil \log n \rceil)$-ruling forest for $\hat{Z}_i$ in $\hat{G}_i$. Each $(i + 1)$-level cluster $C \in \hat{V}_{i+1}$ is formed by merging all clusters of a tree $(T, r) \in \mathcal{F}_i$. For two roots $r, r' \in \hat{Z}_i$ of two distinct trees $(T, r), (T', r') \in \mathcal{F}_i$, the distance between them in $\hat{G}_i$ is at least 3.

Also, since $r, r' \in \hat{Z}_i$, their degrees in $\hat{G}_i$ are at least $n^{1/k}$. Hence the tree (T, r) (respectively, (T', r')) contains at least $n^{1/k}$ distinct i-level clusters which are neighbors of r (resp., r') in $\hat{G}_i$. (If r and r' would have a common neighboring i-level cluster, the distance between them in $\hat{G}_i$ would be at most 2, contradiction.) Hence the size of an $(i + 1)$-level cluster C is at least $n^{1/k}$ multiplied by the minimum size of an i-level cluster, i.e., $|C| \geq n^{1/k} \cdot n^{i/k} = n^{(i+1)/k}$, proving the inductive assertion. The assertion obviously implies the lemma. $\square$

By substituting $i = k - 1$, we derive $|\hat{V}_{k-1}| \leq n^{1/k}$.

We proved that the partition $\mathcal{P} = \mathcal{P}'$ constructed by the algorithm has an orientation μ (also computed by the algorithm) with out-degree at most $n^{1/k}$. By Lemma 3.3, $\chi(\mathcal{G}) \leq n^{1/k} + 1$, where $\mathcal{G}$ is the supergraph induced by the partition $\mathcal{P}$. Observe that each cluster $C \in \mathcal{P}$ has a designated center x_C. Indeed, for a 0-level cluster $C = \{v\} \in \hat{V}_0$, the cluster C is centered at v. For i, $0 \leq i \leq k - 2$, an $(i + 1)$-level cluster C is formed by merging all vertices of the tree (T, r) of $\mathcal{F}_i$ into a single cluster C. The tree (T, r) is rooted at an i-level cluster r. The center of r becomes the center of C as well.

Denote $t = 6 \cdot \lceil \log n \rceil$. In the next lemma we provide an upper bound on the diameters of clusters in $\mathcal{P}$.

Lemma 9.8   *For every $i = 0, 1, ..., k - 1$, a cluster $C \in \hat{V}_i$ (i.e., an i-level cluster C) has strong diameter at most $(t + 1)^{i+1} - 1$.*

Proof. The proof is by induction on i.

Base ($i = 0$): 0-level clusters have diameter 0.

Step: For some i, $0 \leq i \leq k - 2$, suppose that each cluster $C \in \hat{V}_i$ has strong diameter at most $(t + 1)^{i+1} - 1$. Consider an $(i + 1)$-level cluster $\hat{C}$. The cluster $\hat{C}$ is obtained by merging all vertices from i-level clusters C that belong to a tree $(T, r) \in \mathcal{F}_i$. Recall that the radius of the tree (T, r) in $\hat{G}_i$ with respect to the i-level cluster r is at most $t/2 = 3 \cdot \lceil \log n \rceil$, and thus its diameter is at most t.

Let $v, v' \in \hat{C}$ be some two vertices in $\hat{C}$. Let C, C' be the i-level clusters such that $v \in C, v' \in C$. If $C = C'$ then by the induction hypothesis $\text{dist}_{G(\hat{C})}(v, v') \leq \text{dist}_{G(C)}(v, v') \leq (t + 1)^i - 1$, and we are done. Otherwise both clusters C, C' belong to the tree $(T, r) \in \mathcal{F}_i$. whose clusters were merged to obtain $\hat{C}$. The distance between C and C' in (T, r) is at most t. Let $(C = C_0, C_1, ..., C_\ell = C')$, $\ell \leq t + 1$, be the (unique) path connecting C and C' in

(T, r). The superedges $(C_0, C_1), (C_1, C_2), ..., (C_{\ell-1}, C_\ell)$ belong to (T, r), and thus they belong to $\hat{G}_i$. Hence there exist edges $e_{01} = (v'_0, v_1), e_{12} = (v'_1, v_2), ..., e_{\ell-1,\ell} = (v'_{\ell-1}, v_\ell) \in E$ so that $v'_0 \in C_0$, $v_i, v'_i \in C_i$ for $1 \le i \le \ell - 1$, and $v_\ell \in C_\ell$. See Figure 9.1 for an illustration.

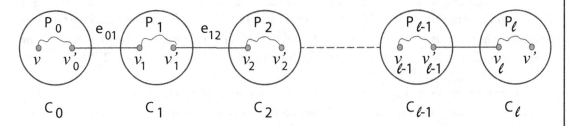

Figure 9.1: A path between two vertices v and v' in an $(i + 1)$-level cluster $\hat{C}$.

Denote also $v_0 = v$ and $v'_\ell = v'$. For i, $0 \le i \le \ell$, let P_i be the shortest path in $G(C_i)$ between V_i and v'_i. By the induction hypothesis, $|P_i| \le (t + 1)^i - 1$. Let $P = P_0 \circ e_{01} \circ P_1 \circ e_{12} \circ ... \circ e_{\ell-1,\ell} \circ P_\ell$ be the concatenation of paths $P_0, P_1, ..., P_\ell$, alternating with edges $e_{01}, e_{12}, ..., e_{\ell-1,\ell}$. Observe that P is a path in $\hat{C}$ connecting v and v'. It follows that

$$
\begin{aligned}
\mathrm{dist}_{G(\hat{C})}(v, v') &\le \sum_{i=0}^{\ell} |P_i| + \ell \le (\ell + 1) \cdot ((t + 1)^i - 1) + \ell \\
&\le (t + 1) \cdot ((t + 1)^i - 1) + t = (t + 1)^{i+1} - 1,
\end{aligned}
$$

proving the lemma. □

Since the level i of clusters in $\mathcal{P}$ is at most $k - 1$, we conclude the strong diameter of $\mathcal{P}$ is at most $(t + 1)^k - 1$.

Theorem 9.9 *[5] The network decomposition algorithm that was described in this section invoked on an n-vertex graph with an integer parameter $k = 1, 2, ...$ constructs a network decomposition with strong diameter $\alpha \le (6 \cdot \lceil \log n \rceil + 1)^k$ and $\beta \le n^{1/k} + 1$. The algorithm requires $O(\log^{k+2} n) \cdot 2^{O(k)}$ deterministic time.*

Proof. It only remains to analyze the running time of the algorithm. In level i, for $i = 0, 1, ..., k - 2$, the algorithm constructs a $(3, 3 \cdot \lceil \log n \rceil)$-ruling forest $\mathcal{F}_i$ in the supergraph $\hat{G}_i$. In a graph such computation requires $O(\log n)$ time. (See Lemma 9.4.) However, in the supergraph $\hat{G}_i$ each node is in fact a cluster of diameter $2^{O(i)} \log^{i+1} n$. Hence the overall running time of this computation is $2^{O(i)} \cdot \log^{i+2} n$. The dominant term in the running time is the term with $i = k$, proving the theorem. □

Given this network decomposition $\mathcal{P}$ it is not difficult also to compute an $O(n^{1/k})$-coloring of the supergraph $\mathcal{G}$ induced by it. Indeed we have a partition of $\mathcal{P} = \hat{U}_0 \cup \hat{U}_1 \cup \ldots \cup \hat{U}_{k-1}$. Within each set $\hat{U}_i$, $0 \leq i \leq k-1$, the maximum degree Δ_i in $\mathcal{G}(\hat{U}_i)$ is at most $n^{1/k}$. Thus an $(n^{1/k}+1)$-coloring φ for $\mathcal{G}(\hat{U}_i)$ can be computed by an algorithm of either [8] or [48]. (See Chapter 6.) The running time of these algorithms is $O(\Delta_i) + \frac{1}{2}\log^* n$. However, since $\mathcal{G}(\hat{U}_i)$ is a supergraph with clusters of diameter $2^{O(i)} \cdot \log^{i+2} n$, simulating a step of an algorithm of [8] or [48] requires $2^{O(i)} \cdot \log^{i+2} n$ time. Hence the total running time of this step is $2^{O(i)} \cdot \log^{i+2} n \cdot n^{1/k} \leq 2^{O(k)} \cdot \log^{k+2} n \cdot n^{1/k}$.

Given the colorings $\varphi_0, \varphi_1, \ldots, \varphi_{k-1}$, we can compute a single $O(n^{1/k})$-coloring ψ for $\mathcal{G}$ by the following recoloring process. (It is closely related to $O(a)$-coloring that requires $O(a \log n)$ time. See Section 5.2.) Clusters of $\hat{U}_{k-1}$ retain their colors. Clusters $C \in \hat{U}_{k-2}$ with $\varphi_{k-2}(C) = 1$ recolor themselves in parallel into an admissible color from the palette $[n^{1/k}+1]$. They can do so because they have at most $n^{1/k}$ neighbors in $\hat{U}_{k-1}$. Then clusters $C \in \hat{U}_{k-2}$ with $\varphi_{k-2}(C) = 2$ do so. (Observe that they have at most $n^{1/k}$ neighboring clusters in $\hat{U}_{k-2} \cup \hat{U}_{k-1}$.) This process continues up until the color classes of $\hat{U}_{k-2}$ are exhausted, and then we recolor color classes of $\hat{U}_{k-3}, \hat{U}_{k-4}, \ldots, \hat{U}_0$. Altogether there are $O(n^{1/k} \cdot k)$ recoloring steps. Since each step involves communication between neighboring clusters of diameter at most $2^{O(k)} \cdot \log^{k+2} n$, it follows that the overall running time of the recoloring phase is $O(k n^{1/k} \cdot 2^{O(k)} \cdot \log^{k+2} n)$.

We summarize this discussion below.

Theorem 9.10   [5] *The network decomposition algorithm invoked on n-vertex graphs with a parameter k, $k = 1, 2, \ldots$, constructs a network decomposition $\mathcal{P}$ with parameters $\alpha \leq 2^{O(k)} \cdot \log^{k+2} n$ and $\beta \leq n^{1/k} + 1$ in deterministic $O(\log^{k+2} n) \cdot 2^{O(k)}$. Moreover, in additional time $2^{O(k)} \cdot O(n^{1/k} \log^{k+2} n)$ it computes an $O(n^{1/k})$-coloring for the supergraph $\mathcal{G}$ induced by $\mathcal{P}$.*

As was argued in Section 9.1 (see Corollary 9.2), given this decomposition one can compute an MIS or a $(\Delta+1)$-coloring of the original graph within additional $\alpha \cdot \beta \leq 2^{O(k)} \cdot \log^{k+2} n \cdot (n^{1/k}+1)$ time. Hence the overall running time for computing an MIS or a $(\Delta+1)$-coloring by this algorithm is $2^{O(k)} \cdot O(\log^{k+2} n \cdot n^{1/k})$. Set $k = \sqrt{\log n / \log \log n}$ to optimize this expression. The resulting running time is $2^{O(\sqrt{\log n \log \log n})}$.

Corollary 9.11   [5] *Using the network decomposition algorithm one can compute an MIS or a $(\Delta+1)$-coloring of an n-vertex graph within $2^{O(\sqrt{\log n \log \log n})}$ deterministic time.*

As was mentioned above, this result was improved by Panconesi and Srinivasan [69]. The running time of their network decomposition (and MIS) algorithm is $2^{O(\sqrt{\log n})}$.

A more extensive treatment of network decompositions of various types can be found in [67].

CHAPTER 10

Introduction to Distributed Randomized Algorithms

In the previous sections we dealt with deterministic algorithms. In the current section we turn to describing randomized ones. The best currently known randomized algorithms for distributed symmetry breaking problems are much more efficient than the best-known deterministic ones (unless the maximum degree of the input graph is very small). However, randomized algorithms have the drawback that with some (very small) probability over the coin tosses of the algorithms they may fail or not terminate within the expected time.

10.1 SIMPLE ALGORITHMS

Many randomized algorithms adhere to the following approach.[1] The algorithm proceeds in phases. In each phase each vertex randomly selects a value from some appropriate set. Based on the selected value and the values of the neighbors, each vertex either makes a final decision (e.g., of a color), or continues to the next phase. All vertices that make their final decision form a subset of a correct solution. Then these vertices are removed from the graph, and the algorithm continues in the same way on the residual subgraph. An important requirement in this approach is that partial solutions should be correct not only inside each subset, but also in the union of all subsets that were removed from the graph, after each phase. Once the algorithm terminates, the union of all subsets forms the input graph with the required solution.

We begin with describing a 2Δ-vertex-coloring algorithm that works according to the approach described above. The algorithm is called *Procedure Rand-2Delta*. It accepts as input a graph G. In each round each vertex v draws uniformly at random (henceforth, *u.a.r.*) a color c_v from the set $[2\Delta] = \{1, 2, ..., 2\Delta\}$. If a vertex selects a color that is different from the selections of all its neighbors, and from the final decisions of all its neighbors, then c_v becomes the final decision of v. In this case v terminates. Otherwise it discards the color c_v, and proceeds to the next round. This completes the description of the procedure. Its pseudocode is provided below. Its properties are analyzed in the following lemmas.

For a vertex $v \in V$, denote by $\varphi(v)$ the final color of v (if v terminates). Otherwise $\varphi(v)$ is undefined.

---

[1]This approach dates back to Luby's randomized $O(\log n)$-time algorithm for the MIS problem [60]. The algorithms we describe in this section can be viewed as simplified variants of the algorithms from [60, 61].

Algorithm 18 Procedure Rand-2Delta(G)

An algorithm for each vertex $v \in V$.

Initially $T_v = \emptyset$, $F_v = \emptyset$, for each $v \in V$.

/* T_v is the set of temporary colors selected by neighbors of v. */

/* F_v is the set of final colors selected by neighbors of v. */

  1: **for** each round **do**

  2:     $T_v = \emptyset$

  3:     $c_v :=$ draw a color from $[2\Delta]$ u.a.r., independently of other vertices

  4:     send the color c_v to all neighbors

  5:     **for** each received color c_u from a neighbor u **do**

  6:        $T_v := T_v \cup \{c_u\}$

  7:     **end for**

  8:     **if** $c_v \notin T_v \cup F_v$ **then**

  9:        send the message "final c_v" to all neighbors

10:        select c_v as the final color φ_v of v and terminate

11:     **else**

12:        **for** each received message "final c_u" from a neighbor u **do**

13:           $F_v := F_v \cup \{c_u\}$

14:        **end for**

15:        discard c_v and continue to the next round

16:     **end if**

17: **end for**

Lemma 10.1   *If all vertices terminate, Procedure Rand-2Delta computes a legal 2Δ-vertex-coloring of the input graph.*

Proof. If all vertices terminate, then each vertex selects a color from the set $[2\Delta]$. Consider a pair of neighbors $u, v \in V$. Let i, j be the rounds in which u and v terminate, respectively. Suppose for contradiction that $\varphi(u) = \varphi(v)$. Then, obviously, $i \neq j$. (Otherwise, in round i it holds that $c_u = c_v$, and thus both vertices continue to round $i + 1$. This is a contradiction.) Suppose without loss of generaility that $i < j$. Then after round i it holds that $\varphi(u) \in F_v$. Therefore, $\varphi(v) \neq \varphi(u)$ since $\varphi(v) \notin T_v \cup F_v$. Again, a contradiction. □

Lemma 10.2   *During the execution of Procedure Rand-2Delta all vertices terminate within $O(\log n)$ rounds with probability $1 - 1/n^c$, for an arbitrarily large constant c.*

Proof. Consider a vertex $v \in V$. We analyze the probability that v terminates in round i, conditioned on that it has not terminated before round i, for any $i > 0$. Notice that the size of the set

$T_v \cup F_v$ is at most Δ, since each neighbor of v contributes at most one color to this set. Consequently, there are at least Δ available colors for v in $[2\Delta] \setminus (T_v \cup F_v)$. Thus, the probability that c_v is such a color is at least $\Delta/2\Delta = 1/2$. Hence, assuming that v did not terminate before round i, it terminates in round i with probability at least $1/2$, independently of all other vertices.

The probability that some given vertex v does not terminate within i rounds is at most $(1/2)^i$. By the union bound, the probability that *there exists* a vertex $v \in V$ that does not terminate within i rounds is at most $n \cdot (1/2)^i$. Hence, after $(c + 1) \cdot \log n$ rounds, with probability at least $1 - n \cdot (1/2)^i \geq 1 - 1/n^c$, *all* vertices terminate. $\qquad\square$

A slight modification of Procedure Rand-2Delta allows computing a $(\Delta + 1)$-coloring within $O(\log n)$ time. To this end, each vertex in each round selects a color from the set $\{0, 1, 2, ..., \Delta + 1\}$. The color 0 is a special color whose selection probability is $1/2$. For any other available color $c \in \{1, 2, ..., \Delta + 1\} \setminus F_v$, the color c is selected with probability $\frac{1}{2(\Delta+1-|F_v|)}$. Note that the colors in F_v are permanently selected by neighbors of v, and, therefore, are not considered for selection by v. (Thus their selection probability is 0). The other steps of the procedure remain the same, except that the color 0 is never set as a final color. A vertex that selects 0 will continue to the next round. The pseudocode of the modified procedure, *Procedure Rand-Delta-Plus1* is provided below.

It can be easily verified that if all vertices terminate then the graph is colored with $(\Delta + 1)$ colors. The next lemma shows that all vertices terminate within $O(\log n)$ rounds with high probability.

Lemma 10.3 *During the execution of Procedure Rand-Delta-Plus1 all vertices terminate within $O(\log n)$ rounds with probability $1 - 1/n^c$, for an arbitrarily large constant c.*

Proof. Consider a vertex $v \in V$. We analyze the probability the v terminates in round i, conditioned on that it has not terminated before round i, for any $i > 0$. This is the probability that v selects a color $c_v > 0$, and that it is different from the selections of all neighbors. Suppose that indeed $c_v > 0$. Then c_v is distinct from all colors in F_v. The probability that a given neighbor u of v selects the same color $c_u = c_v$ in this round is at most $\frac{1}{2(\Delta+1-|F_v|)}$. (Because the probability that u selects a color greater than 0 is $1/2$, and v has $\Delta + 1 - |F_v|$ different colors to select from.) By the union bound, the probability that v selects a color that is equal to a color of some neighbor of v is at most $(\Delta + 1 - |F_v|) \cdot \frac{1}{2(\Delta+1-|F_V|)} = 1/2$. Thus, if v selects a color $c_v > 0$, it is distinct from the colors of its neighbors with probability at least $1/2$. It holds that $c_v > 0$ with probability $1/2$. Thus v terminates with probability at least $1/4$.

The probability that some given vertex v does not terminate within i rounds is at most $(3/4)^i$. By the union bound, the probability that *there exists* a vertex $v \in V$ that does not terminate within i rounds is at most $n \cdot (3/4)^i$. Hence, after $(c + 1) \cdot 4 \log n$ rounds, with probability at least $1 - n \cdot (3/4)^i \geq 1 - 1/n^c$, *all* vertices terminate. $\qquad\square$

Algorithm 19 Procedure Rand-Delta-Plus1(G)

An algorithm for each vertex $v \in V$.

Initially $T_v = \emptyset$, $F_v = \emptyset$, for each $v \in V$.

1: **for** each round **do**
2: $\quad T_v := \emptyset$
3: $\quad c_v :=$ draw u.a.r. a bit from $\{0, 1\}$
4: $\quad$ **if** $c_v = 0$ **then**
5: $\quad\quad$ discard c_v and continue to the next round
6: $\quad$ **else**
7: $\quad\quad c_v :=$ draw u.a.r. a color from $[\Delta + 1] \setminus F_v$, independently of other vertices
8: $\quad\quad$ send the color c_v to all neighbors
9: $\quad\quad$ **for** each received color c_u from a neighbor u **do**
10: $\quad\quad\quad T_v := T_v \cup \{c_u\}$
11: $\quad\quad$ **end for**
12: $\quad\quad$ **if** $c_v \notin T_v \cup F_v$ **then**
13: $\quad\quad\quad$ send the message "final c_v" to all neighbors
14: $\quad\quad\quad$ select c_v as the final color φ_v of v and terminate
15: $\quad\quad$ **else**
16: $\quad\quad\quad$ **for** each received meassage "final c_u" from a neighbor u **do**
17: $\quad\quad\quad\quad F_v := F_v \cup \{c_u\}$
18: $\quad\quad\quad$ **end for**
19: $\quad\quad\quad$ discard c_v and continue to the next round
20: $\quad\quad$ **end if**
21: $\quad$ **end if**
22: **end for**

We summarize this discussion with the following theorem.

Theorem 10.4 *A $(\Delta + 1)$-coloring of a graph G can be computed within $O(\log n)$ time with high probability.*

We conclude this section by presenting an extremely simple algorithm that computes an $O(\log n)$-defective $O(\Delta / \log n)$-coloring within $O(1)$ time. Actually, the algorithm does not require any communication whatsoever. It is called *Procedure Rand-DC*. It consists of one single line. Its pseudocode is provided below.

We analyze the performance of Procedure Rand-DC in the next theorem.

Theorem 10.5 *Procedure Rand-DC computes an $O(\log n)$-defective $O(\Delta / \log n)$-coloring of the input graph G within $O(1)$ time, with probability $1 - 1/n^c$, for an arbitrarily large constant c.*

Algorithm 20 Procedure Rand-DC(G)

An algorithm for each vertex $v \in V$.

1: select a color from the set $\{1, 2, ..., \lceil \deg(v)/(\rho \cdot \log n) \rceil\}$ uniformly at random
/* ρ is a sufficiently large fixed constant. */

Proof. The running time analysis is trivial. Next we prove the correctness of the algorithm. Consider a vertex $v \in V$. If $\deg(v) \leq \rho \cdot \log n$, then v has at most $O(\log n)$ neighbors that have selected the same color as v did, and we are done. Otherwise, for each neighbor u of v, let X_u denote the random indicator variable, such that $X_u = 1$ if u selects the same color as v, and $X_u = 0$ otherwise. Let $X = \sum_{u \in \Gamma(v)} X_u$ be the sum of at most Δ indicator variables. The expected number of neighbors of v that select the same color as v is $\mathbb{E}(X) = \frac{\deg(v)}{\lceil \deg(v)/(\rho \cdot \log n) \rceil} \leq \rho \log n$. Observe also that $\mathbb{E}(X) > \frac{1}{2}\rho \log n$, since $\deg(v) > \rho \cdot \log n$. By Chernoff bound for upper tails (see, e.g., [2], Chapter A.1), for any $\gamma > 0$, it holds that

$$Pr[X > (1 + \gamma)\mathbb{E}(X)] < \left(\frac{e^\gamma}{(1+\gamma)^{1+\gamma}} \right)^{\mathbb{E}(X)} .$$

We set $\gamma \geq 1$. It holds that $Pr[X > 2\mathbb{E}(X)] < (e/4)^{\mathbb{E}(X)} < 1/n^{c+1}$, for a sufficiently large constant ρ. By the union bound the probability that all vertices have at most $2\rho \log n$ neighbors with the same color is $1 - n/n^{c+1} = 1 - 1/n^c$. $\qquad \square$

10.2 A FASTER $O(\Delta)$-COLORING ALGORITHM

In this section we describe a more sophisticated algorithm that achieves a running time of $O(\sqrt{\log n})$ for $O(\Delta)$-vertex-coloring. This result is due to Kothapalli et al. [47], but the algorithm and the analysis that we present here are different from those of [47]. (Interestingly, the algorithm in [47] can be extended within roughly the same running time while communicating only *single-bit* messages between neighboring vertices. This is not the case for the algorithm we present in this section.) The algorithm proceeds in two stages. The first stage is similar to the algorithms described in the previous section, but it is performed for $O(\sqrt{\log n})$ rounds instead of $O(\log n)$. It is probable that as a result some vertices do not terminate by the end of this stage. Nevertheless, the subgraph of remaining vertices has, with high probability, some helpful properties. These properties are used to complete the solution in the second stage. Specifically, given an acyclic orientation of the input graph, in the beginning of the second stage the length of the orientation restricted to the remaining graph is $O(\sqrt{\log n})$ with high probability. This allows one to use Property 3.3 (see Section 3.3) for computing a $(\Delta + 1)$-coloring of the remaining subgraph. If a fresh palette of size $(\Delta + 1)$ is used in the second stage, a legal $O(\Delta)$-coloring for the entire input graph is obtained.

The procedure for computing an $O(\Delta)$-coloring is called *Fast-Rand-Color*. It accepts as input the graph G. In the first stage it computes an acyclic orientation by directing all edges toward endpoints with greater Ids. Then it invokes Procedure Rand-2Delta for $\lceil \rho \sqrt{\log n} \rceil$ rounds, for a sufficiently large constant ρ. In the second stage a $(\Delta + 1)$-coloring is computed using Property 3.3 on the subgraph of remaining vertices (that have not terminated in the previous stage). This completes the description of the algorithm. Its pseudocode is provided below.

Algorithm 21 Procedure Fast-Rand-Color(G)

An algorithm for each vertex $v \in V$.

1: **for** each neighbor u of v **do**
2:     orient the edge (u, v) toward the endpoint with greater Id
3: **end for**
4: **for** round $R = 1, 2, ..., \lceil \rho \sqrt{\log n} \rceil$ **do**
5:     execute an iteration of Rand-2Delta(G)
6: **end for**
7: **if** v has not terminated **then**
8:     compute a coloring using the palette $\{2\Delta + 1, 2\Delta + 2, ..., 3\Delta + 1\}$ by using Property 3.3
9: **end if**

By the correctness of Procedure Rand-2Delta, it follows that Procedure Fast-Rand-Color computes a legal $O(\Delta)$-coloring on the subgraph of vertices that terminate in the first stage (lines 1-6). By Property 3.3, the coloring computed in the second stage (lines 7-9) on the remaining vertices is a legal $(\Delta + 1)$-colorings. Since the palettes used in the two stage are disjoint, the final coloring is a legal $(3\Delta + 1)$-coloring. For the running time analysis, it is sufficient to show that in the beginning of the second stage all consistently-oriented paths have length at most $\sqrt{\log n}$, with high probability. (In this case a $(\Delta + 1)$-coloring can be computed within at most $\sqrt{\log n}$ rounds, by Property 3.3.) We will prove this for graphs with $\Delta < 2^{o(\sqrt{\log n})}$. For graphs with larger degree, a slightly different algorithm (which will be described in the sequel) provides the desired results.

Lemma 10.6   *Suppose that Procedure Fast-Rand-Color is invoked on a graph G with $\Delta < 2^{o(\sqrt{\log n})}$. In the beginning of the second stage (lines 7-9 of Procedure Fast-Rand-Color) all consistently-oriented paths have length at most $\sqrt{\log n}$ with probability $1 - 1/n^c$, for an arbitrarily large constant c.*

Proof. Consider some consistently-oriented path $P = \langle v_1, v_2, ..., v_k \rangle$ in G of length $k = \lceil \sqrt{\log n} \rceil$ (with respect to the orientation computed in lines 1-3). We show that with high probability at least one vertex of P terminates during the first stage. Each vertex of P terminates with probability at least $1/2$ in each round, and remains active with probability at most $1/2$. In any given round $R \in \{1, 2, ..., \lceil \rho \sqrt{\log n} \rceil\}$, for $i = 1, 2, ..., k$, the probability that v_i remains active conditioned on that $v_1, v_2, ..., v_{i-1}$ remain active in round R is at least $1/2$ as well. (One can assume without loss of generality that v_i draws a color after $v_1, v_2, ..., v_{i-1}$ do so.) Thus the probability that all vertices of P remain active during a single round is at most $1/2^k$. For $R \in \{1, 2, ..., \lceil \rho \sqrt{\log n} \rceil\}$, the probability that all vertices of P remain active in round R conditioned on that they all remain active in rounds $1, 2, ..., R - 1$, is $1/2^k$. Thus, the probability of all of them to remain for $\lceil \rho \sqrt{\log n} \rceil$ rounds is at most $1/2^{k \cdot \lceil \rho \sqrt{\log n} \rceil} \leq 1/2^{\rho \cdot \log n} = 1/n^{c+2}$, for a constant $\rho = c + 2$.

The number of different paths of length k is at most $n \cdot \Delta^k \leq n^2$. (Recall that $\Delta < 2^{o(\sqrt{\log n})}$.) Thus, by the union bound, the probability that there exists a consistently-oriented path of length k in which all vertices remain for $\lceil \rho \sqrt{\log n} \rceil$ rounds is at most $n^2 \cdot (1/n^{c+2}) = 1/n^c$. $\square$

To complete the analysis we need to consider the case that $\Delta \geq 2^{\Omega(\sqrt{\log n})}$. In this case before executing Procedure Fast-Rand-Color, we invoke Procedure Rand-DC (see Algorithm 20) that partitions the input graph into $O(\Delta / \log n)$ vertex-disjoint subgraphs with maximum degree $O(\log n)$. By Lemma 10.6, executing Procedure Fast-Rand-Color in all these subgraphs in parallel results in an $O(\log n)$-coloring in each of them with probability $1 - 1/n^c$. By using disjoint palettes, one obtains an $O(\Delta)$-coloring of the input graph. The success probability is at least $(1 - 1/n^c)^n > 1 - 1/n^{c-2}$. We summarize this section with the following theorem.

Theorem 10.7   *An $O(\Delta)$-coloring of an input graph G can be computed in $O(\sqrt{\log n})$ time, with probability $1 - 1/n^c$, for an arbitrarily large constant c.*

This result was recently improved in [11]. Specifically, Barenboim et al. [11] devised a randomized $(\Delta + 1)$-coloring algorithm with running time $O(\log \Delta) + 2^{O(\sqrt{\log \log n})}$. Prior to this result Schneider and Wattenhofer [78] showed that $O(\Delta + \log n)$-coloring can be constructed within $O(\log^* n)$ randomized time. Combining these two results [11] devised a randomized $O(\Delta)$-coloring algorithm with running time $2^{O(\sqrt{\log \log n})}$.

10.3   RANDOMIZED MIS

10.3.1   A HIGH-LEVEL DESCRIPTION

In this section we describe a randomized algorithm that computes an MIS in $O(\log \Delta \sqrt{\log n})$ time. This result is due to [11]. Since for $\Delta = 2^{\Omega(\sqrt{\log n})}$ the algorithm of Luby [60] computes an MIS in time $O(\log n) \leq O(\log \Delta \sqrt{\log n})$, we henceforth assume that $\Delta \leq 2^{\sqrt{\log n}}$. Before we describe the algorithm we introduce a definition that will be useful in this section.

Definition 10.8   *Given a graph $G = (V, E)$ and a vertex set $C \subseteq V$, the* weak radius *of C with respect to a vertex $v \in C$, denoted wrad(C, v), is the maximum distance in G of a vertex $u \in C$ from v. The* weak radius *of C, denoted by wrad(C), is given by*

$$wrad(c) = \min_{v \in C}\{wrad(C, v)\}.$$

The algorithm consists of two main stages. In the first stage it computes an independent set I of the input graph G, which is, however, not necessarily maximal. Nevertheless, with high probability, it satisfies some very helpful properties. Next, the vertices of I and their neighbors are removed from G. Let G' be the subgraph induced by the set of remaining vertices. In the second stage an MIS I' of G' is computed. (Observe that $I \cup I'$ is an MIS of G.) This computation relies upon properties that hold with high probability after the first stage. Specifically, with high probability, all connected components of G' have weak radius $O(\sqrt{\log n})$. Consequently, an MIS of G' can be computed in $O(\sqrt{\log n})$ time.

We start with presenting a high-level description of the algorithm. Initially all vertices are active. During an execution vertices become inactive. In the beginning an empty set U is initialized. During the execution certain active vertices join U. The vertices join in such a way that the set U remains independent throughout the entire execution, and it is an MIS once the execution terminates. A vertex becomes inactive if it joins U, or if at least one of its neighbors joins U. The algorithm terminates once all vertices become inactive.

Suppose first that we are given a procedure *Decide()* that is executed by each vertex and requires one round. Procedure Decide satisfies the following four properties: (1) After a single execution of Procedure Decide by all vertices, each vertex becomes inactive with probability at least ρ, for a constant $0 < \rho < 1$. (2) For a vertex v, denote by $\mathcal{E}(v)$ the event that v becomes inactive as a result of invoking Procedure Decide by all vertices in the same round. For any subset of vertices $X \subseteq V$, such that for any pair x, x' of distinct vertices from X, it holds that $dist_G(x, x') \geq 5$, the events $\{\mathcal{E}(x) \mid x \in X\}$ are mutually independent. (3) If a pair of active neighbors execute Procedure Decide, at most one of them joins U (even if these executions are performed in distinct rounds). (4) If in a certain round a vertex v decides to join U, then in that round all its neighbors decide not to join. (Consequently, v and all its neighbors become inactive.)

Denote $\lambda = \lfloor \log n \rfloor$. In the first stage the algorithm executes Procedure Decide() for $d \cdot \lambda = O(\sqrt{\log n})$ rounds, for a positive constant d to be determined later. In each of these rounds it is executed on the set of remaining active vertices. Let V' denote the set of remaining active vertices once the first stage completes. In the second stage, it computes an MIS of the set V' as follows. Denote the graph induced by V' by $G' = G(V')$. Each active vertex v collects the topology of the connected component in G' that contains v, and computes an MIS of this connected component locally. By the "topology" of a vertex set $Z \in V$ we mean the identities of all vertices of Z, the edge set $E(Z)$, and all local variables of vertices in Z. This completes the high-level description of the algorithm. Its pseudocode is provided below.

Algorithm 22 A high-level description of the randomized MIS algorithm

An algorithm for each vertex $v \in V$. Initially, all vertices are active.

1: **for** $i = 1, 2, ..., d \cdot \left\lfloor \sqrt{\log n} \right\rfloor$ **do**
2:      **if** v is active **then**
3:          Decide()
4:      **end if**
5: **end for**
6: **if** v is active **then**
7:      Denote by G' the subgraph induced by all active vertices
8:      $G'_v :=$ collect the topology of the connected component in G' that contains v
9:      Compute an MIS of G'_v locally
10: **end if**

We assume that all vertices of a connected component G'_v run locally the same centralized deterministic procedure *Central-MIS* for computing an MIS. Since any two vertices u, w in G'_v collect the same topology on line 8 of Algorithm 22, their inputs to Procedure Central-MIS are identical. Thus executions of Procedure Central-MIS on different vertices of G'_v produce the same output. Hence the MIS is computed in a consistent way by different vertices of the same connected component. Finally, each vertex $v \in G'_v$ selects the output for v based on the output for v of Procedure Central-MIS invoked on G'_v.

The correctness of the algorithm follows from the fact that in the first stage (lines 1-5) all inactive vertices are either belong to U, or have a neighbor in U. In addition, by property (3) of Procedure Decide, no two neighbors can join U. In the second stage (lines 6-10) an MIS is computed on connected components of the graph G' induced by the remaining active vertices. Hence each vertex in G' either joins U, or has a neighbor in its connected component that joins U. Moreover, any pair of vertices that belong to distinct connected components and join U, are not connected by an edge. Therefore, all vertices of G either belong to U or have neighbors that belong to U, and no two neighbors in G join U. (A pair of vertices that join U in distinct stages are not connected, because all neighbors of a vertex that joins in the first stage do not join. This is guaranteed by property (4) of Procedure Decide.) Therefore, U is an MIS. We summarize this discussion in the following theorem.

Theorem 10.9 *Algorithm 22 computes a Maximal Independent Set of G.*

Next, we analyze the running time of the algorithm. We will show that all connected components of G' have weak diameter at most $\sqrt{\log n}$ with high probability. In other words, for any pair of vertices u, v, such that $dist_G(u, v) > \sqrt{\log n}$, there is no path in G' connecting u and v. Consequently, each vertex can collect the entire information of its connected component in

$O(\sqrt{\log n})$ time. The next lemma analyzes the probability that all vertices on a certain path remain active after a certain number of rounds. (Recall that $\mathcal{E}(v)$ is the event that a vertex v becomes inactive as a result of executing Procedure Decide, and ρ is a lower bound on the probability that $\mathcal{E}(v)$ occurs, for any $v \in V$.)

Lemma 10.10   *Let P be a path in G that contains k vertices $u_1, u_2, ..., u_k$, such that $\mathcal{E}(u_1), \mathcal{E}(u_2), ..., \mathcal{E}(u_k)$ are independent. Suppose also that all vertices execute Procedure Decide for ℓ rounds. Then the probability that all the vertices of P remain active is at most $(1 - \rho)^{k \cdot \ell}$.*

Proof. Since the events are independent, the probability that $u_1, u_2, ..., u_k$ remain active in a single round is at most $(1 - \rho)^k$. We now prove the assertion of the lemma by induction on ℓ. The induction base, $\ell = 1$, was already shown. For the induction step observe that the probability that $u_1, u_2, ..., u_k$ survive (i.e., remain active) for ℓ rounds conditioned on them surviving for $\ell - 1$ rounds is $\Pi_{i=1}^{k} \mathbb{P}(\mathcal{E}(u_i)) \leq (1 - \rho)^k$. This completes the proof. $\square$

Suppose that a path contains $k \geq 1/5 \cdot \sqrt{\log n}$ vertices $u_1, u_2, ..., u_k$, such that the events $\mathcal{E}(u_1), \mathcal{E}(u_2), ..., \mathcal{E}(u_k)$ are independent. Then the probability that all vertices $u_1, u_2, ..., u_k$ remain active for $d \cdot \sqrt{\log n}$ rounds is at most

$$(1 - \rho)^{1/5 \cdot \sqrt{\log n} \cdot d \cdot \sqrt{\log n}} = ((1 - \rho)^{\log n})^{d/5} \leq 1/n^{c'},$$

for $c' = c'(d)$. The exponent c' can be made as large as one wishes, by increasing the value of d. (Recall that $(1 - \rho) \leq 1$ is a positive constant.) Note also that since $\Delta \leq 2^{\sqrt{\log n}}$, the number of different paths in G of length $\mu = \lfloor \sqrt{\log n} \rfloor$ is at most $n \cdot \Delta^{\sqrt{\log n}} = O(n^2)$.

Let $\mathcal{P}$ be the set containing all the paths P in G of length μ that satisfy the following property: the path P contains $k \geq 1/5 \cdot \sqrt{\log n}$ vertices $u_1, u_2, ..., u_k$, such that the events $\mathcal{E}(u_1), \mathcal{E}(u_2), ..., \mathcal{E}(u_k)$ are independent. By the union bound, the probability that after the first stage there remains a path in $\mathcal{P}$ in which all vertices are active is $O(n^2/n^{c'}) \leq 1/n^{c''}$, for an arbitrarily large constant $c'' > 0$. However, this fact by itself is insufficient to show that all connected components of G' (the graph induced by the active vertices remaining after the first stage) have weak diameter $O(\sqrt{\log n})$. We next prove a stronger claim that says that for each pair of vertices u, v such that $dist_G(u, v) \geq \sqrt{\log n}$, there is no path in G' connecting u and v.

Definition 10.11   *A sequence $Q = (q_0, q_1, ..., q_k)$ of vertices is called a well-spread sequence if there exists a path $R = (r_0, r_1, ..., r_{5k})$ in $G = (V, E)$ such that the following two conditions hold:*
   (1) For every index $j \in [0, k]$, it holds that $r_{5j} = q_j$.
   (2) For every pair of distinct indices $i, j \in [0, k]$, it holds that $dist_G(q_i, q_j) \geq 5$.

Lemma 10.12   *Let P be a simple path between a pair of vertices $u, v \in V$ with $dist_G(u, v) \geq 5k$, for some integer $k \geq 0$. Then P contains a well-spread sequence $Q \subseteq V(P)$ of length $|Q| = k + 1$.*

Proof. Denote $P = (u = w_0, w_1, ..., v = w_t)$, $t \geq 5k$. The proof is by induction on k.

Base ($k = 0$): Set $Q = (q_0 = w_0)$, $R = (r_0 = q_0 = w_0)$. This completes the proof of the induction base.

Step ($k \geq 1$): Let i be the largest index such that $dist_G(w_0, w_i) = 5$. It follows that $dist_G(w_i, w_t) \geq dist_G(w_0, w_t) - dist_G(w_0, w_i) \geq 5(k-1)$. Let $\sigma = (r_0 = w_0, r_1, r_2, r_3, r_4, r_5 = w_i)$ be an arbitrary shortest path between w_0 and w_i in G. Let $P' = (w_i, w_{i+1}, ..., w_t)$. Denote also $q_0 = w_0$. By the choice of i, for every index $j \in [i, t]$, $dist_G(q_0, w_j) \geq 5$. By the induction hypothesis, there exists a well-spread sequence $Q' = (q'_0, q'_1, ..., q'_{k-1})$, $Q' \subseteq V(P')$. Hence there exists a path $R' = (r'_0, r'_1, ..., r'_{5(k-1)})$ with $r'_{5j} = q'_j$, for every $j \in [0, k-1]$. We form the well-spread sequence $Q = (q_0) \circ Q'$, by concatenating the sequence (q_0) with the sequence Q'. The respective path R is formed by $R = \sigma \circ R'$. Observe that $q_{j+1} = q'_j$, for every index $j \in [0, k-1]$, and $r_{5+i} = r'_i$, for every $i \in [0, 5(k-1)]$. See Figure 10.1 for an illustration.

By induction hypothesis, for every pair of distinct indices $i, j \in [1, k]$, $dist_G(q_i, q_j) = dist_G(q'_{i-1}, q'_{j-1}) \geq 5$. Also, since for every index $j \in [1, k]$, $q_j = q'_{j-1} \in V(P')$, it follows that $dist_G(q_0, q_j) \geq 5$ as well. $\square$

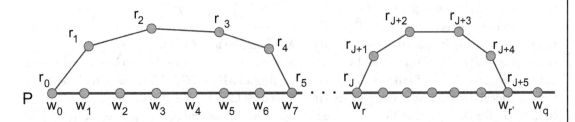

Figure 10.1: Obtaining the path $\langle r_0, r_1, ..., r_{5k} \rangle$. The vertex r_{j+5} equals to $w_{r'}$, for the maximum r' such that $dist_G(r_j, w_{r'}) = 5$. The path P is depicted by a thick line.

Recall that for a well-spread sequence $Q = (q_0, q_1, ..., q_k)$, the events $\{\mathcal{E}(q_j) \mid j \in [0, k]\}$ are mutually independent. (See the properties of Procedure Decide in the beginning of this section.)

Corollary 10.13 *A path P that satisfies the conditions from the assertion of Lemma 10.12 contains a sequence $Q \subseteq V(P)$, $Q = (q_0, q_1, ..., q_k)$ such that the events $\{\mathcal{E}(q_j) \mid j \in [0, k]\}$ are mutually independent.*

Let $\mathcal{R}$ denote the set of all paths of length $\mu = \lfloor \sqrt{\log n} \rfloor$ in $G = (V, E)$. Let $\mathcal{Q}'$ denote the set of well-spread sequences of length $\lfloor \mu/5 \rfloor$. Observe that $|\mathcal{R}| \leq n \cdot \Delta^\mu \leq n^2$, and so

$$|\mathcal{Q}'| \leq n \cdot \Delta^\mu \leq n^2 \tag{10.1}$$

as well. The probability that after the first stage there remains a path P that connects two vertices at distance at least μ whose all vertices are active is at most the probability that there remains a well-spread sequence $Q \in \mathcal{Q}'$ of length $\lfloor \mu/5 \rfloor$ with all vertices active. The latter probability is at most $1/n^{c''}$, for an arbitrary large constant $c'' > 0$. (Because the probability of all these vertices to remain active is at most $(1 - \rho)^{1/5 \cdot \sqrt{\log n} \cdot d \cdot \sqrt{\log n}} = ((1 - \rho)^{\log n})^{d/5}$, for a large constant d.) Hence, after the first stage, with high probability, there is no path P in G consisting of active vertices, that connects a pair of vertices u, v such that $dist_G(u, v) \geq \sqrt{\log n}$. Thus, the graph G' induced vertices that remain active after the first stage has weak diameter smaller than $\sqrt{\log n}$, with high probability. We summarize this discussion in the following lemma.

Lemma 10.14   *After the first stage of Algorithm 22 (lines 1–5) the weak diameter of the subgraph G' induced by the remaining active vertices is smaller than $\sqrt{\log n}$, with high probability.*

For a graph G' with weak diameter $K < \sqrt{\log n}$, an MIS is computed within K rounds in the following way. For $i = 1, 2, ..., K$, suppose that before the beginning of round i, each vertex v knows its entire $(i-1)$-hop neighborhood $\hat{\Gamma}_{i-1}(v, G)$ *with respect to G*. On round i, each vertex v sends the representation of $G(\hat{\Gamma}_{i-1}(v, G))$ to all its neighbors *in G*. Once v receives a message from all its neighbors it computes the representation of $G(\hat{\Gamma}_i(v, G))$. In round $\hat{k}$ each vertex v computes the representation of $G(\hat{\Gamma}_K(v, G))$. Denote by G'_v the connected component of v in G'. For any $u \in G'_v$ it holds that $dist_G(v, u) \leq K$. Therefore $u \in \hat{\Gamma}_K(v)$. Hence G'_v is a subgraph of the graph $G(\hat{\Gamma}_K(v, G))$ induced by $\hat{\Gamma}_K(v, G)$. Next, v computes G'_v from $\hat{\Gamma}_K(v)$, and runs a deterministic local centralized algorithm for computing an MIS on G'_v. All vertices in G'_v perform the same local deterministic computation (run Procedure Central-MIS), resulting in an identical MIS of G'_v for all vertices in this connected component. In particular, for each vertex in G'_v this computation determines whether it should join the MIS.

To summarize, the second stage of Algorithm 22 (lines 6–10) requires, with high probability, $O(\sqrt{\log n})$ time as well. We summarize the properties of Algorithm 22 in the following theorem.

Theorem 10.15   *Given Procedure Decide that satisfies the four properties mentioned above and has running time τ, Algorithm 22 computes an MIS in $O(\sqrt{\log n} \cdot \tau)$ time, for an input graph G with maximum degree $\Delta \leq 2^{\sqrt{\log n}}$.*

As was mentioned above, for $\Delta > 2^{\sqrt{\log n}}$ the running time of $O(\log \Delta \cdot \sqrt{\log n})$ follows trivially from Luby's logarithmic bound of $O(\log n)$.

10.3.2   PROCEDURE DECIDE

In this section we describe a variant of Procedure Decide that is used in conjunction with Algorithm 22. This variant, however, does not compute an MIS for the entire input graph, but rather for the subraph of G induced by vertices with degree at least $\Delta/2$. (Although the MIS may include some vertices of G with smaller degrees.) This computation eliminates the vertices with large degrees, and the residual subgraph has maximum degree at most $\Delta/2$. This stage is repeated for $\log \Delta$ iterations to eliminate all vertices. As a result we obtain an MIS for the entire input graph.

Procedure Decide accepts an input a parameter $\gamma > 1$. It draws a biased random bit, with 1 having probability $\frac{1}{\gamma+1}$, and 0 having probability $1 - \frac{1}{\gamma+1}$. Denote this probability distribution by $\mathcal{D}(\gamma)$. Each vertex sends its random bit to all its neighbors. Once a vertex receives the bits of all its neighbors, it decides to join the MIS (and becomes inactive) if it has drawn 1 and all its neighbors have drawn 0. In this case its neighbors decide not to join, and become inactive as well. If a vertex does not decide to join, and none of its neighbors decides to join, then it remains active. This completes the description of the procedure. Its pseudocode is provided below.

Algorithm 23 Procedure Decide(γ)

An algorithm for each vertex $v \in V$.
1: $b :=$ draw a bit from $\mathcal{D}(\gamma)$
2: send b to all neighbors
3: **for** all active neighbors u of v in parallel **do**
4:    $b_u :=$ receive a bit from u
5: **end for**
6: **if** $b = 1$ **and** for all active neighbors u of v it holds that $b_u = 0$ **then**
7:    v joins the MIS
8:    v sends "joined MIS" to all neighbors and becomes inactive
9: **end if**
10: **if** v receives the message "joined MIS" from a neighbor **then**
11:    v does not join the MIS and becomes inactive
12: **end if**

Next, we describe a variant of Algorithm 22 that employs Procedure Decide. This algorithm is called *Procedure Compute-MIS*. The algorithm proceeds in phases. For $j = 0, 1, ..., \lfloor \log \Delta \rfloor$, in phase j the algorithm invokes Procedure Decide with the parameter $\gamma = \Delta/2^j$ for $O(\sqrt{\log n})$ times. As a result, with high probability, all connected components in the subgraph induced by active vertices with sufficiently large number of active neighbors have weak diameter $O(\sqrt{\log n})$. (Specifically, it holds for the subgraph induced by active vertices with at least $\gamma/2$ active neighbors each. Henceforth, we call the number of active neighbors of a vertex v *the active degree of v*, and denote it actdeg(v).) Next, an MIS is computed in these connected components, and all their vertices become inactive. Consequently, the remaining active vertices induce a subgraph with maximum degree at most $\gamma/2$. After phase $\lfloor \log \Delta \rfloor$, with high probability, all remaining active vertices have active degree 0. Thus, they constitute an independent set. All these remaining vertices join the MIS, and the algorithm terminates. The pseudocode of Procedure Compute-MIS is provided below.

Algorithm 24 Procedure Compute-MIS()

An algorithm for each vertex $v \in V$. Initially, all vertices are active.

1: **for** $j = 0, 1, ..., \lfloor \log \Delta \rfloor$ **do**
2:     $\gamma = \Delta / 2^j$
3:     **for** $i = 1, 2, ..., d \cdot \lfloor \sqrt{\log n} \rfloor$ **do**
4:                                    /* d is a large constant */
5:         **if** v is active **then**
6:             Decide(γ)   /* See Algorithm 23 */
7:         **end if**
8:     **end for**
9:     **if** v is active **then**
10:        Denote by G' the subgraph induced by active vertices u with actdeg(u) $\geq \gamma/2$
11:        **if** $v \in G'$ **then**
12:            $G'_v :=$ collect the topology of the connected component in G' that contains v
13:            Compute an MIS of G'_v locally
14:        **end if**
15:        **if** v joins the MIS **or** a neighbor of v joins the MIS **then**
16:            v becomes inactive
17:        **end if**
18:    **end if**
19: **end for**
20: **if** v is active and has no active neighbors **then**
21:    v joins the MIS and becomes inactive
22: **end if**

Observe that if at the beginning of iteration j of the external for-loop of Algorithm 24 (lines 1-19) (henceforth, *phase j*), for $j = 0, 1, ..., \lfloor \log \Delta \rfloor$, the graph induced by the active vertices has maximum degree $\gamma_j = \Delta / 2^j$, then in the end of phase j the graph induced by the active vertices has maximum degree at most $\gamma_j / 2$. (Because an MIS is computed on the subgraph G' induced by the active vertices that have at least $\gamma_j / 2$ active neighbors each. See lines 10-14 of Algorithm 24. Consequently, all vertices of G' become inactive.) Thus, once the algorithm terminates, no active vertices remain. This implies the correctness of the algorithm, because each inactive vertex either belongs to the MIS or has a neighbor in the MIS, and no two neighbors join the MIS. This discussion is summarized in the following theorem.

Theorem 10.16   *Procedure Compute-MIS computes an MIS of the input graph.*

For the procedure to be efficient, collecting the information of connected components should require $\sqrt{\log n}$ rounds. Thus, the following requirement to Algorithm 24 has to be added. *Line 12 of Algorithm 24 must terminate in $\mu = \left\lfloor \sqrt{\log n} \right\rfloor$ rounds.* If it does not terminate on time, then the algorithm fails to produce an MIS. Fortunately, it is possible to show that with high probability all such computations terminate on time. To this end we will show that with high probability weak diameters of all connected components in G' are smaller than $\sqrt{\log n}$, for any phase j. (Observe also that if this is indeed the case, then the vertices can devote exactly $\left\lfloor \sqrt{\log n} \right\rfloor$ rounds for performing lines 9-18. Consequently, all vertices start a phase j in the same time, for all $j = 0, 1, ..., \lfloor \log \Delta \rfloor$.)

Let $\hat{G}_j$ denote the subgraph induced by the vertices that are active in the beginning of phase j, and that have active degree at least $\gamma_j / 2 = \frac{\Delta/2^j}{2}$. The maximum degree of $\hat{G}_j$ is at most γ_j. First, we show that Procedure Decide that accepts γ_j as input satisfies the following four required properties.

Lemma 10.17   *Suppose that Procedure Decide(γ_j) is executed by all active vertices. Then the following four assertions hold.*
(1) Each vertex v in $\hat{G}_j$ becomes inactive with probability ρ, for a constant $0 < \rho < 1$.
(2) For any well-spread sequence $Q = (u_1, u_2, ...u_k) \subseteq V$, for some integer $k > 0$, the events $\mathcal{E}(u_1), \mathcal{E}(u_2), ..., \mathcal{E}(u_k)$ are independent.
(3) If a pair of active neighbors execute Procedure Decide, at most one of them joins the MIS.
(4) If a vertex v decides to join the MIS, then all its neighbors decide not to join. Consequently, v and all its neighbors become inactive.

Proof. (1) A vertex $v \in \hat{G}_j$ has k active neighbors, for some integer k, $\gamma_j / 2 \leq k \leq \gamma_j$. The vertex v becomes inactive if either it joins the MIS or one of its neighbors joins the MIS. In other words, it becomes inactive if either (a) v draws $b_v = 1$ and all its active neighbors draw 0, or (b) v draws $b_v = 0$, an active neighbor w of v draws $b_w = 1$, and all the active neighbors of w draw 0.

Denote by $\{w_1, w_2, ..., w_k\}$ the set of active neighbors of v. Denote $\gamma = \gamma_j$. First, we compute the probability that exactly one of the vertices $\{v, w_1, w_2, ..., w_k\}$ draws 1 and all the rest draw 0. We denote this event by $\mathcal{E}$. The probability of $\mathcal{E}$ is

$$\mathbb{P}(\mathcal{E}) = (k+1) \cdot \frac{1}{\gamma + 1} \cdot \left(1 - \frac{1}{\gamma + 1}\right)^k \geq \left(\frac{\gamma}{2} + 1\right) \cdot \frac{1}{\gamma + 1} \cdot \left(1 - \frac{1}{\gamma + 1}\right)^{\gamma + 1} \geq \frac{1}{8}.$$

Consider a vertex $w \in \{v, w_1, w_2, ..., w_k\}$. Let $\mathcal{E}'(w)$ denote the event that all active neighbors of w that are not in $\{v, w_1, w_2, ..., w_k\}$ have drawn 0. The probability of $\mathcal{E}'(w)$ is

$$\mathbb{P}(\mathcal{E}'(w)) \geq \left(1 - \frac{1}{\gamma + 1}\right)^{\gamma} \geq 1/4. \tag{10.2}$$

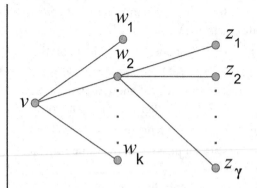

Figure 10.2: In this example w_2 is the only vertex in $\hat{\Gamma}(v)$ that has drawn 1. All its neighbors $z_1, z_2, ..., z_\gamma$ have drawn 0.

See Figure 10.2 for an illustration.

Recall that b_w denotes the bit that w has drawn. Observe that

$$
\begin{aligned}
\mathbb{P}(v \text{ becomes inactive}) \quad &\geq \quad \mathbb{P}(\mathcal{E} \wedge (\exists w \text{ such that } ((b_w = 1) \wedge \mathcal{E}'(w)))) \\
&= \quad \mathbb{P}(\exists w \text{ such that } ((b_w = 1) \wedge \mathcal{E}'(w)) \mid \mathcal{E}) \cdot \mathbb{P}(\mathcal{E}) \\
&\geq \quad \frac{1}{8} \cdot \mathbb{P}(\exists w \text{ such that } ((b_w = 1) \wedge \mathcal{E}'(w)) \mid \mathcal{E}).
\end{aligned}
$$

Observe that conditioned on $\mathcal{E}$, there necessarily exists a vertex $w \in \{v, w_1, w_2, ..., w_k\}$ with $b_w = 1$. Also, by (10.2), for this vertex w it holds that $\mathbb{P}(\mathcal{E}'(w)) \geq 1/4$. Hence

$$\mathbb{P}(\exists w \text{ such that } ((b_w = 1) \wedge \mathcal{E}'(w)) \mid \mathcal{E}) \geq 1/4.$$

Hence $\mathbb{P}(v \text{ becomes inactive}) \geq 1/32$. Hence the first assertion holds with $\rho = 1/32$.

(2) The decision of a vertex $q \in \{u_1, u_2, ..., u_k\}$ whether to become inactive depends only on bits drawn by vertices from its 2-neighborhood $\hat{\Gamma}_2(q)$. Therefore, the event $\mathcal{E}(q)$ that q becomes inactive is independent from each of the events $\mathcal{E}(x)$ for $x \in \{\{u_1, u_2, ..., u_k\} \setminus q\}$, since each of these vertices x is at distance at least 5 from q in G. (Hence $\hat{\Gamma}_2(q) \cap \hat{\Gamma}_2(x) = \emptyset$.)

(3) A vertex joins the MIS only if it draws 1 and all its neighbors draw 0. Therefore, a pair of neighbors cannot join the MIS.

(4) By description of Procedure Decide, if a vertex v decides to join the MIS, then all its neighbors decide not to join.   □

Next, we show that all connected components in G' (which is defined in line 10 of Algorithm 24) have weak diameter smaller than $\sqrt{\log n}$ with high probability. (This does not follow directly from Lemma 10.14, because $\hat{G}_j$ does not contain all active vertices of G in the beginning of phase j. Rather it contains only those of them that have active degree at least $\gamma_j/2$. Therefore, certain modifications in the proof are required. However, the general idea of the proof is similar to that of Lemma 10.14.)

Lemma 10.18   *For $j = 0, 1, ..., \lfloor \log \Delta \rfloor$, and $\gamma = \gamma_j = \Delta/2^j$, in phase j of Algorithm 24, consider the graph G' induced by the active vertices that have active degree at least $\gamma_j/2$. (See line 10 of Algorithm 24.) All connected components of G' have weak diameter smaller than $\sqrt{\log n}$, with high probability.*

Proof. Consider the subgraph $\hat{G}_j$ of vertices that are active in the beginning of iteration j and that have at least $\gamma_j/2$ active neighbors each. The graph G' which was mentioned in the statement of this lemma is the graph obtained from $\hat{G}_j$ by running the internal for-loop (lines 3-8) of Algorithm 24 on iteration j of the external for-loop (lines 1-19) of the algorithm. Recall that $\mathcal{Q}'$ is the set of all well-spread sequences of length $\lfloor \mu/5 \rfloor$, $\mu = \lfloor \sqrt{\log n} \rfloor$. Recall also that by (10.1), it holds that $|\mathcal{Q}'| = O(n^2)$. By Lemma 10.12, for any pair of vertices $u, v \in V(\hat{G}_j)$, such that $dist_G(u, v) \geq \sqrt{\log n} \geq \mu$, and any path P in $\hat{G}_j$ that connects u and v, there exists a well-spread sequence $Q \in \mathcal{Q}'$ of length $\lfloor \mu/5 \rfloor$ with $Q \subseteq V(P)$. Also, by Corollary 10.13, the events $\{\mathcal{E}(q) \mid q \in Q\}$ are mutually independent. Thus, by union bound, the probability that after $d \cdot \mu$ iterations there remains a well-spread sequence $Q \in \mathcal{Q}'$, $Q \subseteq V(P)$, whose all vertices $q \in Q$ are active and have at least $\gamma_j/2$ active neighbors each is at most $O(n^2) \cdot (1 - \rho)^{d \cdot \mu \cdot \lfloor \mu/5 \rfloor}$.

Let c' be an arbitrarily large constant. For a sufficiently large constant d it holds that $O(n^2) \cdot ((1 - \rho)^{\log n})^{d/5} \leq 1/n^{c'}$. (Recall that $\rho = \frac{1}{32}$. See the proof of Lemma 10.17 (1).) Therefore, once the internal for-loop of Algorithm 24 (lines 3-8) is completed, with high probability, no path P that satisfies all the following properties survives. (a) All vertices of P are active, (b) each vertex of P has at least $\gamma_j/2$ active neighbors, and (c) the endpoints of P have distance (in G) at least $\sqrt{\log n}$ one from another. Therefore, in line 10 of Algorithm 24, all connected components of G' have weak diameter smaller than $\sqrt{\log n}$ with high probability. $\square$

Lemma 10.18 implies that, with high probability, a single phase of Algorithm 24 (that is, a single iteration of the external for-loop, lines 1-19 of Algorithm 24) terminates successfully within $d \cdot \mu + \mu$ rounds, for a constant d. Specifically, lines 3-8 require at most $d \cdot \mu$ rounds, and lines 9-18 require at most μ rounds. Next, we analyze the success probability of the entire algorithm. Let c' be an arbitrarily large constant. For any $\hat{c} > c'$, for a sufficiently large n, it holds that $(1 - 1/n^{\hat{c}})^{\log \Delta} \geq 1 - 1/n^{c'}$. Thus, with probability at least $1 - 1/n^{c'}$, for an arbitrarily large constant c', all phases complete successfully within overall time $\lfloor \log \Delta \rfloor \cdot (d \cdot \mu + \mu) + O(1)$. Recall that $\mu = \lfloor \sqrt{\log n} \rfloor$. We summarize this discussion in the following theorem.

Theorem 10.19   *Procedure Compute-MIS computes, with high probability, an MIS of a graph G with degree $\Delta \leq 2^{\sqrt{\log n}}$ in time $O(\log \Delta \sqrt{\log n})$.*

We remark that when $\Delta > 2^{\sqrt{\log n}}$, the running time of the algorithm of Luby [60] is $O(\log n) = O(\log \Delta \sqrt{\log n})$. Hence we derive the following corollary.

Corollary 10.20 *An MIS on n–vertex graphs wiht maximum degree at most Δ can be computed, with high probability, within $O(\log \Delta \sqrt{\log n})$ time.*

The above result is due to [11]. It is also shown in [11] that if Δ is at most polylogarithmic in n, then an MIS can be computed, with high probability, in time $2^{O(\sqrt{\log \log n})}$. We remark that the algorithm for computing MIS that was described in this section requires sending large messages. This is also the case for the MM algorithm presented in the next section. Devising algorithms with a similar time complexity that employ only short (say, $\log n$-bit sized) messages is an open problem.

10.4 RANDOMIZED MAXIMAL MATCHING

In this section we describe a randomized Maximal Matching algorithm due to [11] with running time $O(\sqrt{\log n} + \log \Delta)$, for graphs with maximum degree Δ, for the entire range $1 \leq \Delta \leq n$. The general framework of the algorithm is similar to Algorithm 22 (Section 10.3.1). In the first stage vertices execute a procedure, called *Procedure Decide-Match*, for $O(\sqrt{\log n} + \log \Delta)$ rounds. In each round some edges are matched, and become inactive. Edges incident to the matched ones become inactive as well. A vertex becomes inactive once all the edges it belongs to become inactive. Thus, once an edge is matched, its endpoints become inactive.

Like in Section 10.3, here too we refer to the number of active edges incident on a vertex as its *active degree*. Procedure Decide-Match guarantees that the active degree of a vertex is reduced by a multiplicative constant factor in each round, with high probability, for sufficiently large degrees. Once the first stage completes, with high probability, all connected components of the subgraph induced by active vertices with sufficiently large degree have weak diameter $O(\sqrt{\log n} + \log \Delta)$. The subgraph induced by remaining active vertices satisfies certain properties. These properties enable us to compute a Maximal Matching of this subgraph within additional $O(\sqrt{\log n} + \log \Delta)$ time. The pseudocode of Procedure Decide-Match is provided below.

Next, we describe *Procedure Compute-MM* that employs Procedure Decide-Match to compute a Maximal Matching of the input graph G. First, it completes the first stage, in which Procedure Decide-Match is invoked in each round. Next, it computes a Maximal Matching of the subgraph G' of active vertices with active degrees greater than Δ', for a parameter Δ' that will be determined later. In the sequel we show that the subgraph G' has weak diameter $O(\sqrt{\log n} + \log \Delta)$, with high probability. This property enables us to compute a Maximal Matching of G' in $O(\sqrt{\log n} + \log \Delta)$ time. After this stage the subgraph induced by the set X of yet remaining active vertices decomposes as $X = Z \cup Y$, where Z is an independent set of unmatched vertices which are left after the previous stages, and Y is a set of vertices that induce a subgraph with maximum active degree at most Δ'. In the sequel we show that a Maximal Matching for X can be computed in $O(\Delta' + \log^* n)$ time. The procedure that computes a maximal matching for such a graph will be called *Procedure Complete-MM*. Once it is computed, all ver-

---

Algorithm 25 Procedure Decide-Match()

An algorithm for each vertex $v \in V$.

1: Initialize the forest F_1 and the matching MM by $F_1 := \emptyset$ and MM $:= \emptyset$
2: Select uniformly at random an active neighbor u of v, and add the arc $\langle v, u \rangle$ to F_1
3: /* We say that v *selected* u. */
4: **if** v has indegree at least 1 in F_1 **then**
5:    /* if v is selected */
6:    Select an arbitrary incoming neighbor w, and insert the arc $\langle w, v \rangle$ into F_2
7:    /* F_2 is a vertex disjoint set of oriented paths and cycles. */
8: **end if**
9: Toss a random bit $b(v)$
10: **if** $b(v) = 0$ **and** there is an edge $\langle v, u \rangle$ in F_2 such that $b(u) = 1$ **then**
11:    $\langle v, u \rangle$ joins MM
12:    $\langle v, u \rangle$ and all edges incident on it become inactive
13: **end if**

---

tices and edges become inactive, and the algorithm terminates. The pseudocode of the procedure Compute-MM is provided below. The notation $f(n, \Delta)$ stands for $\max\{\sqrt{\log n}, \log \Delta\}$.

In what follows we show that once the first stage (lines 1-6 of Algorithm 26) completes, all connected components in the subgraph G' (defined in line 8) have weak diameter $O(f(n, \Delta))$, with high probability. The main idea is that the probability that the active degree of a vertex v remains greater than $\Delta' = \Theta(f(n, \Delta))$ after $\ell = \lfloor c_\ell \cdot f(n, \Delta) \rfloor$ rounds is, roughly speaking, $\exp\{-\ell\} = \exp\{-\lfloor c_\ell \cdot f(n, \Delta) \rfloor\}$. Consequently, the probability that for a path $\hat{P}$ connecting the vertices u, v such that $dist_G(u, v) \geq f(n, \Delta)$, all vertices of $\hat{P}$ have active degrees greater than Δ', is at most $p = \exp\{-\ell \cdot f(n, \Delta)\} = \exp\{-c_\ell \cdot \max\{\sqrt{\log n}, \log \Delta\}^2\}$. The number of different paths of length $f(n, \Delta)$ in G is at most $D = n \cdot \Delta^{f(n, \Delta)} = \exp\{\log n + \log \Delta \cdot f(n, \Delta)\}$. Hence, by the union bound, the probability that some path $\hat{P}$ as above survives is at most $p \cdot D \leq 1/\text{poly}(n)$.

We will use the following variant of Chernoff's bound (see, e.g., [2], Chapter A.1).

Theorem 10.21   *Let Y be the sum of mutually independent indicator random variables, with $\mu = \mathbb{E}(Y)$. Let $t \geq \mu$ be a real. Then for all $\epsilon > 0$,*

$$\mathbb{P}(Y > \mu + \epsilon(t + 1)) < 2 \cdot \exp\{-c_\epsilon \cdot t\},$$

where $c_\epsilon > 0$ depends only on ϵ.

For a fixed vertex $v \in V$ and index $i \in [\ell]$ of an iteration, let $\deg^{(i)}(v)$ denote the active degree of v at the beginning of iteration i. We say that v is *in Case 3 in iteration i* if during

---

Algorithm 26 Procedure Compute-MM(Δ')

An algorithm for each vertex $v \in V$. Initially, all vertices and edges are active.

1: $\ell := \lfloor c_\ell \cdot f(n, \Delta) \rfloor$ /* c_ℓ is a large constant */
2: **for** $i = 1, 2, ..., \ell$ **do**
3:      **if** v is active **then**
4:          Decide-Match()
5:      **end if**
6: **end for**
7: **if** v is active **then**
8:      Denote by G' the subgraph induced by active vertices u, with actdeg(u) $> \Delta'$
9:      /* The parameter Δ' will be determined in the sequel */
10:      **if** $v \in G'$ **then**
11:          $G'_v :=$ collect the topology of the connected component in G' that contains v
12:          Compute a Maximal Matching M of G'_v locally
13:      **end if**
14:      **if** v belongs to an edge e that joins the Maximal Matching (i.e., $e \in M$) **then**
15:          The vertex v and all edges that are incident on it become inactive
16:      **end if**
17: **end if**
18: Compute a Maximal Matching of the remaining active edges (by Procedure Complete-MM that will be described in the sequel)

---

iteration i the active degree of v becomes smaller than Δ'. We say that v is *in Case 1 in iteration i* if it is not in Case 3, and the number of neighbors of v that were selected in iteration i by some vertex other than v is at least $\deg^{(i)}(v)/2$. (See line 2 of Algorithm 25 for the definition of "selected.") If in iteration i the vertex v is not in Case 3 and not in Case 1, we say that v is *in Case 2 in iteration i*.

For an active vertex u at the beginning of iteration i, let $I_{i+1}(u)$ be the indicator random variable which is equal to 1 if u survives the ith iteration (i.e., does not get matched on this iteration).

Denote by $\Gamma^{(i)}(v)$ the set of (immediate) active neighbors of v at the beginning of iteration i. By definition, $|\Gamma^{(i)}(v)| = \deg^{(i)}(v)$.

Denote by $S_i(v)$ (respectively, $U_i(v)$) the subset of $\Gamma^{(i)}(v)$ of neighbors of v that were selected (resp., were not selected) on iteration i by some vertex other than v. If the vertex v is in Case 1 in iteration i, then $|S_i(v)| \geq \deg^{(i)}(v)/2$.

Next, we analyze the probability that the active degree of a vertex in Case 1 or Case 2 is reduced by some multiplicative factor.

Case 1

In this section we assume that the vertex v is in Case 1 in iteration i.

Consider a pair of distinct neighbors $u, u' \in S_i(v)$, $u \neq u'$, of v. If u and u' belong to different connected components (i.e., paths of cycles) of F_2, then $I_{i+1}(u)$ and $I_{i+1}(u')$ are independent random variables. Moreover, if u and u' belong to the same connected component of F_2 and the distance between them in F_2 is at least 3, then these random variables are independent as well.

Next, we construct a subset $S_i'(v) \subseteq S_i(v)$ of neighbors of v, such that the set $\{I_{i+1}(u) \mid u \in S_i'(v)\}$ of their respective random variables is independent. The set $S_i'(v)$ is initialized as an empty set. Then we pick an arbitrary neighbor $u \in S_i(v)$ of v and add it to $S_i'(v)$. Also, all other neighbors $u' \in S_i(v)$ of v that are at distance at most 2 from u in F_2 are removed from $S_i(v)$. We iterate this until the set $S_i(v)$ becomes empty. (We remark that the set $S_i'(v)$ is constructed only for the analysis. The algorithm itself does not construct this set.)

It is easy to see that the set $\{I_{i+1}(u) \mid u \in S_i'(v)\}$ is a set of independent random variables. Moreover, since the degree of any vertex in F_2 is at most 2, the size $s_i'(v)$ of $S_i'(v)$ is at least a constant fraction of the size $s_i(v)$ of $S_i(v)$. Specifically, $s_i'(v) \geq s_i(v)/5$. Since the vertex v is in Case 1 in iteration i, it follows that $s_i(v) \geq \deg^{(i)}(v)/2$, and so $s_i'(v) \geq \deg^{(i)}(v)/10$.

The degree of v after iteration i, $\deg^{(i+1)}(v)$, satisfies

$$\deg^{(i+1)}(v) \leq \sum_{u \in \Gamma^{(i)}(v)} I_{i+1}(u) \leq \sum_{u \in \Gamma^{(i)}(v)} I_{i+1}'(u), \tag{10.3}$$

where

$$I_{i+1}'(u) = \begin{cases} 1, & u \in \Gamma^{(i)}(v) \setminus S_i'(v), \\ I_{i+1}(u), & u \in S_i'(v). \end{cases} \tag{10.4}$$

Observe that when $u \in S_i'(v)$, the random variable $I_{i+1}'(u)$ depends upon the random bit $b(u)$ and upon at most two additional random bits $b(x)$ and $b(y)$, where x and y are the neighbors of u in (an unoriented version of) F_2. (Since each connected component of F_2 is a path or cycle, u has at most 2 neighbors in F_2.)

Denote by

$$\deg'^{(i+1)}(v) = \sum_{u \in \Gamma^{(i)}(v)} I_{i+1}'(u). \tag{10.5}$$

By (10.3), $\deg'^{(i+1)}(v)$ stochastically dominates $\deg^{(i+1)}(v)$. Then

$$\deg'^{(i+1)}(v) = (\deg^{(i)}(v) - s_i'(v)) + \sum_{u \in S_i'(v)} I_{i+1}'(u).$$

Hence

$$\mathbb{E}(\deg'^{(i+1)}(v)) = (\deg^{(i)}(v) - s_i'(v)) + \sum_{u \in S_i'(v)} \mathbb{E}(I_{i+1}'(u)).$$

(The expectation above is taken over the random bits that determine random variables $I'_{i+1}(u)$, for $u \in S'_i(v)$. In other words, on this stage $\deg^{(i)}(v)$ and $s'_i(v)$ are already fixed.)

For $u \in S'_i(v)$, $\mathbb{E}(I'_{i+1}(u)) = \mathbb{P}(I'_{i+1}(u) = 1)$. It is easy to verify that if u has two neighbors in F_2 then this probability is 1/2, and if it has just one neighbor (i.e., if it is an endpoint of a path) then this probability 3/4. Hence $\mathbb{E}(\deg'^{(i+1)}(v)) = \deg^{(i)}(v) - s'_i(v)(1 - \rho)$, for $1/2 \leq \rho \leq 3/4$. Since v is in Case 1 in iteration i, it follows that $s'_i(v) \geq \deg^{(i)}(v)/10$. Hence

$$\mathbb{E}(\deg'^{(i+1)}(v)) \;\leq\; \deg^{(i)}(v)\frac{9 + \rho}{10} \;\leq\; \frac{39}{40}\deg^{(i)}(v) . \tag{10.6}$$

This completes the analysis for Case 1.

Case 2

Next, we consider a vertex v that is in Case 2 in iteration i.

In this case v has at least $\deg^{(i)}(v)/2$ neighbors that were not selected by any vertex other than v. If v selects one of them (and it does so with probability at least 1/2), then this selected neighbor u has no choice but to insert the edge $\langle u, v \rangle$ into F_2. Hence the vertex v reachs $V(F_2)$ on iteration i with probability at least 1/2. If it does, then with probability at least 1/4 it gets matched.

Denote the event "v selects one of these $\deg^{(i)}(v)/2$ neighbors on iteration i" by $\alpha_{i+1}(v)$, and the event "v gets matched on iteration i" by $M_{i+1}(v)$. Denote also by $M'_{i+1}(v)$ the event that v gets matched in the particular way that was described above. Specifically, that v selects one of its neighbors that were not selected by any vertex other than v, and gets matched by a matching computed for F_2. Observe that $M'_{i+1}(v) \subseteq M_{i+1}(v)$, and therefore $\mathbb{P}(M'_{i+1}(v)) \leq \mathbb{P}(M_{i+1}(v))$.

It follows that $\mathbb{P}(\alpha_{i+1}(v)) \geq 1/2$, and $\mathbb{P}(M'_{i+1}(v) \mid \alpha_{i+1}(v)) \geq 1/4$. Hence

$$\begin{aligned} \mathbb{P}(M_{i+1}(v)) \;&\geq\; \mathbb{P}(M'_{i+1}(v)) \geq \mathbb{P}(\alpha_{i+1}(v) \text{ and } M'_{i+1}(v)) \\ &=\; \mathbb{P}(M'_{i+1}(v) \mid \alpha_{i+1}(v)) \cdot \mathbb{P}(\alpha_{i+1}(v)) \geq 1/8, \end{aligned} \tag{10.7}$$

i.e., the probability of v to get matched in this case is at least 1/8.

Consider a subset $W \subseteq V$ of vertices that are in Case 2 in iteration i. Assume that for every pair of vertices $u, w \in W$, $dist_G(u, w) \geq 3$. (The subset W will be later constructed in a way that satisfies this assumption.) Then the events $\{M'_{i+1}(u) \mid u \in W\}$ are (mutually) independent. This is because an event $M'_{i+1}(v)$ is determined by random bits tossed by the vertex v and some of its (immediate) neighbors. On the other hand, for a set W as above and two vertices $u, w \in W$, the neighborhoods $\Gamma(u)$ and $\Gamma(v)$ are disjoint. This completes the analysis for Case 2.

We now return to the analysis of Algorithm 26. The next lemma shows that after the first stage of Algorithm 26 (lines 1-6), with high probability, all connected components of the graph induced by remaining active vertices with sufficiently large degrees have weak diameter $O(\sqrt{\log n} + \log \Delta)$.

Lemma 10.22 *After the first stage of Algorithm 26, with probability at least $1 - 1/poly(n)$, for all pairs $u, v \in V$ of vertices such that $dist_G(u, v) \geq k$, for $k = \Theta(\sqrt{\log n} + \Delta)$, each path between u and w contains a vertex whose active degree is at most $\Delta' = O(\sqrt{\log n} + \log \Delta)$.*

Proof. Denote $f = f(n, \Delta) = \max\{\sqrt{\log n}, \log \Delta\}$, $\Delta' = c_\Delta \cdot f$, $k = \lfloor c_{\hat{Q}} \cdot f \rfloor$, $\ell = \lfloor c_\ell \cdot f \rfloor$, where $c_\Delta, c_{\hat{Q}}, c_\ell$ are positive constants to be determined later. Denote by $\deg_i(v) = \deg^{(i)}(v)$ the active degree of a vertex $v \in V$ in the beginning of iteration i of Algorithm 26 (lines 2-5). Denote also $\deg'_{i+1}(v) = \deg'^{(i+1)}(v)$ (see (10.5)).

Fix a pair of vertices u, v with $dist_G(u, v) \geq k$, and a path P between them. Let $\hat{Q} = \hat{Q}(P) \subseteq V(P)$ be a well-spread sequence of length at least $\lfloor k/5 \rfloor$. Such a sequence exists, by Lemma 10.12.

Denote by $\hat{Q}_3(i) \subseteq \hat{Q}$ the set of vertices q with $\deg_i(q) \leq \Delta' = c_\Delta \cdot f$ (i.e., vertices in Case 3 in iteration i). Denote by $\hat{Q}_1(i) \subseteq \hat{Q}$ the set of vertices q *not* in Case 3 that are in Case 1 in iteration i (i.e., at least $\frac{1}{2} \deg_i(q)$ of q's neighbors were selected by someone else). Denote by $\hat{Q}_2(i) \subseteq \hat{Q}$ the set of vertices q *not* in Case 3 that are in Case 2 in iteration i (i.e., less than $\frac{1}{2} \deg_i(q)$ of q's neighbors were selected by someone else).

We say that *an iteration i is of type 3* if $\hat{Q}_3(i) \neq \emptyset$. *An iteration i is of type 1* if it is not of type 3 and $|\hat{Q}_1(i)| \geq \frac{\hat{Q}}{2}$. *An iteration i is of type 2* if it is not of type 3 and $|\hat{Q}_2(i)| > \frac{\hat{Q}}{2}$.

Our analysis now splits into a number of cases, depending on the type of iteration i.

(1) For an iteration i of *type 1*:

By inequality (10.6), for every vertex $q \in \hat{Q}_1(i)$, it holds that $\mathbb{E}\left(\deg'_{i+1}(q)\right) \leq \frac{39}{40} \deg_i(q)$. By Chernoff's bound (applicable because $\deg'_{i+1}(q) = \sum_{u \in \Gamma^{(i)}(v)} I'_{i+1}(u)$ is a sum of independent indicator random variables),

$$\mathbb{P}\left(\deg'_{i+1}(q) \geq \frac{79}{80} \deg_i(q)\right) \leq \exp\{-\Omega(\deg_i(q))\} \leq \exp\{-\Omega(\Delta')\} = \exp\{-\Omega(c_\Delta \cdot f)\}.$$

It follows that

$$\mathbb{P}\left(\exists q \in \hat{Q}_1(i) \text{ such that } \deg'_{i+1}(q) > \frac{79}{80} \deg_i(q)\right) \leq |\hat{Q}| \cdot \exp\{-\Omega(c_\Delta \cdot f)\} \quad (10.8)$$
$$\leq c_{\hat{Q}} \cdot f \cdot \exp\{-\Omega(c_\Delta \cdot f)\}$$
$$\leq \exp\{-\Omega(c_\Delta \cdot f)\}.$$

(Because $f = f(n, \Delta)$ tends to infinity when n tends to infinity. Note that, we can assume without loss of generality that $\Delta = \omega(1)$, because for $\Delta = O(1)$ there is an existing very fast algorithm by Panconesi and Rizzi [68] for computing a maximal matching. The latter algorithm requires $O(\Delta + \log^* n)$ time.)

An iteration i of type 1 is called *bad* if the event $\left\{\exists q \in \hat{Q}_1(i) \text{ such that } \deg'_{i+1}(q) > \frac{79}{80}\deg_i(q)\right\}$ occurs. Denote by $Bad(i)$ the event that iteration i is bad, and by $T_1(i)$ (respectively, $T_2(i)$; respectively, $T_3(i)$) the event that iteration i is of type 1 (resp., of type 2; resp., of type 3). Inequality (10.8) implies that $\mathbb{P}(Bad(i) \mid T_1(i)) \leq \exp\{-\Omega(c_\Delta \cdot f)\}$.

(2) For an iteration of type 2:

We say that a vertex is *eliminated* if it is matched or all its neighbors are matched. For an iteration i of type 2, it holds that $|\hat{Q}_2(i)| \geq |\hat{Q}|/2$. Also, recall that by (10.7), for a vertex $q \in \hat{Q}_2(i)$, $\mathbb{P}(q \text{ is not matched}) \leq 7/8$. Hence

$$
\begin{aligned}
\mathbb{P}(\forall q \in \hat{Q}_2(i), q \text{ is not eliminated}) \quad &\leq \quad \mathbb{P}(\forall q \in \hat{Q}_2(i), q \text{ is not matched}) \\
&\leq \quad \left(\frac{7}{8}\right)^{|\hat{Q}_2(i)|} \leq \left(\frac{7}{8}\right)^{|\hat{Q}|/2} \\
&= \quad \exp\{-\Omega(|\hat{Q}|)\} = \exp\{-\Omega(c_{\hat{Q}} \cdot f)\}.
\end{aligned}
$$

An iteration of type 2 is called *bad* if neither of the vertices of $\hat{Q}_2(i)$ is eliminated. It follows that $\mathbb{P}(Bad(i) \mid T_2(i)) \leq \exp\{-\Omega(c_{\hat{Q}} \cdot f)\}$.

(3) An iteration of type 3 is never bad.

Hence $\mathbb{P}(Bad(i) \mid T_3(i)) = 0 < \exp\{-\Omega(\min\{c_\Delta, c_{\hat{Q}}\} \cdot f)\}$.

Thus

$$
\mathbb{P}(Bad(i)) \quad = \quad \sum_{j=1}^{3} \mathbb{P}(Bad(i) \mid T_j(i)) \cdot \mathbb{P}(T_j(i)) \tag{10.9}
$$

$$
\leq \quad \exp\{-\Omega(\min\{c_\Delta, c_{\hat{Q}}\} \cdot f)\} \cdot \sum_{j=1}^{3} \mathbb{P}(T_j(i)) = \exp\{-\Omega(\min\{c_\Delta, c_{\hat{Q}}\} \cdot f)\}.
$$

Lemma 10.23 $\mathbb{P}(\exists \ell/2 \text{ bad iterations}) \leq \binom{\ell}{\ell/2} \cdot \exp\{-\Omega(\frac{\ell}{2} \cdot \min\{c_\Delta, c_{\hat{Q}}\} \cdot f)\}$.

Proof. For given $\ell/2$ iterations $i_1, i_2, ..., i_{\ell/2}$, for each i_j among them

$$
\mathbb{P}(Bad(i_j) \mid Bad(i_1), Bad(i_2), ..., Bad(i_{j-1})) \leq \exp\{-\Omega(\min\{c_\Delta, c_{\hat{Q}}\} \cdot f)\}.
$$

Indeed, the analysis that results in inequality (10.9) applies even when the event $Bad(i)$ is conditioned on the event $(Bad(i_1) \wedge ... \wedge Bad(i_{j-1}))$, for $i_1, ..., i_{j-1} < i$. The meaning of the event $(Bad(i_1) \wedge ... \wedge Bad(i_{j-1}))$ is the following one. First, it means that no vertex of $\hat{Q}$ was eliminated on iterations $i_1, i_2, ..., i_{j-1}$, and that no vertex of $\hat{Q}$ ended up having active degree below Δ' on any of these iterations. In addition, the event $(Bad(i_1) \wedge ... \wedge Bad(i_{j-1}))$ means that in each iteration $h \in \{i_1, i_2, ..., i_{j-1}\}$ that was of type 1, there exists a vertex $q^{(h)} \in \hat{Q}$ whose active degree did not decrease in iteration h by a factor $\frac{79}{80}$ or less.

Hence
$$\mathbb{P}(Bad(i_1), Bad(i_2), ..., Bad(i_{\ell/2}))$$

$$
\begin{aligned}
&= \mathbb{P}(Bad(i_{\ell/2}) \mid Bad(i_1), Bad(i_2), ..., Bad(i_{\ell/2-1})) \cdot \mathbb{P}(Bad(i_1), Bad(i_2), ..., Bad(i_{\ell/2-1})) \\
&= \exp\{-\Omega(\min\{c_\Delta, c_{\hat{q}}\} \cdot f)\} \cdot \mathbb{P}(Bad(i_1), Bad(i_2), ..., Bad(i_{\ell/2-1})) \\
&\leq \exp\{-\Omega(\frac{\ell}{2} \cdot \min\{c_\Delta, c_{\hat{q}}\} \cdot f)\} = \exp\{-\Omega(f^2 \cdot c_\ell \cdot \min\{c_\Delta, c_{\hat{q}}\})\}.
\end{aligned}
$$

Hence

$$
\begin{aligned}
\mathbb{P}(\exists \ell/2 \text{ bad iterations}) &\leq 2^\ell \cdot \exp\{-\Omega(f^2 \cdot c_\ell \cdot \min\{c_\Delta, c_{\hat{Q}}\})\} \\
&= \exp\left\{c_\ell \cdot f - \Omega(f^2 \cdot c_\ell \cdot \min\{c_\Delta, c_{\hat{Q}}\})\right\} \\
&= \exp\left\{-\Omega(f^2 \cdot c_\ell \cdot \min\{c_\Delta, c_{\hat{Q}}\})\right\}
\end{aligned}
$$

$$\square$$

By Lemma 10.12, each such path P contains a well-spread sequence of length $\lfloor k/5 \rfloor + 1$. Let $\mathcal{P}$ denote the set of all paths whose endpoints u, v satisfy $dist_G(u, v) > k$. Let $\hat{Q}$ be the set of well-spread sequences of length $\lfloor k/5 \rfloor + 1$. Then for each path $P \in \mathcal{P}$ there is a well-spread sequence $\hat{Q} \in \hat{\mathcal{Q}}, \hat{Q} \subseteq V(P)$. Since the size of $\hat{\mathcal{Q}}$ is at most $n \cdot \Delta^{5k+5} \leq n \cdot \Delta^{O(c_{\hat{\varrho}} \cdot f)}$. Hence, by the union bound,
$\mathbb{P}(\exists$ path P between some pair of vertices u, v such that $dist_G(u, v) > k$, such that

$$\exists \ell/2 \text{ bad iterations for } \hat{Q} = \hat{Q}(P)) \leq n \cdot \Delta^{O(c_{\hat{\varrho}} \cdot f)} \cdot \exp\left\{-\Omega(f^2 \cdot c_\ell \cdot \min\{c_\Delta, c_{\hat{Q}}\})\right\}. \tag{10.10}$$

The right-hand side of (10.10) is at most

$$\exp\left\{\log n + O(\log \Delta \cdot c_{\hat{Q}} \cdot f) - \Omega(f^2 \cdot c_\ell \cdot \min\{c_\Delta, c_{\hat{Q}}\})\right\}$$

$$
\begin{aligned}
&\leq \exp\left\{\log n + O(c_{\hat{Q}} \cdot f^2) - \Omega(f^2 \cdot c_\ell \cdot \min\{c_\Delta, c_{\hat{Q}}\})\right\} \\
&= \exp\left\{-\Omega(f^2 \cdot c_\ell \cdot \min\{c_\Delta, c_{\hat{Q}}\})\right\} \leq 1/poly(n),
\end{aligned}
$$

for a large constant c_ℓ and $c_\Delta \geq c_{\hat{Q}}$. (Because $f = \max\{\log \Delta, \sqrt{\log n}\}$.)
Hence with probability at least $1 - 1/poly(n)$, for all well-spread sequences $\hat{Q}$ of length at least $\lfloor k/5 \rfloor + 1$ there at least $\ell/2$ good iterations.

Consider again a fixed pair of vertices u, v with $dist_G(u, v) \geq k$, a path P between them, and the well-spread sequence $\hat{Q} = \hat{Q}(P)$ of this path. If there is at least one good iteration of type 3 for $\hat{Q}$, then we are done (one of the vertices of $\hat{Q}$ gets degree at most Δ'). If there is at least one good iteration of type 2, then one of the vertices of $\hat{Q}$ gets matched, and we are again done. So we are left with the case that there are at least $\ell/2$ good iterations of type 1.

Denote by $i_1, i_2, ..., i_{\ell/2}$ the indices of the first $\ell/2$ such iterations. For each index $j \in [\ell/2]$, denote $\hat{Q}^{(j)} = \hat{Q}_1(i_j)$. Denote $\ell' = \ell/2, k = |\hat{Q}|$. We know that for all $j \in [\ell']$,

$$|\hat{Q}^{(j)}| = |\hat{Q}_1(i_j)| \geq \frac{|\hat{Q}|}{2} = k/2.$$

Also for every $q \in \hat{Q}^{(j)} = \hat{Q}_1(i_j)$, $\deg'_{i_j+1}(q) \leq \frac{79}{80} \cdot \deg_{i_j}(q)$. (Because i_j is a good iteration of type 1, and all vertices of $\hat{Q}_1(i_j)$ are vertices of type 1 in iteration i_j.) The overall number D of distinct pairs (q, j) such that $q \in \hat{Q}^{(j)}$ is at least $\ell' \cdot \frac{|\hat{Q}|}{2}$. For a given $q \in \hat{Q}$ denote by $D(q)$ the number of pairs (q, j) as above that involve the particular vertex q. Note that $D(q)$ is the number of sets $\hat{Q}^{(j)}$ to which q belongs. Hence

$$D = \sum_{q \in \hat{Q}} D(q) \geq \ell' \cdot \frac{|\hat{Q}|}{2}.$$

By the pigeonhole principle, there exists a vertex $q \in \hat{Q}$ with $D(q) \geq \frac{\ell'}{2}$. In other words, there exists a vertex $q \in \hat{Q}$ that belongs to at least $\ell'/2 = \ell/4$ sets $\hat{Q}^{(j)}$.

Fix a specific vertex $q \in \hat{Q}$ with $D(q) \geq \ell/4$. Let $p_1, p_2, ..., p_{\ell/4}$ denote the indices of distinct iterations such that $q \in \hat{Q}^{(p_1)}, q \in \hat{Q}^{(p_2)}, ..., q \in \hat{Q}^{(p_{\ell/4})}$. For each $p_j, j \in [\ell/4]$, it holds that $\deg'_{p_j+1}(q) \leq \frac{79}{80} \cdot \deg_{p_j}(q)$. Denote by $\widehat{\deg}(q)$ the active degree of q after all these iterations. Then $\widehat{\deg}(q) \leq (\frac{79}{80})^{\ell/4} \cdot \deg(q)$. Set ℓ so that $(\frac{79}{80})^{\ell/4} < \frac{1}{\Delta}$. (We set $\ell = \lfloor c_\ell \cdot f \rfloor$, for a sufficiently large constant c_ℓ. Specifically, $c_\ell > \frac{4}{\log(80/79)}$.)

It follows that $\widehat{\deg}(q) < \frac{1}{\Delta} \cdot \deg_0(q) \leq 1$. Hence $\widehat{\deg}(q) = 0$. Hence with probability at least $1 - \exp\{-\Omega(f^2)\}$, for all well-spread sequences $\hat{Q}$, at least one of the vertices of $\hat{Q}$ is either eliminated (due to all its neighbors being matched, or because it itself got matched), or its degree becomes at most Δ'. (The latter happens if there is a good iteration of type 3.) Hence with probability at least $1 - 1/poly(n)$, for all pairs $u, v \in V$ of vertices such that $dist_G(u, v) \geq k$, $k = \Theta(|\hat{Q}|) = \Theta(c_{\hat{Q}} \cdot f)$, each path between u and w contains a vertex whose active degree is at most Δ'. This completes the proof of Lemma 10.22.   □

By Lemma 10.22, once the first stage of Algorithm 26 terminates, all connected components induced by vertices with active degree greater than Δ' have weak diameter $O(\sqrt{\log n} + \log \Delta)$, with high probability. In the next stage, the algorithm computes a Maximal Matching in these connected components. This is done in the same way as in the algorithm for computing an MIS. Specifically, each vertex v collects the topology of its $O(\sqrt{\log n} + \log \Delta)$-neighborhood. Consider the graph G' induced by vertices that have active degree at least Δ' at this stage. The vertex v computes locally the topology of the connected component G'_v of G' to which v belongs.

Then v computes locally a Maximal Matching for G'_v. This matching is computed by the same centralized procedure by all vertices u in G'_v. Therefore, the resulting matching is computed consistently by all vertices. Consequently, with high probability, for each edge e that remains after this stage (henceforth, *active edge*) at least one of the endpoints of e has active degree at most Δ'. Let X denote the set of remaining active vertices once lines 1-16 of Algorithm 26 complete. Let Y be the subset of X containing all vertices with active degree at most Δ'. Let $Z = X \setminus Y$. Since for each remaining active edge, at least one of its endpoints belongs to Y, the set Z is an independent set.

To successfuly complete Algorithm 26, we need to compute a Maximal Matching of $G(X)$ in line 17. Next, we describe Procedure Complete-MM that performs this task. This procedure starts with invoking the algorithm of Panconesi and Rizzi [68] on $G(Y)$, and removing all matched edges, and the edges incident on them. This invocation requires $O(\Delta' + \log^* n)$ time. Consequently all edges whose both endpoints belong to Y become inactive. Therefore, the yet remaining edges have one endpoint in Y and one endpoint in Z. In other words, the subgraph induced by the remaining active vertices is a bipartite graph, where all vertices in Y have active degree at most Δ'. A Maximal Matching in such graph can be computed in $O(\Delta')$ rounds in the following way. In each round, a vertex from Y selects an arbitrary neighbor from Z. Next, each selected neighbor from Z selects an arbitrary neighbor from Y that has selected it. All edges selected by vertices from Z become matched, and, therefore, these edges and the edges incident to them become inactive. Consequently, the active degree of each vertex v in Y decreases, either because v is matched and becomes inactive, or because the neighbor selected by v becomes matched. Hence, after $O(\Delta')$ rounds, the active degree of all vertices in Y become zero, and no active edges remain in the graph. We summarize this discussion in the following theorem.

Theorem 10.24   *Algorithm 26 (Procedure Compute-MM), invoked with the input parameter $\Delta' = O(\sqrt{\log n} + \log \Delta)$, computes a Maximal Matching of the input graph, with high probability, in time $O(\sqrt{\log n} + \log \Delta)$.*

It is instructive to compare this result with the lower bound of Kuhn et al. [50, 52]. The latter lower bound shows that there are (infinitely many) n-vertex graphs with maximum degree $\Delta = 2^{\Theta(\sqrt{\log n})}$, on which any algorithm for Maximal Matching requires $\Omega(\sqrt{\log n}) = \Omega(\log \Delta)$ time. This result implies that Maximal Matching requires $\Omega(\min\{\sqrt{\log n}, \log \Delta\})$ time. Therefore, the upper bound in Theorem 10.24 is tight up to constant factors, for $\Delta = 2^{\Theta(\sqrt{\log n})}$.

Finally, we remark that the current state-of-the-art randomized algorithm for the MM problem requires $O(\log \Delta + \log^4 \log n)$ time [11].

10.5 GRAPHS WITH BOUNDED ARBORICITY

In this section we describe randomized MIS and MM algorithms for graphs with bounded arboricity. These algorithms are based on a randomized reduction that transforms a graph with arboricity at most a into a graph with maximum degree at most $t \cdot a$, for some parameter $t \geq 1$, within $O(\log_t n)$ rounds. An MIS or MM in the resulting graph gives rise to an MIS or MM in the original graph. This reduction and its corollaries are due to [11].

Theorem 10.25   *Let $G = (V, E)$ be a graph of arboricity a. Let $t \geq \max\{11^8 \cdot a^8, (4(c+1)\ln n)^7\}$ be a parameter, where c is a sufficiently large positive constant. In $O(\log_t n)$ time one can find a matching $M \subseteq E$ (or an independent set $I \subseteq V$) so that with probability at least $1 - 1/n^c$, the maximum degree of the graph $G(V \setminus V(M))$ (or $G(V \setminus \hat{\Gamma}(I))$) is at most $t \cdot a$.*

Proof. In $O(\log_t n)$ phases, each of which lasts for $O(1)$ rounds, we commit edges to M (or vertices to I) and remove all incident edges (or incident vertices). Let G be the graph still under consideration before some phase and let $\mathcal{H} = \{v \in V \mid \deg_G(v) \geq t \cdot a\}$ be the remaining set of high-degree vertices. Our goal is to reduce the size of $\mathcal{H}$ by a roughly $t^{1/7}$ factor within one phase. As a result, after $O(\log_t n)$ phases (and rounds) no high-degree vertices will be left in the graph. Let $\mathcal{J} = \{v \in \mathcal{H} \mid \deg(v, \mathcal{H}) \geq \frac{t \cdot a}{2}\}$, i.e., $\mathcal{J}$ is the subset of $\mathcal{H}$ that contains all vertices whose "inner" degree (degree into $\mathcal{H}$) is at least $\frac{t \cdot a}{2}$. Let $\mathcal{H}' = \mathcal{H} \setminus \mathcal{J}$. For a vertex $v \in \mathcal{H}'$, $\deg(v, \mathcal{H}) \leq \frac{t \cdot a}{2}$ and $\deg(v) \geq \frac{t \cdot a}{2}$. Hence $\deg(v, V \setminus \mathcal{H}) \geq \frac{t \cdot a}{2}$, for $v \in \mathcal{H}'$. We form an edge set $\tilde{E} \subseteq E(\mathcal{H}', V \setminus \mathcal{H})$ by picking, for every $v \in \mathcal{H}'$, some arbitrary $\frac{t \cdot a}{2}$ edges incident on v whose other endpoint is in $V \setminus \mathcal{H}$. Hence $|\tilde{E}| = \frac{t \cdot a}{2} \cdot |\mathcal{H}|$.

For an edge set A and a vertex u, let $\deg_A(u)$ denote the number of edges in A incident on u. Under this terminology, $\deg_{\tilde{E}}(v) = \frac{t \cdot a}{2}$, for every $v \in \mathcal{H}'$. See Figure 10.3 for an illustration.

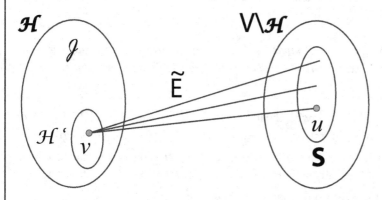

Figure 10.3: The sets $\mathcal{H}, \mathcal{H}', \mathcal{J}, \tilde{E}$ and S.

Let $S = \{u \mid v \in \mathcal{H}', (v, u) \in \tilde{E}\}$ be the neighborhood of $\mathcal{H}'$ with respect to $\tilde{E}$. Observe that $|S| \leq \frac{t \cdot a}{2} \cdot |\mathcal{H}'|$. Let $\beta = t^{1/7}$. We define bad vertices of S, bad edges of $\tilde{E}$ and bad vertices of $\mathcal{H}'$, as follows. The set B_S of *bad vertices* of S is given by

$$B_S = \{u \in S \mid \deg_{\tilde{E}}(u) \geq \beta \text{ or } \deg(u, S) \geq \beta^2\}.$$

(These vertices of S either have a too large degree in $\tilde{E}$, or a too large degree in S. If we are only interested in the MM problem, the second condition can be dropped.) Also, let

$$
\begin{aligned}
B^1_{\tilde{E}} &= \{(v, u) \in \tilde{E} \mid u \in B_S, \deg_{\tilde{E}}(u) \geq \beta\}, \\
B^2_{\tilde{E}} &= \{(v, u) \in \tilde{E} \mid u \in B_S, \deg(u, S) \geq \beta^2\}.
\end{aligned}
$$

We also write $B_{\tilde{E}} = \{(v, u) \in \tilde{E} \mid u \in B_S\}$. Observe that $B_{\tilde{E}} = B^1_{\tilde{E}} \cup (B^2_{\tilde{E}} \setminus B^1_{\tilde{E}})$. (The set $B_{\tilde{E}}$ is the set of *bad edges* of $\tilde{E}$.) Finally, the set of *bad vertices in* $\mathcal{H}'$ is given by $B_{\mathcal{H}'} = \{v \in \mathcal{H}' \mid \deg_{\tilde{E} \setminus B_{\tilde{E}}}(v) < \frac{a \cdot t}{4}\}$.

Consider an edge $(v, u) \in B^1_{\tilde{E}}$. Then $\deg_{\tilde{E}}(v) = \frac{t \cdot a}{2}$ and $\deg_{\tilde{E}}(u) \geq \beta = t^{1/7}$, i.e., the degrees in $\tilde{E}$ of both endpoints are at least β. Hence, by Lemma 2.28, $|B^1_{\tilde{E}}| \leq \frac{a \cdot |\tilde{E}|}{\beta - a} \leq \frac{a}{\beta - a} \cdot |\mathcal{H}'| \cdot \frac{t \cdot a}{2}$. Also, by Lemma 2.28, the number of vertices u in S with $\deg(u, S) \geq \beta^2$ is at most $\frac{a \cdot |S|}{\beta^2 - a}$. Each of these vertices contributes to $B^2_{\tilde{E}} \setminus B^1_{\tilde{E}}$ less than β edges. (Because if for $u \in S$, $\deg_{\tilde{E}}(u) \geq \beta$, then the $\tilde{E}$-edges incident on u are in $B^1_{\tilde{E}}$.) Hence

$$
|B^2_{\tilde{E}} \setminus B^1_{\tilde{E}}| \leq \frac{a \cdot |S|}{\beta^2 - a} \cdot (\beta - 1) \leq \frac{a}{\beta^2 - a} \cdot (\beta - 1) \cdot \frac{t \cdot a}{2} \cdot |\mathcal{H}'|.
$$

In total, since $\beta \geq 11^{8/7} a^{8/7}$, we have

$$
\begin{aligned}
|B_{\tilde{E}}| &\leq |B^1_{\tilde{E}}| + |B^2_{\tilde{E}}| \leq |\mathcal{H}'| \cdot \frac{t \cdot a}{2} \left(\frac{a}{\beta - a} + \frac{a}{\beta^2 - a} \cdot (\beta - 1) \right) \\
&\leq 1.1 \cdot |\mathcal{H}'| \cdot \frac{a^2 t}{\beta} = \frac{2.2a}{\beta} \cdot (t \cdot a \cdot \frac{|\mathcal{H}'|}{2}) = \frac{2.2a}{\beta} \cdot |\tilde{E}|.
\end{aligned}
$$

To summarize, the size of the set of bad edges $B_{\tilde{E}}$ is just a small fraction of $|\tilde{E}|$.

A bad vertex $v \in \mathcal{H}'$ is incident to more than $\frac{t \cdot a}{4}$ edges in $B_{\tilde{E}}$ (because $\deg_{\tilde{E}}(v) = \frac{t \cdot a}{2}$ and $\deg_{\tilde{E} \setminus B_{\tilde{E}}}(v) \leq \frac{t \cdot a}{4}$). Hence, by Lemma 2.28, $|B_{\mathcal{H}'}| < \frac{|B_{\tilde{E}}|}{t \cdot a/4} < 4.4 \cdot \frac{a}{\beta} \cdot |\mathcal{H}'|$, i.e., the size of the set of bad vertices $B_{\mathcal{H}'}$ is also a small fraction of $|\mathcal{H}'|$. Moreover, recall that $\mathcal{J} = \{v \in \mathcal{H} \mid \deg(v, \mathcal{H}) \geq \frac{t \cdot a}{2}\}$ and $\mathcal{H} = \{v \in V \mid \deg_G(v) \geq t \cdot a\}$. Hence for every $v \in \mathcal{H}' = \mathcal{H} \setminus \mathcal{J}$, it holds that $\deg(v, V \setminus \mathcal{H}) \geq \frac{t \cdot a}{2}$. Also, by Lemma 2.28, $|\mathcal{J}| \leq \frac{\mathcal{H} \cdot a}{\frac{t \cdot a}{2} - a} = \frac{\mathcal{H}}{t/2 - 1}$.

Hence $|\mathcal{J}|$ is a small fraction of $|\mathcal{H}|$, i.e., most of the vertices of $\mathcal{H}$ are in $\mathcal{H}'$. Moreover, $|B_{\mathcal{H}'}|$ is a small fraction of $\mathcal{H}'$, i.e., most of the vertices of $\mathcal{H}$ are in $\mathcal{H}' \setminus B_{\mathcal{H}'}$. The latter vertices v satisfy $\deg_{\tilde{E} \setminus B_{\tilde{E}}}(v) \geq \frac{a \cdot t}{4}$. Specifically, denote $\mathcal{H}'' = \mathcal{H}' \setminus B_{\mathcal{H}'}$. Then

$$
|\mathcal{H}''| \geq (1 - 4.4 \cdot \frac{a}{\beta}) \cdot |\mathcal{H}'| \geq \left(1 - \frac{1}{t/2 - 1}\right) \left(1 - \frac{4.4a}{t^{1/7}}\right) \cdot |\mathcal{H}|, \tag{10.11}
$$

and for every $v \in \mathcal{H}''$, it holds that $\deg_{\tilde{E} \setminus B_{\tilde{E}}}(v) \geq \frac{a \cdot t}{4}$. Recall that $B_{\tilde{E}} = \{(v, u) \in \tilde{E} \mid u \in B_S\}$, i.e., each $v \in \mathcal{H}''$ has at least $\frac{a \cdot t}{4}$ edges of $\tilde{E} \setminus B_{\tilde{E}}$ incident on it that lead to $S' = S \setminus B_S$. In addition for every $u \in S'$ it holds that $\deg_{\tilde{E}}(u) < \beta$ and $\deg(u, S) < \beta^2$. Observe that S' is not empty; indeed, otherwise $S = B_S$ and so $B_{\tilde{E}} = \tilde{E}$. However, we saw that $|B_{\tilde{E}}| \leq \frac{2 \cdot 2a}{\beta} \cdot |\tilde{E}|$, a contradiction. Finally, note that vertices of S' can locally recognize that they belong to S'.

Our algorithm and its analysis splits here into two cases. The first is the case of MIS, and the second is the case of MM.

MIS: Each vertex $u \in S'$ selects a random number and joins the MIS if it holds a local maximum in S'. Observe that for every $u \in S'$, it holds that $\deg(u, S') < \beta^2$. Hence

$$\mathbb{P}(u \text{ joins } MIS) = \frac{1}{\deg(u, S') + 1} \geq \frac{1}{\beta^2}.$$

The event $\{u \text{ joins MIS}\}$ is independent of all events $\{u' \text{ joins MIS}\}$ for u and u' at distance at least 3 in $G(S')$. Recall that for all $v \in \mathcal{H}''$, it holds that $\deg_{\tilde{E} \setminus B_{\tilde{E}}}(v) \geq \frac{t \cdot a}{4}$. Hence the neighborhood of each $v \in \mathcal{H}''$ within S' contains at least $\frac{t \cdot a}{4 \cdot \beta^4}$ vertices, each pair of which are at distance at least 3 in $G(S')$. The probability that no neighbor of v joins the MIS is at most

$$\left(1 - \frac{1}{\beta^2}\right)^{\frac{t \cdot a}{4\beta^4}} < e^{-\frac{t \cdot a}{4\beta^6}} = e^{-\frac{a \cdot \beta}{4}} \leq \frac{1}{n^{c+1}}.$$

(Recall that $t \geq (4(c+1) \ln n)^7$, $\beta = t^{1/7}$.) Hence, with high probability, all vertices of $\mathcal{H}''$ are knocked off, i.e., the set $\mathcal{H}$ of high-degree vertices is decimated by a factor of (see (10.11)) $\frac{1}{\Omega(t^{1/56})}$. Therefore, after $O(\log_t n)$ phases all vertices in the residual graph have degrees at most $t \cdot a$, as required.

MM: Here each vertex $u \in S'$ chooses an edge (v, u) from $\tilde{E} \setminus B_{\tilde{E}}$ uniformly at random and proposes to v to include (v, u) in the matching. Any vertex $v \in \mathcal{H}'' = \mathcal{H}' \setminus B_{\mathcal{H}'}$ that receives a proposal accepts an arbitrary one among the proposals and becomes matched.

Recall that a vertex $v \in \mathcal{H}''$ has $\deg_{\tilde{E} \setminus B_{\tilde{E}}}(v) \geq \frac{t \cdot a}{4}$ neighbors in S'. Each of the latter neighbors has less than β neighbors in $\mathcal{H}'$ (with respect to edges of $\tilde{E}$). The probability that none of them proposes to v is at most

$$\left(1 - \frac{1}{\beta}\right)^{\frac{t \cdot a}{4}} < e^{-\frac{t \cdot a}{4\beta}} = e^{-\frac{t^{6/7}a}{4}} \leq O\left(\frac{1}{n^{c+1}}\right).$$

Hence, with high probability, all vertices of $\mathcal{H}''$ are matched, and so the number of high-degree vertices is decimated by a factor of $\frac{1}{\Omega(t^{1/56})}$. Within $O(\log_t n)$ phases all high-degree vertices are eliminated, and we are done. $\square$

The reduction given by Theorem 10.25 is very powerful. Next we show how it can be used in conjunction with the MIS and MM algorithms from Sections 10.3 and 10.4 to obtain fast MIS and MM algorithms for graphs of bounded arboricity.

For the MM problem in graphs with arboricity a we start with running the reduction with $t = \exp\{\sqrt{\log n}\}$. As a result, in $O(\sqrt{\log n})$ rounds the problem reduces to the MM problems in graphs with $\Delta \leq \exp\{\sqrt{\log n}\} \cdot a$, with high probability. By running the MM algorithm from Section 10.4 in this graph we get an MM within additional time of $O(\log \Delta + \sqrt{\log n}) = O(\log a + \sqrt{\log n})$, again with high probability. We summarize this argument in the next corollary.

Corollary 10.26   *[11] The MM problem on n–vertex graphs with arboricity a can be solved in randomized $O(\log a + \sqrt{\log n})$ time.*

In particular, for graphs with $a \leq \exp\{O(\sqrt{\log n})\}$, the running time of this algorithm is $O(\sqrt{\log n})$. Recall that the best deterministic algorithms for graphs of small arboricity a run in $O(\frac{\log n}{\log \log n})$ time for $a < \log^{1-\epsilon} n$, for some arbitrarily small constant $\epsilon > 0$. So the randomized algorithm from Corollary 10.26 is almost quadratically faster than that, and applies to a much wider family of graphs. Moreover, in view of the lower bound of [11] that shows that the MM problem in unoriented trees requires $\Omega(\sqrt{\log n})$ time, it follows that for $a \leq \exp\{O(\sqrt{\log n})\}$ the result of Corollary 10.26 is tight up to constant factors!

For the MIS problem we set $t = \exp\{\log^{1/4} n\}$. As a result within $O(\log^{3/4} n)$ time we obtain a graph with $\Delta \leq a \cdot \exp\{\log^{1/4} n\}$. Running the algorithm from Section 10.3 in this graph constructs an MIS within additional $O(\log \Delta \sqrt{\log n}) = O((\log a + \log^{1/4} n) \cdot \sqrt{\log n})$ time.

Corollary 10.27   *[11] The MIS problem in n–vertex graphs with arboricity a can be solved in randomized $O(\log a \cdot \sqrt{\log n} + \log^{3/4} n)$ time.*

In particular, for $a \leq \exp\{O(\log^{1/4} n)\}$ this results in an MIS algorithm with running time $O(\log^{3/4} n)$. For small (e.g., constant) values of arboricity, there exists a faster randomized algorithm for MIS [11]. That algorithm requires $O(\log^{2/3} n)$ time.

CHAPTER 11

Conclusion and Open Questions

11.1 PROBLEMS THAT CAN BE SOLVED IN POLYLOGARITHMIC TIME

In this monograph we made an effort to reflect and make accessible to the reader the significant progress that was achieved in the area of distributed symmetry breaking in recent years. On the other hand, many central problems in this field are open, and some of these problems are wide open. In this chapter we will overview the main open questions in this area.

Perhaps the most fundamental open problem in this field is to understand the power and limitations of randomization. For centralized algorithms there is a powerful methodology for derandomizing randomized algorithms, i.e., converting them into deterministic ones while incurring only a bounded overhead. (See, e.g., [2], Chapter 16, and the references therein.) The situation is similar for many distributed shared-memory models, such as PRAM. However, in the distributed message-passing model there is currently no generic derandomization technique known. Developing such a technique, even for a limited spectrum of algorithms, would be a very interesting advance. This leads us to our first open problem.

Open Problem 11.1 *Develop a general derandomization technique for the distributed message-passing model.*

The most notable specific problem that has to do with derandomization is whether the symmetry-breaking problems, specifically the MIS and the $(\Delta + 1)$-coloring problems, can be solved in deterministic polylogarithmic time. Solving an MIS appears to be more dificult (or at least no easier) than solving a $(\Delta + 1)$-coloring, as demonstrated by Luby's reduction (see Section 3.9). Hence it is natural to approach the $(\Delta + 1)$-coloring problem first. For both problems the state-of-the-art upper bound is the deterministic algorithm by Panconesi and Srinivasan [69]. This algorithm requires $2^{O(\sqrt{\log n})}$ time. It is based on the network decomposition approach.

In the lower bound front, the state-of-the-art is $\Omega(\sqrt{\log n})$, due to Kuhn et al. [50, 52]. Narrowing this gap is probably the most outstanding problem in this area. We state this open problem below.

Open Problem 11.2 *Devise a deterministic polylogarithmic time algorithm for the MIS problem, or rule it out. As an intermediate state, narrow the gap between the upper bound of $2^{O(\sqrt{\log n})}$ due to [69]* *and the lower bound of $\Omega(\sqrt{\log n})$ due to [50, 52]. The same question for the $(\Delta + 1)$-coloring is as interesting, and is even more widely open than this one. (See below.)*

In fact, for the $(\Delta + 1)$-coloring problem the gap is even larger than for the MIS problem. The lower bound of [50, 52] is not known to apply to the $(\Delta + 1)$-coloring problem, and thus, one can hope to come up with a $\log^* n$-time deterministic algorithm for $(\Delta + 1)$-coloring.

The $(\Delta + 1)$-coloring problem can be naturally relaxed, and one can ask whether $f(\Delta)$-coloring can be computed in deterministic polylogarithmic time, for some mildly growing super-linear function $f(\cdot)$. Linial [55] initiated the study of this relaxed question, and showed that $O(\Delta^2)$-coloring can be computed in $\log^* n + O(1)$ time. He also asked if one can compute a coloring within significantly less than Δ^2 colors in deterministic polylogarithmic time. The authors of the current monograph answered this question in the affirmative in [9], and showed that $\Delta^{1+O(1)}$-coloring can be computed in deterministic polylogarithmic time. Specifically, in [9] we presented a $\Delta \cdot 2^{O(\log \Delta / \log \log \Delta)}$-coloring in $\log n \cdot \log^{1+\epsilon} \Delta$ time, for an arbitrarily small constant $\epsilon > 0$. (See Chapter 7.) Improving the number of colors in this result would be very interesting.

Open Problem 11.3   *Devise a $\Delta \cdot polylog(\Delta)$-coloring in deterministic polylogarithmic time. As an intermediate step, improve upon the result of [9].*

Another related variant of the $(\Delta + 1)$-coloring problem is the $(2\Delta - 1)$-edge-coloring problem. As we saw in Chapter 8 any algorithm for the former problem translates into an algorithm with roughly the same running time for the latter. The best currently known deterministic algorithm for the $(2\Delta - 1)$-edge-coloring problem is still the network-decomposition algorithm of [69], which requires $2^{O(\sqrt{\log n})}$ time. The situation with lower bounds is as appalling as for the $(\Delta + 1)$-vertex-coloring problem.

One can try to use slightly more colors, and get deterministic polylogarithmic time. There are two results along these lines known. The first one is a deterministic $O(\Delta \cdot \log n)$-edge-coloring algorithm by Czygrinow et al. [21] which requires $O(\log^4 n)$ time. The second one is an algorithm from [10] which provides a $\Delta \cdot 2^{O(\log \Delta / \log \log \Delta)}$-edge-coloring within $O(\log^{1+\epsilon} \Delta + \log^* n \frac{\log \Delta}{\log \log \Delta})$ time, for an arbitrarily small constant $\epsilon > 0$. We summarize this problem below.

Open Problem 11.4   *Devise or rule out a deterministic $(2\Delta - 1)$-edge-coloring algorithm that runs in polylogarithmic time. As an intermediate step, improve upon the aforementioned results of [10, 21]. Specifically, devise a $\Delta \cdot polylog(\Delta)$-edge-coloring in deterministic polylogarithmic time.*

Another closely related problem is the MM problem. Unlike its sister symmetry breaking problems (the MIS, the $(\Delta + 1)$-vertex-coloring, and the $(2\Delta - 1)$-edge-coloring), there is a polylogarithmic deterministic algorithm for the MM problem. The algorithm is due to Hanckowiak et al. [35], and it requires $O(\log^4 n)$ time. As we saw in chapter 8 the MM problem reduces to the MIS problem in graphs with neighborhood independence bounded by 2. However, for the latter problem there is no known deterministic polylogarithmic algorithm. Solving it would be a good stepping stone toward the MIS problem in general graphs.

Open Problem 11.5   *Devise or rule out a deterministic polylogarithmic algorithm for the MIS problem in graphs with neighborhood independence bounded by 2.*

Another related open question is to improve the upper bound of [35] for the MM problem. (It is $O(\log^4 n)$.)

11.2 PROBLEMS THAT CAN BE SOLVED IN (SUB)LINEAR IN Δ TIME

The complexity of all the abovementioned problems was studied also in terms of the maximum degree parameter Δ. Specifically, Panconesi and Rizzi [68] showed that the MM and the $(2\Delta - 1)$-edge-coloring problems can be solved in $O(\Delta) + \log^* n$ time. (See Section 8.1.) The authors of the current monograph [7] and Kuhn [48] showed that this is also the case for the MIS and the $(\Delta + 1)$-vertex-coloring problems. (See Chapter 6.) In the lower bounds front the $\Omega(\log^* n)$ lower bound is due to Linial [55], and for the MIS and the MM problems there is also a lower bound of $\Omega(\log \Delta)$ due to Kuhn et al. [50, 52].

Open Problem 11.6   *Devise or rule out an algorithm with running time $o(\Delta) + \log^* n$ for one of these problems.*

Interestingly, in contrast to the previous problems, for Open Problem 11.6 there is no known *randomized* algorithm that achieves the desired bound (of $o(\Delta) + \log^* n$).

The $(\Delta + 1)$-coloring algorithms of [8, 48] are based on defective coloring (see Section 2.4 and Chapter 6). Lovasz showed that in a graph with maximum degree Δ, for any parameter p, $1 \leq p \leq \Delta$, there exists a (Δ/p)-defective p-coloring [58]. The known distributed counterparts of this result are substantially weaker. Specifically, Kuhn [48] showed that a (Δ/p)-defective $O(p^2)$-coloring can be computed in $O(\log^* n)$ deterministic time. (See also [8] for a weaker result obtained by a different technique.)

Open Problem 11.7   *Devise an efficient distributed algorithm for computing a (Δ/p)-defective $O(p)$-coloring.*

We remark that for graphs with bounded neighborhood independence such a result is known [10]. It was used in [10] to devise a $\Delta^{1+\epsilon}$-edge-coloring algorithm that requires $O(\log \Delta) + \log^* n$ time. Answering Open Problem 11.7 in the affirmative would lead to a similar result for vertex-coloring. This, in turn, would be a significant improvement over the best currently-known vertex-coloring algorithms [9, 11].

11.3   ALGORITHMS FOR RESTRICTED GRAPH FAMILIES

Instead of graphs of bounded degree it is often instructive to consider graphs of bounded arboricity. In [7] the authors of this monograph showed that for graphs with arboricity $a \leq \text{polylog}(n)$, all these problems are solvable in deterministic polylogarithmic time.

Open Problem 11.8 *Devise or rule out a deterministic polylogarithmic algorithm for one of these problems, for graphs with a $\gg \text{polylog}(n)$. For example, for a $= \exp\{\log^{\epsilon} n\}$, for some fixed constant $\epsilon > 0$.*

In the context of graphs with bounded arboricity it is also natural to look on the logarithmic barrier. In [7] we showed that the MIS and the $(\Delta + 1)$-coloring problems can be solved in deterministic time $O(\frac{\log n}{\log \log n})$, as long as $a \leq \log^{1/2-\epsilon} n$, and the MM and the $(2\Delta - 1)$-edge-coloring problems can be solved within the same time for $a \leq \log^{1-\epsilon} n$. (In both cases $\epsilon > 0$ is a fixed arbitrarily small constant.)

Open Problem 11.9 *Devise a sublogarithmic deterministic algorithm for the MIS and the $(\Delta + 1)$-coloring problems for graphs with a $< t(n)$, for some $t(n) = \Omega(\sqrt{\log n})$, and for the MM and the $(2\Delta - 1)$-edge-coloring problems for graphs with a $\leq s(n)$, for some $s(n) = \Omega(\log n)$.*

Closely related to Open Problem 11.9 are numerous questions regarding $f(a)$-coloring of graphs with arboricity at most a, for various functions $f(\cdot)$. Those questions, in turn, are closely related to the problem of computing forest decompositions. Recall that for a graph of arboricity a one can compute a decomposition into $(2 + \epsilon) \cdot a$ forests in $O(\log n)$ time. One can also compute a $2a$-forest-decomposition in $O(a \log n)$ time [7]. However, by Nash-Williams's theorem, there exists a forest decomposition into a forests. This leads to the following open question.

Open Problem 11.10 *Devise or rule out an efficient distributed algorithm for computing a decomposition of a graph with arboricity a into less than 2a forests.*

A progress in this question will probably lead to a progress for Open Problem 11.8, and for the $f(a)$-coloring problems. One notable problem from the latter category is the following one.

Open Problem 11.11 *There exists a deterministic $O(a^2)$-coloring algorithm that requires $O(\log n)$ time [7]. Can one use significantly less than a^2 colors, and still stay within deterministic $O(\log n)$ time?*

This question is open even for randomized algorithms, though a significant progress in this direction was recently achieved by Kothapalli and Pemmaraju [45]. On the other hand, it is known that $O(a^2)$-coloring requires $\Omega(\log n)$ time, and more generally, for a positive parameter $q < n^{1/4}/a$, computing $O(a \cdot q)$-coloring requires $\Omega(\frac{\log n}{\log a + \log q})$ time [7, 55]. Therefore, the running time of $O(\log n)$ cannot be improved if one wishes to employ $O(a^2)$ colors, but it may be possible to improve the palette size, while spending only $O(\log n)$ time.

11.4 RANDOMIZED ALGORITHMS

Randomized complexity of symmetry breaking problems also poses major challenges. For the MIS problem Luby [60] and Alon et al. [1] devised $O(\log n)$-time randomized algorithms. Barenboim et al. [11] have recently devised an $O(\sqrt{\log n}\log \Delta)$-time algorithm for this problem. (See Section 10.3.) For $\Delta \leq \text{polylog}(n)$ the algorithm of [11] performs even better. Specifically, its running time in this case is $2^{O(\sqrt{\log \log n})}$. Kuhn et al. [50, 52] proved a lower bound of $\Omega(\min\{\sqrt{\log n}, \log \Delta\}$ time for this problem.

Open Problem 11.12 *Devise or rule out a randomized algorithm for the MIS problem in general graphs with running time $O(\sqrt{\log n})$. More generally, pin down the randomized complexity of this fundamental problem.*

The randomized complexity of the MIS problem was also studied for graphs with bounded arboricity a. Barenboim et al. [11] devised an algorithm with running time $O(\log a \sqrt{\log n} + \log^{3/4} n)$ for this problem. Moreover, for $a \leq \log^{1/3} n$ their algorithm requires just $O(\log^{2/3} n)$ time. For $a = 1$ (the case of unoriented trees) Lenzen and Wattenhofer [54] devised an MIS algorithm with running time $O(\sqrt{\log n}\log \log n)$. This was marginally improved to $O(\sqrt{\log n \log \log n})$ in [11].

Open Problem 11.13 *Improve the results of [11, 54] for the MIS problem in graphs with bounded arboricity.*

For the closely related MM problem the classical $O(\log n)$-time randomized algorithm of Israeli and Itai [39] was recently improved to $O(\log \Delta + \log^4 \log n)$ by [11].

Open Problem 11.14 *Devise or rule out an $O(\sqrt{\log n})$-time randomized algorithm for the MM problem.*

In graphs of arboricity a the MM problem can be solved in $O(\log a + \sqrt{\log n})$ time [11]. The problem is also known to require $\Omega(\sqrt{\log n})$ time even for unoriented trees [11, 50, 52]. Therefore, this is tight for $a = 2^{O(\sqrt{\log n})}$. Remarkably, this lower bound is not known to apply to the MIS problem in unoriented trees.

Open Problem 11.15 *Pin down the randomized complexity of the MIS problem in unoriented trees. We conjecture that it is $\Theta(\sqrt{\log n})$. For an upper bound of $\tilde{O}(\sqrt{\log n})$ see [11, 54].*

The randomized complexity of the $(\Delta + 1)$-coloring problem was also subject of intensive research. The algorithms of Luby [60] and of Alon et al. [1], in conjunction with the reduction from coloring to MIS (see Section 3.9), provide an $O(\log n)$-time randomized algorithm for the $(\Delta + 1)$ coloring problem. An explicit $(\Delta + 1)$-coloring algorithm is given in [61]. This result was recently improved by Schneider and Wattenhofer [78] to $O(\sqrt{\log n} + \log \Delta)$, and consequently improved by Barenboim et al. [11] to $O(\log \Delta) + 2^{O(\sqrt{\log \log n})}$. Remarkably, the lower bounds of [50, 52] do not apply to the $(\Delta + 1)$-coloring problem, and therefore, the current state of knowledge does not preclude $(\Delta + 1)$-coloring in $\frac{1}{2} \log^* n$ time!

Open Problem 11.16   *Determine the randomized complexity of the $(\Delta + 1)$-coloring problem. Specifically, either improve the $O(\log \Delta) + 2^{O(\sqrt{\log \log n})}$ upper bound from [11], or prove a lower bound stronger than $\frac{1}{2} \log^* n$ (due to [55]).*

The related variant of the randomized $(\Delta + 1)$-coloring problem in which we allow $O(\Delta)$ colors is also of great interest. Kothapalli et al. [47] devised an $O(\sqrt{\log n})$ time algorithm for this problem. Schneider and Wattenhofer [78] showed that if $\Delta > \log^{1+\epsilon} n$, for an arbitrarily small constant $\epsilon > 0$, then $O(\Delta)$-coloring can be computed in randomized $O(\log^* n)$ time. Barenboim et al. [11] devised an $O(\Delta)$-coloring algorithm with running time $2^{O(\sqrt{\log \log n})}$.

Open Problem 11.17   *Can the randomized $O(\Delta)$-coloring algorithm of [78] that runs in $O(\log^* n)$ time be extended to sublogarithmic values of Δ?*

Obviously, this list of open problems is by any means not exhaustive. Many other very good open problems are left out. We however hope that it illustrates how much work is still left to be done in this area. We invite the reader to roll up his sleeves, and indulge in solving them!

Bibliography

[1] N. Alon, L. Babai, and A. Itai. A fast and simple randomized parallel algorithm for the maximal independent set problem. *Journal of Algorithms*, 7(4):567–583, 1986. DOI: 10.1016/0196-6774(86)90019-2. 55, 147

[2] N. Alon, and J. Spencer. *The probabilistic method.* Wiley, 3rd ed., 2008. DOI: 10.1002/9780470277331. 8, 115, 129, 143

[3] K. Appel, and W. Haken. The solution of the four color map problem. *Scientific American*, 237(4): 108–121, 1977. DOI: 10.1038/scientificamerican1077-108. 17

[4] H. Attiya, and J. Welch. *Distributed Computing: Fundamentals, Simulations, and Advanced Topics.* Wiley, 2nd ed., 2004. 1

[5] B. Awerbuch, A. V. Goldberg, M. Luby, and S. Plotkin. Network decomposition and locality in distributed computation. In *Proc. of the 30th Annual Symposium on Foundations of Computer Science*, pages 364–369, 1989. DOI: 10.1109/SFCS.1989.63504. vi, 2, 4, 103, 105, 106, 109, 110

[6] L. Barenboim. On the locality of some NP-complete problems. In *Proc. of the 39th International Colloquium on Automata, Languages, and Programming*, part II, pages 403–415, 2012. DOI: 10.1007/978-3-642-31585-5_37. 103

[7] L. Barenboim, and M. Elkin. Sublogarithmic distributed MIS algorithm for sparse graphs using Nash-Williams decomposition. In *Proc. of the 27th ACM Symp. on Principles of Distributed Computing*, pages 25–34, 2008. DOI: 10.1145/1400751.1400757. vi, 3, 4, 55, 62, 66, 97, 145, 146

[8] L. Barenboim, and M. Elkin. Distributed $(\Delta + 1)$-coloring in linear (in Δ) time. In *Proc. of the 41th ACM Symp. on Theory of Computing*, pages 111–120, 2009. vi, 3, 4, 25, 39, 67, 68, 70, 73, 110, 145

[9] L. Barenboim, and M. Elkin. Deterministic distributed vertex coloring in polylogarithmic time. In *Proc. 29th ACM Symp. on Principles of Distributed Computing*, pages 410–419, 2010. DOI: 10.1145/1835698.1835797. vi, 2, 3, 4, 25, 26, 81, 91, 144, 145

[10] L. Barenboim, and M. Elkin. Distributed deterministic edge coloring using bounded neighborhood independence. In *Proc. of the 30th ACM Symp. on Principles of Distributed Com-*

puting, pages 129 - 138, 2011. DOI: 10.1145/1993806.1993825. 4, 25, 93, 97, 101, 144, 145

[11] L. Barenboim, M. Elkin, S. Pettie, and J. Schneider. The locality of distributed symmetry breaking. In *Proc. of the 53rd Annual Symposium on Foundations of Computer Science*, pages 321–330, 2012. DOI: 10.1109/FOCS.2012.60. vi, 3, 4, 49, 117, 128, 137, 138, 141, 145, 147, 148

[12] M. Bellare, O. Goldreich, and M. Sudan. Free bits, PCPs, and nonapproximability - towards tight results. *SIAM Journal on Computing*, 27(3):804–915, 1998. DOI: 10.1137/S0097539796302531. 7

[13] B. Bollobas. *Modern Graph Theory*. Springer, corrected edition, 1998. DOI: 10.1007/978-1-4612-0619-4. 7, 14, 27

[14] B. Bollobas. *Random Graphs*. Cambridge University Press, 2nd ed., 2001. DOI: 10.1017/CBO9780511814068. 12

[15] B. Chen, M. Matsumoto, J. Wang, Z. Zhang, and J. Zhang. A short proof of Nash-Williams' theorem for the arboricity of a graph. *Graphs and Combinatorics*, 10(1): 27–28, 1994. DOI: 10.1007/BF01202467. 19

[16] F. Chierichetti, and A. Vattani. The Local Nature of List Colorings for Graphs of High Girth. *SIAM Journal on Computing*, 39(6), 2232–2250. DOI: 10.1007/978-3-540-70575-8_27. 5

[17] R. Cole, and L. Kowalik. New linear-time algorithms for edge-coloring planar graphs. *Algorithmica*, 50(3): 351–368, 2008. DOI: 10.1007/s00453-007-9044-3. 27

[18] R. Cole, and U. Vishkin. Deterministic coin tossing with applications to optimal parallel list ranking. *Information and Control*, 70(1):32–53, 1986. DOI: 10.1016/S0019-9958(86)80023-7. vi, 2, 3, 4, 32, 34, 55, 93

[19] L. Cowen, R. Cowen, and D. Woodall. Defective colorings of graphs in surfaces: partitions into subgraphs of bounded valence. *Journal of Graph Theory*, 10:187–195, 1986. DOI: 10.1002/jgt.3190100207. 25

[20] L. Cowen, W. Goddard, and C. Jesurum. Coloring with defect In *Proc. of the 8th ACM-SIAM Symp. on Discrete Algorithms*, pages 548–557, 1997. 25

[21] A. Czygrinow, M. Hanckowiak, and M. Karonski. Distributed O(Delta logn)-edge-coloring algorithm. In *Proc. of the 9th Annual European Symposium on Algorithms*, pages 345–355, 2001. 144

[22] B. Descartes. Solution to advanced problem No. 4526. *American Mathematical Monthly*, 61, page 532, 1954. 10

[23] R. Diestel. *Graph Theory*. Springer, 4th ed., 2010. DOI: 10.1007/978-3-642-14279-6. 7

[24] D. Dubhashi, D. Grable, and A. Panconesi. Nearly-optimal distributed edge-colouring via the nibble method. *Theoretical Computer Science, a special issue for the best papers of ESA95*, 203(2):225–251, 1998. DOI: 10.1016/S0304-3975(98)00022-X. 5

[25] D. Dubhashi and A. Panconesi. *Concentration of Measure for the Analysis of Randomized Algorithms*. Cambridge University Press, 2009. DOI: 10.1017/CBO9780511581274. 5

[26] P. Erdős. Graph theory and probability. *Canadian Journal of Mathematics*, 11: 34–38, 1959. DOI: 10.4153/CJM-1959-003-9. 11

[27] P. Erdős, P. Frankl, and Z. Füredi. Families of finite sets in which no set is covered by the union of r others. *Israel Journal of Mathematics*, 51:79–89, 1985. DOI: 10.1007/BF02772959. 41, 43, 44

[28] T. Gallai. On directed graphs and circuits. *Theory of Graphs (Proceedings of the Colloquium Tihany 1966), New York: Academic Press*, pages 115–118, 1968. 30, 31

[29] M. Garey, and D. Johnson. The complexity of near-optimal graph coloring. *Journal of ACM*, 23(1): 43–49, 1976. DOI: 10.1145/321921.321926. 7

[30] B. Gfeller, and E. Vicari. A randomized distributed algorithm for the maximal independent set problem in growth-bounded graphs. In *Proc. of the 26th ACM Symp. on Principles of Distributed Computing*, pages 53–60, 2007. DOI: 10.1145/1281100.1281111. vi, 3, 5

[31] A. Goldberg, S. Plotkin, and G. Shannon. Parallel symmetry-breaking in sparse graphs. *SIAM Journal on Discrete Mathematics*, 1(4):434–446, 1988. DOI: 10.1137/0401044. vi, 2, 3, 4, 32, 34, 37, 39, 55, 105

[32] D. Grable, and A. Panconesi. Nearly optimal distributed edge colouring in O(log log n) rounds. *Random Structures and Algorithms*, 10(3): 385–405, 1997. DOI: 10.1002/(SICI)1098-2418(199705)10:3%3C385::AID-RSA6%3E3.3.CO;2-3. 5

[33] D. Grable, and A. Panconesi. Fast distributed algorithms for Brooks-Vizing colourings. In *Proc. of the 9th Annual ACM-SIAM Symposium on Discrete Algorithms*, pages 473–480, 1998. 5

[34] H. Grotzsch. Zur Theorie der diskreten Gebilde, VII: Ein Dreifarbensatz fur dreikreisfreie Netze auf der Kugel. *Wiss. Z. Martin-Luther-U., Halle-Wittenberg, Math.-Nat. Reihe* 8: 109–120, 1959. 8

[35] M. Hanckowiak, M. Karonski, and A. Panconesi. On the distributed complexity of computing maximal matchings. *SIAM Journal on Discrete Mathematics*, 15(1):41–57, 2001. DOI: 10.1137/S0895480100373121. 2, 103, 144, 145

[36] F. Harary, and K. Jones. Conditional colorability II: Bipartite variations. *Congressus Numer*, 50:205–218, 1985. 25

[37] G. Hardy, and E. Wright. *An introduction to the theory of numbers*. Oxford university press, 5th edition, 1980. 44

[38] J. Hastad. Clique is Hard to Approximate Within $n^{1-\epsilon}$. In *Proc. of the 37th Annual Symposium on Foundations of Computer Science*, pages 627–636, 1996. DOI: 10.1109/SFCS.1996.548522. 7

[39] A. Israeli, and A. Itai. A fast and simple randomized parallel algorithm for maximal matching. *Information Processing Letters*, 22(2):77–80, 1986. DOI: 10.1016/0020-0190(86)90144-4. vi, 2, 147

[40] A. Israeli, and Y. Shiloach. An Improved Parallel Algorithm for Maximal Matching. *Information Processing Letters*, 22(2):57–60, 1986. DOI: 10.1016/0020-0190(86)90144-4. vi, 2

[41] S. Janson, T. Luczak, and A. Rucinski. *Random Graphs*. Wiley-Interscience, 2000. DOI: 10.1002/9781118032718. 12

[42] Ö. Johansson. Simple distributed $(\Delta + 1)$-coloring of graphs. *Information Processing Letters*, 70(5):229–232, 1999. DOI: 10.1016/S0020-0190(99)00064-2.

[43] R. Karp Reducibility among combinatorial problems. *Complexity of Computer Computations*, New York: Plenum Press, pages 85–103, 1972. DOI: 10.1007/978-1-4684-2001-2_9. 7

[44] A. Korman, J. Sereni, and L. Viennot. Toward more localized local algorithms: removing assumptions concerning global knowledge. In *Proc. of the 30th ACM Symp. on Principles of Distributed Computing*, pages 49–58, 2011. DOI: 10.1007/s00446-012-0174-8. 66, 67

[45] K. Kothapalli, and S. Pemmaraju. Distributed graph coloring in a few rounds. In *Proc. of the 30th ACM Symp. on Principles of Distributed Computing*, pages 31–40, 2011. DOI: 10.1145/1993806.1993812. 146

[46] K. Kothapalli, and S. Pemmaraju. Super-Fast 3-Ruling Sets. In *proc. of the 32nd IARCS Annual Conference on Foundations of Software Technology and Theoretical Computer Science*, pages 136–147, 2012. 2

[47] K. Kothapalli, C. Scheideler, M. Onus, and C. Schindelhauer. Distributed coloring in $O(\sqrt{\log n})$ bit rounds. In *Proc. of the 20th International Parallel and Distributed Processing Symposium*, 2006. DOI: 10.1109/IPDPS.2006.1639281. vi, 3, 4, 115, 148

[48] F. Kuhn. Weak graph colorings: distributed algorithms and applications. In *Proc. of the 21st ACM Symposium on Parallel Algorithms and Architectures*, pages 138–144, 2009. DOI: 10.1145/1583991.1584032. vi, 3, 4, 25, 39, 67, 68, 70, 73, 85, 99, 110, 145

[49] F. Kuhn, T. Moscibroda, T. Nieberg, and R. Wattenhofer. Fast deterministic distributed maximal independent set computation on growth-bounded graphs. In *Proc. of the 19th International Symposium on Distributed Computing*, pages 273–287, 2005. DOI: 10.1007/11561927_21. vi, 3, 5

[50] F. Kuhn, T. Moscibroda, and R. Wattenhofer. What cannot be computed locally! In *Proc. of the 23rd ACM Symp. on Principles of Distributed Computing*, pages 300–309, 2004. DOI: 10.1145/1011767.1011811. vi, 5, 49, 137, 143, 144, 145, 147, 148

[51] F. Kuhn, T. Moscibroda, and R. Wattenhofer. On the locality of bounded growth. In *Proc. of the 24th ACM Symp. on Principles of Distributed Computing*, pages 60 -68, 2005. DOI: 10.1145/1073814.1073826. vi, 3, 5

[52] F. Kuhn, T. Moscibroda, and R. Wattenhofer. Local Computation: Lower and Upper Bounds. *http://arXiv.org/abs/1011.5470*, 2010. vi, 5, 49, 137, 143, 144, 145, 147, 148

[53] F. Kuhn, and R. Wattenhofer. On the complexity of distributed graph coloring. In *Proc. of the 25th ACM Symp. on Principles of Distributed Computing*, pages 7–15, 2006. DOI: 10.1145/1146381.1146387. 3, 38

[54] C. Lenzen and R. Wattenhofer. MIS on trees. In *Proc. of the 30th ACM Symp. on Principles of Distributed Computing*, pages 41–48, 2011. DOI: 10.1145/1993806.1993813. 147

[55] N. Linial. Distributive graph algorithms: Global solutions from local data In *Proc. of the 28th Annual Symp. on Foundation of Computer Science*, pages 331–335, 1987. vi, 1, 2, 4, 32, 34, 39, 40, 41, 43, 44, 47, 51, 53, 79, 81, 91, 144, 145, 146, 148

[56] N. Linial. Locality in distributed graph algorithms. *SIAM Journal on Computing*, 21(1):193–201, 1992. DOI: 10.1137/0221015. 65, 72, 75, 79

[57] N. Linial and M. Saks. Low diameter graph decomposition. *Combinatorica* 13: 441 - 454, 1993. DOI: 10.1007/BF01303516. 103

[58] L. Lovász. On decompositions of graphs. *Studia Sci. Math. Hungar.*, 1:237–238, 1966. 25, 68, 145

[59] A. Lubotzky, R. Phillips, and P. Sarnak. Ramanujan graphs. *Combinatorica*, 8(3): 261–277, 1988. DOI: 10.1007/BF02126799. 11, 47

[60] M. Luby. A simple parallel algorithm for the maximal independent set problem. *SIAM Journal on Computing*, 15:1036–1053, 1986. DOI: 10.1137/0215074. vi, 2, 4, 40, 41, 55, 111, 117, 127, 147

[61] M. Luby. Removing randomness in parallel computation without a processor penalty. In *Proc. of the 29th Annual Symposium on Foundations of Computer Science*, pages 162–173, 1988. DOI: 10.1109/SFCS.1988.21934. vi, 2, 4, 55, 111, 147

[62] N. Lynch. *Distributed Algorithms*. Morgan Kaufmann, 1996.

[63] B. Mohar and C. Thomassen. *Graphs on Surfaces*. Johns Hopkins University Press, 2001. 1

[64] J. Mycielski. Sur le coloriage des graphes. *Colloq. Math.* 3: 161–162, 1955. 14

[65] M. Naor. A lower bound on probabilistic algorithms for distributive ring coloring. *SIAM Journal on Discrete Mathematics*, 4(3):409–412, 1991. DOI: 10.1137/0404036. 8

[66] C. Nash-Williams. Decompositions of finite graphs into forests. *J. London Math*, 39:12, 1964. DOI: 10.1112/jlms/s1-39.1.12. 51, 53

[67] D. Peleg. *Distributed Computing: A Locality-Sensitive Approach*. SIAM, 2000. DOI: 10.1137/1.9780898719772. 17

[68] A. Panconesi, and R. Rizzi. Some simple distributed algorithms for sparse networks. *Distributed Computing*, 14(2):97–100, 2001. DOI: 10.1007/PL00008932. 1, 2, 110

[69] A. Panconesi, and A. Srinivasan. On the complexity of distributed network decomposition. *Journal of Algorithms*, 20(2):581–592, 1995. DOI: 10.1006/jagm.1996.0017. 4, 36, 55, 93, 133, 137, 145

[70] A. Panconesi, and A. Srinivasan. The local nature of Δ-coloring and its algorithmic applications. *Combinatorica*, 15(2):255–280, 1995. DOI: 10.1007/BF01200759. 2, 4, 55, 103, 110, 143, 144
5

[71] A. Panconesi, and A. Srinivasan. Randomized Distributed Edge Coloring via an Extension of the Chernoff-Hoeffding Bounds. *SIAM Journal on Computing*, 26(2):350–368, 1997. DOI: 10.1137/S0097539793250767. 5

[72] D. Sanders, and Y. Zhao. Planar Graphs of Maximum Degree Seven are Class I. *Journal of Combinatorial Theory, Series B*, 83(2):201–212, 2001. DOI: 10.1006/jctb.2001.2047. 27

[73] N. Santoro. *Design and Analysis of Distributed Algorithms*. Wiley, 2006. DOI: 10.1002/0470072644. 1

[74] M. Szegedy, and S. Vishwanathan. Locality based graph coloring. In *Proc. of the 25th ACM Symp. on Theory of Computing*, pages 201–207, 1993. DOI: 10.1145/167088.167156. 3, 34, 39, 43, 44, 79

[75] V. Vizing. On an estimate of the chromatic class of a p-graph. *Metody Diskret. Analiz*, 3: 25–30, 1964. 27

[76] V. Vizing. Critical graphs with given chromatic index. *Metody Diskret. Analiz*, 5: 9–17, 1965. 27

[77] J. Schneider, and R. Wattenhofer. A log-star distributed Maximal Independent Set algorithm for Growth Bounded Graphs. In *Proc. of the 27th ACM Symp. on Principles of Distributed Computing*, pages 35–44, 2008. DOI: 10.1145/1400751.1400758. vi, 3, 5

[78] J. Schneider, and R. Wattenhofer. A new technique for distributed symmetry breaking. In *Proc. of the 29th ACM Symp. on Principles of Distributed Computing*, pages 257–266, 2010. DOI: 10.1145/1835698.1835760. vi, 3, 117, 148

[79] D. Zuckerman. Linear Degree Extractors and the Inapproximability of Max Clique and Chromatic Number. *Theory of Computing*, 3(1):103–128. 2007. DOI: 10.4086/toc.2007.v003a006. 7

Authors' Biographies

MICHAEL ELKIN

Michael Elkin received his Ph.D. in Computer Science and Mathematics from the Weizmann Institute, Rehovot, Israel, in 2002. He held positions in the Institute for Advanced Study in Princeton and in Yale University, before joining the Ben-Gurion University of the Negev in 2004. He is an Associate Professor in the Computer Science department in the Ben-Gurion University. His main research interests are distributed algorithms, graph algorithms and metric embeddings.

LEONID BARENBOIM

Leonid Barenboim performed his Ph.D. research in Computer Science in Ben-Gurion University of the Negev. His research deals with distributed algorithms for symmetry-breaking and synchronization. His research interests also include graph theory, randomized algorithms and approximation algorithms. He served as a lecturer of a course on implementation of distributed algorithms and a course on object oriented programming. In 2013 he was accepted to the joint research program of Berkeley and I-CORE that deals with the theory of big data analysis and large-scale networks.

Printed in the United States
by Baker & Taylor Publisher Services